The Withered Garland

Reflections and Doubts of a Bomber

The Withered Garland

Reflections and Doubts of a Bomber

Peter Johnson

Also by Peter Johnson

Neutrality: *A Policy for Britain*
The Hinge of Opportunity: a Security System for Europe

Published in the United Kingdom in 1995 by
New European Publications Limited
14 – 16 Carroun Road
Vauxhall
London SW8 1JT
England

Cover Design Lloyd Allen
Project Management Margaret Allen
Typesetting Margaret Allen
Proof-reading John Rattray

British Library Cataloguing in Publication Data

ISBN 1–872410–04–9

Printed and bound in Great Britain by Biddles Limited Guildford Surrey

For Anne . . . who wanted this book.

"Withered is the garland of the war . . . "

Antony and Cleopatra
Act IV Sc. 13

Contents

Illustrations

The Way we Were. – The author and his brother the late Sir John Johnson, 6th Baronet of New York, at Brightwell, 1912

The author, members of his air and ground crews and their Lancaster 'D' of 97 (Pathfinder) Squadron

Rare photograph of a Lancaster dropping a 4,000lb bomb and incendiaries, 1944

Rare photograph of a Lancaster aircraft on its way to attack targets in Northern France

View of the Town Centre of Essen taken by a German photographer, 1943

Essen, 1943

Joseph Bato's drawing of St Paul's Cathedral standing proudly above the destruction of the 'Blitz' on London

Hitler and the Young Idea

The Entrance to Belsen, June 1945

Belsen, April 1945

A typical Raid Schedule of 97 (Pathfinder) Squadron

Foreword

This book is an autobiography of the full career of a Royal Air Force pilot in peace and war. It is eminently readable, finding some unusually interesting aspects of a long and varied career. Among the subjects which have received little coverage elsewhere is the interwar period, when the RAF, poorly and unsuitably equipped for the task, attempted sporadically to play a part in the generally ineffective political reaction to Mussolini's successful African aggressions. The RAF had no cause to be ashamed of this deplorable performance; the politicians had plenty.

If any good came out of this sad performance, it was the belated realisation by those politicians that the coming of major war was inevitable, and the need to re-arm our forces, both in quality and quantity, was urgent and essential. By the grace of God this re-armament was launched and developed in the nick of time.

Because of his age and experience the author was employed on specialised flying instruction for some long time after the outbreak of war, and established for himself a well-earned reputation for initiative and efficiency. When he at last forced himself into operational flying with Bomber Command, this stood him in good stead; and he became one of the leading exponents of the Pathfinder Technique. Nevertheless he always demonstrated a gift for philosophical analysis of those operations and their justification, and of the leaders responsible for them.

Many readers will have learnt of the internecine squabbles that beset wartime Fighter Command; it is interesting to know of the comparable rivalry and contention among the Bomber leaders, particularly among the Group Commanders.

Anyone interested in the history of those dangerous years will find this a most worthwhile account.

Air Chief Marshal Sir Christopher Foxley-Norris
GCB, DSO, OBE, RAF (Ret'd.)

Acknowledgements

This will record my gratitude to John Coleman who, with Sir Richard Body MP, persuaded me to publish this book and who has done so much towards its final appearance.
Also to Margaret Allen for her fast and efficient editing of a pretty scrappy text.

1

Early Days

Childhood and War

I was born five years after that marvellous contraption of wire and fabric emerged from the Wright brothers' bicycle shed at Kittyhawk, North Carolina and, powered by its own motor, struggled off the ground and forward a few yards in the air before subsiding to earth. Wilbur Wright had made the first flight. In England the first coherent attempts to fly were made in the year of my birth, so virtually all British aviation and nearly all the world's experience of flight has taken place in my lifetime. I was not quite six when the First World War burst on the world and almost thirty-one when Hitler provoked and Mr Chamberlain proclaimed the Second.

So it is not altogether surprising that war and flying dominated the first forty years of my life. It is with war and flying, with the relation between them and the corruption of both, that this book is concerned. I have not wished to intrude more than can be helped of my unimportant self upon the tale, but since I am the hook upon which the themes must necessarily hang, and since the happenings I record are seen through my eyes and filtered through my sensibilities, the reader will inevitably walk by my side through the events I have to relate.

Of the two unbottled genies, war and flying, which have so affected my generation, it was war which first disturbed my childish consciousness. This was in September 1914 when my father, who was a Captain in the Royal Navy, was killed.

I knew very little of him since for most of my short life he had been away at sea. In my memory he was little more than an occasional visitor to the home in which he supported my mother and three children in a reasonable degree of comfort. In July 1914 I knew that he had quite suddenly been appointed to a new ship. At the time we lived in a village not far from Portsmouth, "we", in order of importance in my life, being Nanny, my brother, the cook, the house parlourmaid, my mother and my baby sister. When my father brought his ship, the ill-fated *HMS Cressy*, into Portsmouth Harbour to prepare for the great review of the British fleet by King George V, my mother, my brother and I were allowed to go on board. The Captain's pinnace was sent to fetch us and we were lifted into the shining, spotless launch by respectful sailors, chugging past a seemingly endless array of ships to the obscure arm of the huge harbour where the *Cressy* was anchored. I have vague memories of clambering clumsily up and down steel ladders, seeing huge engines rumbling uneasily in the lower regions and having tea and cakes in the Captain's day cabin, which was a large room and not like a ship at all.

I thought the *Cressy*, with her four tall funnels belching black smoke from coal-burning furnaces, the most marvellous ship in the world. Much later I came to know that she was a failure, dug out of reserve where she had been rusting for years since her design was a failure. In particular, the cruiser class to which she belonged was totally unfitted for any kind of North Sea operation, which was her war assignment, where she and her sisters were to be known throughout the Service as the "Live Bait Squadron". She was slow, clumsy, without underwater protection and could not even fire her heavy guns in a high sea. Naturally I knew nothing of this. All I knew when war started was that my father was going in his wonderful ship to fight and conquer the dreadful Germans who had attacked poor little Belgium which was our friend.

The fact was that the *Cressy*, the *Hogue* and the *Aboukir* sailed out to their fatal cruise off the Dutch coast where my father, who was one of the earliest submarine enthusiasts when the Royal Navy despised such craft as useless, must have known perfectly well that he and his companions were sitting ducks for the U-boats, whose base was only a few miles from their patrol line.

As often happened when my father was at sea, I was sent that August to stay with my mother's sister, my godmother. She and my uncle, having no children of their own, treated me as a favourite son and at Brightwell Park, the country house in Oxfordshire where they lived in some style, I was spoilt and cosseted by family, house guests, of whom there were many, and most of the considerable staff.

It was at Brightwell that I spent the happiest times of my boyhood. I loved the big house with its wide staircase and luxurious smells. I loved the view from the window of my bedroom which, although only a "dressing room" by Brightwell standards, was twice the size of my parents' bedroom at home. The most exciting thing was to look down from that great height and hear and see the horse-drawn mower on the lawn below.

I loved the country and the freedom of the garden and grounds with the Home Farm close by, peopled by respectful men whose Oxfordshire talk I could not understand but who were always pleased to interrupt their work to show me the pigs or the cows or the turkeys. One of the working spaniels was my particular favourite and I would take him to help me build a house in the undergrowth of the nearby wood. Almost best of all, perhaps, were the silkworms, everlastingly consuming bayleaves on a green table in the sunshine and miraculously spinning their magical threads. It seems now that there was always sunshine at Brightwell. In the kitchen garden where the silkworms lived I would often be given a lovely white-fleshed peach or a warm, ripe tomato from one of the damp greenhouses. From the kitchen garden it was only a short way to the stable yard where the groom would let me pat the horses and give them carrots. My particular friend was Ogilvy the chauffeur who, utterly contemptuous of horses, would sometimes take me out in one of the cars which he needed to check, or would let me watch him tend the big diesel engine which charged the row of glass-sided batteries, each taller than me, that supplied the house with electric light.

Once a week or so I would go to the dairy and see the butter being made and be allowed surreptitiously to dip a spoon into one of the vats of thick, golden cream waiting to go into the barrel of the handworked churn. While I loved my mother and my brother, the life with them in our own small house could not compare with the variegated delights of staying, without Nanny, at my godmother's.

Brightwell was not a "great" house but it and the houses we visited nearby were luxurious on a scale far beyond what I knew at home. It is now, alas, a ruin and only the stables and a smaller adjoining house, built as a servant's quarters, survive. Pevsner was dismissive of it, saying that it had "no particular architectural interest". Maybe. There are, of course, dozens of such Georgian manors in England but for me it was, and remains, the most beautiful house I have ever known.

My godmother, who was not stupid, enjoyed music and the arts when she was not occupied with high living, racing and gambling. The pianist Moiseiwitch was a frequent visitor to Brightwell and I would sometimes creep out of my room to the top of the stairs to listen to the faint sounds of him playing to the company after dinner. When there was no house party my uncle would take me into the big drawing room and there play the pianola. This now forgotten instrument was a perpetual fascination. Poor relation to the magnificent, shiny grand which was retuned every time that Moiseiwitch came, the pianola was only a humble upright, but its open belly showed a magic white roll of paper with a pattern of tiny slits which somehow controlled the movements of the ivory keys rising and falling as if played by an invisible and infallible hand. My uncle would sit working the pedals and operating two silver hand keys with his thumbs. I never understood the function of these keys even when later I was allowed to operate them myself, but my uncle clearly regarded them as vital to the performance and himself as a skilful operator of their mystery. I think that even as a child I faintly understood the pathos of this rich and successful man who had so much but yearned for a musical talent he could not buy. At the pianola he would sway and nod and hunch his shoulders to the music as I had seen Moiseiwitch do, and I believe that, in a wistful way, my uncle made himself believe that the sounds he produced were comparable to those he loved when the great man played for him.

The golden summer of 1914 had passed, the harvest was in and there was partridge shooting on the stubbles. For England there had not been a full-scale war since Waterloo, ninety-nine years before. The long years of the French wars, and the many lesser conflicts which had littered the years of England's greatness, had not really disrupted the way of life of Brightwell and its peers. That was part of being an island with a huge Navy and being the apex of an Empire three times the size of the Roman, controlling the resources of a quarter of the earth. The confidence of all the years of safety was still deeply ingrained at Brightwell and its peers in 1914.

That is not to say that the war with Germany made no impact. It was increasingly clear, even to my childish observation, that important and unpleasant things were afoot. The arrival of the daily papers was awaited with increasing tension, voices were sometimes hushed as if to gloss over distress or failure, then raised in angry criticism and hatred of the Germans. The words "Hun" and "Boche" were increasingly heard and uttered with growing venom. Gallant little Belgium and gallant little Serbia were on all tongues. Life went on, but it wasn't the same. It was in this new atmosphere, which seemed in a way to bewilder even the grown-ups, that, for the first time, I had contact, true and close contact, with the reality of war.

This happened in the hall which, as was usual in such houses, was not only an avenue for entry and exit but a main living room, in fact the hub and focal point of the house. A long table ran almost the length of the room, scattered about were comfortable chairs and occasional tables ready to support glasses or discarded newspapers. Against a wall was a sideboard with a mahogany posting box and a tantalus. Beside it an elegant HMV gramophone representing modernity, its record cupboard containing many "sacred" records, a term which included all classics, but also a couple of "ragtimes" and songs by George Robey, which I didn't find funny, and Sir Harry Lauder of which I couldn't understand a word. These were only too often played for my benefit and I had to pretend that I enjoyed them and try to laugh. What I really liked was *Drink to me only with thine Eyes* sung by Dame Clara Butt.

The arrival of the day's newspapers, brought up from the village by pony cart, was the key event of the day and, when there was no shooting, most of the house party would wait in the hall for the delivery, chatting and gossiping, and pretending not to be watching the drive up which the little cart would appear. Normally I avoided the hall at these times, not liking the noise and the crowded room, but on this September morning I had been searching everywhere for my godmother without success and finally braved the bustle and loud discussion which always followed the distribution of the newspapers. Hoping not to be noticed I wriggled my way round the wall to the place by the gramophone where my aunt often sat and was relieved to catch the familiar scent of the eau-de-cologne she always used. As she looked up and saw me, she gave a sudden little cry and all at once it seemed that everyone in the room had turned to look at me. The babble of voices stopped as abruptly as if a curtain had descended and for a long moment the only sounds in the room were sharp intakes of breath and the faint rustle of papers. I remember being really frightened. What did they want? What had I done? It was clear that whatever had caused the silence had to do with me. I rushed to my godmother and hid my face in her skirts. Anything to get away from all those eyes, from that silence. I probably began to cry but, as she comforted me and I looked up, the faces were turned away, the newspapers were raised and the voices resumed, but now in low, murmurous tones. Through my tears I glimpsed in the paper my aunt was holding the photograph of a great, dark, four-funnelled ship.

I doubt if I understood much of what I was then told. My father, so often away at sea, made such rare appearances at home that he was a kind of god-like figure, invisible and intangible but nevertheless powerful. "I'll tell your father" or "What will your father say?" were potent spells freely used by our strict Scottish nanny, but I have no memory whatever of him as a person. For a time at least his death had only an indirect effect on me in having caused the utter collapse of my mother which led to the assumption of dictatorial power in the house by Nanny. Our Nanny was an unusual specimen of that usually loveable breed, being a martinet and not even a just one. She loved to punish us and never gave a word of approval let alone praise. Love had no place in her vocabulary. I'm sure my brother and I were headstrong and difficult children but I am equally sure we could have been "managed" a great deal better with a modicum of affection and understanding.

She used my father's ghost ruthlessly as a primary weapon of discipline. I am sure my mother knew nothing of the genuine cruelty with which Nanny often treated my brother and myself, but she was so broken by her husband's death that for a year or more she seldom appeared and the Scottish gorgon, whom we grew actively to hate, had virtually complete control. As a genuinely religious woman of her era, my mother supported Nanny in convincing me, for a time at least, that my father was watching my every action and monitoring my innermost thoughts from above the skies. It was quite some time before this unfortunate concept ceased to play an active part in my life and when it was eventually discarded I think it left a wound made by the thought that I had been deliberately deceived. In retrospect, this may have been unjust since religious people in those times were quite capable of accepting such an idea without too much questioning about its physical implications. I am sure that the idea that she would eventually "rejoin" my father was a powerful influence in my mother's life for many years.

The real impact of the death of my father on me was twofold, one component temporary, the other a lasting factor. Immediately, I was very conscious of a change in the attitude of grown-ups towards me. The house guests took to fondling and kissing me, (poor little fellow, no father!). This was awful. Even worse was the effect on my friends among the staff who played such an important part in my blissful life at Brightwell. Gone was that mixture of fun, intimacy and respect which makes such idyllic relationships for privileged children lucky enough to win the love of nice servants. Instead there were whisperings, head-pattings, endless sympathy, hushed voices. All eyes seemed to be on the black armbands sewn on my clothes and the black tie I wore every day. No one made jokes or told me stories. At home my mother wore widow's weeds and inky black. The writing paper had a thick black edge and there were no parties, no expeditions, no fun.

So, younger than most, I had some experience of the reality of war. But these things wore off with time. How, indeed, could you really love, and therefore really mourn, someone you never really knew? A much more lasting effect was the inculcation in me of hatred for the German enemy. The gap in my life left by my father's death was more negative than positive. Other boys had a father, I had not. Fathers provided money, background, vigour and life. Our home was quietly dominated by my mother's mourning and the weakness in her which the shock had engendered, leading to the odious dictatorship of Nanny. But the loathing of the enemy whose underhand methods had brought all this about was real and increasing. At Brightwell I often overheard accounts of the brutality and deliberate flouting of all civilised standards by the abominable Hun, personified in caricatures and cartoons by the Emperor, the odious "Kaiser Bill", the very essence of the evil of his degraded people. His son, "Little Willy" the Crown Prince, was always portrayed as an effeminate weakling with spindly legs encased in shiny jackboots, well tarred with his father's brush and certainly not a whit better, a coward as well as a bully and a murderer. I doubt if I knew that these two were direct descendants of our good Queen Victoria.

The Kaiser's War probably outshone all its predecessors in the use of propaganda by Governments to whip up popular hatred of the enemy. The medium of the popular press exposed a far greater proportion of people to this persuasion than had been the case in previous wars, and the fear and vilification of "Old

Boney", aroused in Napoleonic time, was far surpassed by the outburst of loathing for the Germans in 1914/15. This was occasioned by tales of the torpedoing of helpless merchant ships (bringing us the sinews of war), of seamen left to drown, of the bayoneting of civilians and women, and of looting and rape. At Brightwell my godmother took in, as it was fashionable and patriotic to do, a "Belgian refugee", a young and very pretty girl who not unnaturally glamorised the real sufferings of her countrymen in the eyes of an impressionable child. I was horrified by her tales, retailed to me at second hand by the servants, of how the Germans had entered her village, killed her father, commandeered their house, forced her mother and herself to wait at table and scrub the floors, and had beaten her mother for inefficiency and then herself for trying to protect her mother.

Such tales were rife even among such rational people as the Brightwell house parties' guests and, although I didn't really understand what was being discussed, the spirit of the time was powerfully conveyed to me. Every dandelion whose head I struck off with my stick was a German soldier beheaded by my sword. My sponge, dragged down to the bottom of the bath, was a German battleship sunk by guns in revenge for my father. The deep ha-ha, which separated the lawn from the park, was the moat of a fort attacked by Germans whom only I could repulse, inflicting enormous casualties. The stones I threw at a bottle perched on a wall were my bullets aimed at the heart of Kaiser Bill and when at last I hit the bottle its disintegration represented to me the death of the arch-villain himself.

The grip of the war gradually tightened on ordinary people. Not all disasters could be concealed and the ghastly casualty lists affected every household in the land. The certainty of ultimate success was still not in doubt because the English, according to the history books, always "won in the end". But now the lives of everyone, squires and workpeople, housewives and farmers, schoolboys and their tutors, all came to be dominated by the fact of war. Not equally, of course, but at least universally. My widowed mother, who had moved our modest establishment into Southsea, the residential and seaside area of Portsmouth, was hauled before a court and fined for having allowed a tiny chink of light to appear from one of our windows. Since these faced the sea, this was a fairly heinous crime and the magistrate, undeterred by her widow's weeds, sadistically reduced her to tears with censure of lack of patriotism and putting the whole naval base at risk.

My brother and I, fired with an obsessive patriotism, did not blame her but felt that we shared her guilt. As a measure of atonement, on hearing that the Government was calling for scrap metal, and especially for lead, we melted down our whole magnificent collection of toy soldiers over the nursery fire. One by one we put them on to the flat coal shovel, melting the Highlanders, upright Guardsmen, colourful Zouaves, bush-hatted Australians, prancing Lifeguards, and dozens of other regiments, all in their glorious uniforms. The paint burnt in the shovel, held carefully over the red hot coals, and all these brave and beautiful creatures shrivelled into shapeless lumps of dull silver metal which I suppose we somehow conveyed to an unheeding Government. I do not remember getting any thanks or acknowledgement and afterwards sometimes wondered whether the tiny burst of machine gun fire which our sacrifice might have produced managed to kill any Germans. I passionately hoped so.

During the war I was sent to my first preparatory school, very small, very expensive, very exclusive, the choice of my godmother who was paying. I hated it. I was unpopular, bullied, always bottom of the class, despised by masters and boys alike. I remember being known as "bread and butter eater" which, for a reason which now escapes me, was a term of considerable contempt and abuse. After a couple of terms there was apparently some hiccup in my godmother's finances and, much to my relief, I was removed to Stubbington, a less expensive school where my brother, eighteen months my senior, was well ensconced.

My father had been at Stubbington at the same time as Captain Scott of the Antarctic and the school was imbued with deep naval and patriotic traditions. As sons of a hero, or at least a casualty, of the current war my brother and I had some reflected glory from his demise. We were quite unaware that the sinking of the

Cressy and her sisters was a disaster only too typical of the early stages of a war when peacetime ignorance and indolence persists in the services and in their civilian masters, in this case Mr Winston Churchill. As the war developed we were all caught up in the huge emotional currents of passionate patriotism which were ruthlessly whipped up by the press and retailed to us by the staff who, too old or debilitated to serve themselves, were as fervently warlike as any recruiting sergeant.

My own hatred of the "Boche", fuelled by my status as the son of a victim of German low cunning and barbarous methods, was deep and genuine. I read avidly every book about the war I could lay hand on and took it as a matter of course that the Great British Empire provided all the heroes, our French allies were second-raters who didn't always really try, and the Germans, Austrians and Turks were villains incapable of fair fight, whose knavish tricks, and especially underwater exploits, were exposed and defeated by such outstanding figures as my father would have been had he survived.

German spies were in especial hate and the target of a great deal of invective in the press. Their machinations were perceived everywhere and any foreign accent was grounds for suspicion. The Stubbington languages master, a middle-aged Frenchman called M. Guillemot, was a prime target for us juvenile spy hunters. He had no capacity for discipline since he spoke English indifferently and we would pretend that the despairing orders he gave in French were incomprehensible so we ragged and disrupted his classes to our hearts' content.

Finding out that he lodged in Portsmouth during the holidays, my brother and I would track him from a distance, finding all his peregrinations highly suspicious. If he stood on the beach looking out to sea, perhaps yearning for his native land, we were sure that he was amassing information about passing ships for transmission to Germany. By stretching a piece of black cotton across the front door of his lodgings we established to our satisfaction that he went out after dark, clearly to transmit nefarious messages to his odious masters. We discussed endlessly how we should convey our evidence to the police but did not quite dare and the good M. Guillemot left the school, under what we were convinced were very suspicious circumstances, before our dossier was complete.

I believe that mass hatred, such as was inoculated into my generation against the Germans, can and usually does become a permanent part of the psyche. Even if a life is devoted to the cultivation of reason and moderation, and I cannot claim that mine has been, there will always be a thin membrane of distaste stretched over that part of the brain which controls dealings with the erstwhile enemy. In my own case I am pretty sure that some at least of the prefabricated hatred of Germany and Germans which engulfed almost all of England trickled into my subconscious and remained with me through the years of peace when sensible English people were trying to restrain the excesses of France and give some comfort and support to the struggling Weimar Republic.

War or no war, school life still had to proceed. The staff used our youthful enthusiasm to get into the fight to encourage us to greater efforts in the classroom and on the playing fields. All the boys, I think, yearned as I did to be able to take some active part in the great struggle against the hated enemy and when at last America, infuriated by unrestricted submarine warfare and attacks on American ships, declared war I think I was secretly rather disappointed. Everyone said that the American decision meant that the war would be won more quickly. For me and my friends it meant that the glory would be shared and that it was unlikely we would play any part.

Apart from an always vivid imagination by which I was enabled to translate stories and newspaper reports into exploits of my own in the future, the nearest the war came in reality was one night in the holidays when a Zeppelin appeared over, or at least near, Portsmouth. I do not remember hearing either bombs or anti-aircraft fire and the alien thing moved tranquilly away. The other and more frequent manifestation of the struggle across the water was the almost constant activity out of the nearby aerodrome of Gosport, only a couple of miles from Stubbington.

School and aerodrome have now, alas, been submerged into the remorseless march of suburban housing.

Gosport was then the main base for the training of Royal Flying Corps pilots and, rudimentary as such training was, the demand for pilots, whose life on active service in France might be only a few days, was infinite and the aerial activity, subject only to weather, was constant. I suppose that, as in my own war a quarter of a century on, the urge to get every possible machine and trainee pilot into the air as often and for as long as possible was remorseless. At the time of course I knew nothing of such things. But keen as I was on cricket and football, my memories of the lovely Stubbington playing fields on which we pursued our outdoor activities, are as much concerned with watching complicated manoeuvres high in the sky above as with the successes I managed to achieve at the games we played.

Even in those early days when flying was still regarded as something of a miracle, pilots were able to coax their fragile steeds into quite sensational manoeuvres, many of which took place directly above us. I had no idea of how or why they performed these extraordinary "stunts" as they were then called. Whether it was simply from high spirits generated by the exhilaration of flight or whether these were officially sanctioned and prescribed exercises was of no concern to me. What mattered was simply the wonderful spectacle provided on most fine afternoons when we were at games. I loved the varying sounds which emanated from these acts of skill and daring. In class I often listened, frustrated, to the prolonged increasing roar of a steep dive and, hearing the inevitable sequel of the ear-splitting "waaaaaaoow" that followed. I imagined that I could see, as we did on the playing field, the machine pulled up in a vertical climb, perhaps completing the loop or other manoeuvre at the top. I loved the suspense of the moments of silence as the engine cut out or was throttled back and the spitting and banging and bursts of black smoke as the pilot strove to regain power from his not unnaturally recalcitrant motor. Of course I then understood nothing of the technicalities of flying and I had never been within sight of an aeroplane on the ground. But I never tired of gazing upwards at the endless variety of weaving and turning, climbing and diving, inverting, rolling and looping achieved by the unknown heroes who were to me, quite literally, "those magnificent men in their flying machines".

Because I was young there was not quite the same miraculous element about this conquest of the air as there might have been to older people who had known a time when powered flight seemed impossible. What was exciting was that here was a whole new world which might grow and develop and bring an element into the lives of me and my generation which our fathers and mothers had never even guessed at. But, beyond a vague and impersonal hero worship of the unknowns who performed over our playing fields, I had no inkling of the part that the successors to the fragile aircraft I saw over Stubbington would play in the world or in my own life. My main interests, apart from the war, were cricket and football and, some way behind, Latin, arithmetic and, a new feature of increasing importance, my introduction to the elements of Greek.

This stemmed from my godmother's offer to finance a public school education for me at Winchester, preferably with a scholarship which it was believed I could achieve. For this an examination in Greek was compulsory. From Winchester, provided my academic abilities fulfilled their early promise, I would go to Oxford and enter the great world from as privileged a starting place as any in the land. Because of this plan I had to take private lessons in Greek which was not part of the normal curriculum, Stubbington being best known for its abilities to squeeze difficult cases through the entrance exam for Dartmouth and the Royal Navy.

My Greek lessons took place in the small, smelly, smoke-filled study of the classics master, a small, smelly, pipe-smoking figure, the least popular of all the masters. It is fair to say that his unpopularity stemmed less from his personal characteristics than from the fact that he personified Latin, which most boys simply loathed. Luckily, I did not share this distaste and even had a certain elementary appreciation of the orderliness and sonority of the language and its literature.

When I got over my revulsion to the mustiness and smell of his study, I found Mr Turner to be a character of great gentle charm and, I suspect, to be no mean scholar. His room was lined with overfilled bookshelves and more books were piled on the floor and scattered about on the few rickety chairs. Two or three volumes were usually open on his desk and more on the floor, but what advantage he gained from having so many books in use at the same time I never discovered. In spite of the disorder, he always seemed to know where everything was and he could infallibly lay his hand immediately on any passage he needed to demonstrate a point. I do not imagine that any of the school maids ever set foot in that room, whose layers of dust would surely have baffled the greediest vacuum cleaner, let alone a prep school tweeny with her dustpan and brush.

Although I was a beginner at Greek, bewildered by the new alphabet and unfamiliar pronunciation, Mr Turner had the knack of making me feel that the effort required for the first steps would be more than repaid when I began to sample the infinity of the riches beyond. He managed to enliven the difficult new grammar by bringing to life, through the strength of his enthusiasm and imagination, some of the magic of the tales which lay waiting for me when I should get beyond the elementary drudgery.

In the event, it was not to be, but in later life, with no classical education beyond the bare elements I learnt from Mr Turner, I would often think of the shabby little man in his musty study and remember those lines of Yeats:

> . . . But I, being poor, have only my dreams;
> I have spread my dreams under your feet;
> Tread softly, because you tread upon my dreams.

I think he had no one to whom he could confess his dreams and little in his life altogether except his books, and perhaps tobacco. But out of his books had come such dreams as are unknown to those many of us who are not capable of evoking a world of imagination out of the genius of dead poets in an idiom now known to few. Something of these dreams he managed, I think, to convey to me as far as my unsophisticated mind was capable of absorbing them. They were dreams of a Greece of the Iliad and the Odyssey, of the great philosophers, of the heroic defence of Athens against the Persians, of the pride of Empire and the disaster at Syracuse, of the marvellous drama and comedy of the plays that have survived and of the simple, sometimes effective, democracy. This was where Mr Turner lived. While we worked together in the foul, smoke-ridden study, he breathed the pure Grecian air of the time of Pericles. The Peloponnesian War and its heroes and villains were probably more real to him in the words of Thucydides than were the daily newspaper reports of the Herculean struggles across the Channel which absorbed everyone else. I began to look forward to my private lessons and had little or no fear that I would fail to achieve the Winchester scholarship which would be my stepping stone to a wider world.

Alas, it did not happen. The Greek lessons stopped suddenly and I heard later that three insuperable barriers had intervened to block the rose-coloured plans for my future. They were my brother's eyesight, my mother's poverty and my godmother's proclivity for gambling and alcohol.

It had been planned that my brother should go from Stubbington to the Royal Naval College, Dartmouth where, as the son of a Naval Officer killed on active service, he would be educated free. He failed the eyesight test, an essential for the Navy of those times, and my mother had to send him to a public school which entailed fees she could barely afford. It would have been out of the question for her to support me at Winchester at the same time, even with a scholarship, and it now became apparent to her that the fulfilment of her sister's promise to pay the Winchester fees and send me to Oxford was looking increasingly precarious. I knew nothing of this at the time, but apparently there were ominous stories about her gambling and about my uncle's finances. My mother took the decision that the risk of being landed with fees she could not possibly afford, and therefore of having to remove me to a cheaper school, was too great. So, willy-nilly, I had to take my brother's place as a non fee-paying cadet at The Royal Naval College, Dartmouth. In the event she was probably right. My uncle and aunt had sold up at Brightwell within ten years which seemed to imply some financial crisis. I never knew the details but I'm sure she wouldn't have seen me through Winchester and Oxford.

What I knew for certain, enormous as the reputation and prestige of the Royal Navy was, it was not the career I would have chosen. Whether there was some connection with my father's death I am not sure, but ships and the sea had no attraction for me. I was an adequate swimmer but I always avoided the robust horseplay inseparable from boys' bathing. I hated being "ducked" and even putting my head under water. This, I am sure, stemmed from my too vivid imagination of what had actually happened when my father, his ship torpedoed by a German submarine, died by drowning.

I hated the prospect of Dartmouth but had no alternative on offer. Accordingly, I attended the much dreaded "interview" in London at which three or four senior naval officers inspected, cross-questioned and bullied prospective candidates for the Dartmouth exam to ensure their suitability, at the ripe age of thirteen, for His Majesty's Commission in the Royal Navy. Many and frightening were the stories of trick questions asked and silly traps set for nervous boys by these hardened old sea dogs. I don't remember my own ordeal so I suppose it was made easy for me since the Admirals would probably have known my father. I passed and duly sat the exam a few weeks later.

Awaiting the result, and believing with a dull resentment that I was inexorably destined for Dartmouth, life at Stubbington, even as Head Boy and Captain of the school cricket and football teams, seemed a bit dull. Accordingly I enlivened it by leading night time roof climbing expeditions over the mostly flat roofs of the jerry-built buildings which were attached to the old house where the school had originated. There was a night watchman, a slow moving, slow thinking character called Bevis whose other job was to shovel into a cart the daily accumulation from the mediaeval pattern earth based lavatory which served one hundred and thirty boys. I still remember the unpleasant exposed feeling when one was heavily engaged there and heard the horse and cart clattering up behind you for Bevis to perform his daily task.

From the roofs we used to track poor Bevis as he did his conscientious perambulations round the buildings at night and we had great difficulty in restraining our laughter at his bewilderment at the apparent supernatural phenomenon of small stones dropping from the sky on the path of his regular round. When we were eventually caught, naturally the rumpus was immense and the whole little world of the school was rocked to its foundations.The other nocturnal prowlers were soundly thrashed for their misdemeanours and as far as I know survived without permanent injury. There was, however, some difficulty about how to treat me as the ringleader, Head Boy, captain of cricket and football, top of the school and, worst of all, awaiting the result of the Dartmouth entrance exam. The normal punishment would have been expulsion, which meant being sent home in total disgrace, a pariah with career prospects severely damaged, if not permanently ruined. The snag, however, from the school's viewpoint, was the Dartmouth entry. Stubbington was well-known as a preparatory school for the Navy, but of late the number of successes had dropped seriously. If I had been sacked it would have been necessary to cancel my candidacy for the Dartmouth entry and the school had no wish to lose even a single success. In the event, I was stripped of my various offices and privileges, not allowed to play any games nor to associate with the other boys except in class. In leisure and recreation times I had to stay in a detention room and write out Latin verse, a regime which was to continue until the exam results came in. I would have much preferred to have been thrashed with the others.

When the Dartmouth exam results came through, there were three successes from Stubbington, more than any other school. Those who had passed were not listed in order of merit but, for some reason the name of the candidate who came first was published and who should this be but that nocturnal miscreant, myself. The school authorities heaved a sigh of relief that they had not expelled me and I was packed off home forthwith where I was able to represent to my mother that my early arrival before the term was finished was a reward for coming first in the exam.

My sojourn at Dartmouth was predictably disastrous. In spite of some proficiency in both work and games, my hostility to the over strict discipline coupled with an instinctive distaste for a career at sea resulted in the Royal Navy, much to my relief, dispensing with my services.

2

Learning to Fly

A Peacetime Disaster

For two years I did sweated labour with a firm of chartered accountants in London, combining this with "doing the season". As I was paid nothing and found some difficulty with the laundry bills for white tie and stiff shirt two or three times a week, let alone with competing with the *jeunesse dorée* in taking out the more attractive debutantes, my financial position grew steadily weaker. Eventually I cancelled my articles in favour of trying my luck as a jackeroo in the Australian outback.

That soon became a bit dull and I found myself back in England where, in 1929, conditions for an unqualified young man looking for a job were about as bad as could be.

It wasn't surprising, therefore, that the work I did find rapidly drove me up the wall. But it was better than nothing. After all I had nothing to offer an employer. My naval career had been a disaster and I had thrown in the sponge after only two years of chartered accountancy which clearly indicated a lack of stamina. Having danced with a lot of debs and having been a special constable at the age of seventeen in the general strike were splendid experiences but little recommendation in the employment market. Unsurprisingly prospective employers were inclined to put my applications to revitalise their operation in the waste paper basket.

So in 1929 I was lucky to have the job I had. It was not well paid, but, with a little of my own, I "got by" and there were supposed to be "prospects".

The firm, a medium sized manufacturer of grocery products, had advertised for two young men of public school background to get experience in all branches of the business with a view to executive positions. Ultimately we could expect to relieve the ageing directors of some of their responsibilities and proceed steadily if slowly to the top of a not very exalted tree. Cards were printed for me showing my status as a member of the firm's "Directors' Office".

After a few weeks my companion trainee left in disgust and I was desperately unhappy. My employers, while still implying that a managerial desk awaited me, kept me rigidly on the sales side which I loathed and for which I had less than no talent. I was particularly involved with a new "line" which they seemed to hope might prop up what I began to see as a somewhat rickety business. The product was a singularly nasty breakfast cereal, soggy and tasteless, called "Aviator Wheat Flakes". The name was justified by the picture of a contemporary pilot with helmet and goggles, wearing a leather coat and breeches, which appeared on every packet, large or small. When, unsurprisingly, the horrible concoction failed to sell, there was devised an advertising scheme which it was hoped would save the situation and put this palpably inferior cereal on every breakfast table in the land.

The idea was to advertise in a local paper that "The Aviator" was in the district covered by the paper. He would call on a number of homes and, if he were shown a packet of the odious flakes, the lucky housewife would be rewarded with a ten shilling note, which was a useful addition to a family budget at a time when you could feed a person quite well on a pound a week. It rapidly transpired that I (who else?) was to be "The Aviator" and, armed with a wad of new ten shilling notes, I had to spend several weeks knocking at doors and trying to explain the scheme to bewildered ladies who had never heard of Aviator Wheat Flakes or, if they had, cordially disliked them. Many were actively rude, clearly suspecting that I was really after their grandmother's silver candlesticks. Small wonder that, when I heard that the Royal Air Force was calling for educated young men to be trained as pilots, I began seriously to consider applying.

"If you join the Air Force," said Chabot, "you'll just be AN aviator. Now you're THE Aviator."

I laughed. Chabot was my friend, a chubby, pink, twinkling man, small in height, large in heart, happy in disposition. He scraped a living out of the manufacture of a special kind of soap powder used for the scouring of the planks of ships' decks. At that time many decks were of wood and their whiteness was a matter of special pride, reflecting the morale and efficiency of the ship and her Master. Chabot's soap was apparently unrivalled in this function. He plied his trade from a derelict shed built out over the river in Limehouse and at high water the black and oily Thames was clearly visible through gaps in the floorboards. Chabot said that at low water he had more than once seen the bodies of discarded babies stranded on the mud under the warehouse. There was nothing he could do about them and they were presumably borne away towards the estuary by the next tide.

Chabot was fifteen years my senior but that made no difference to our friendship. We would talk endlessly on every subject under the sun. Our backgrounds as well as our ages were dissimilar but we had everything else in the present and the future to discuss so why should we bother with the past? He called me by my Christian name but I never even knew his. Everyone seemed to call him Chabot so I did the same. It was only lately that I had discovered that he had been a pilot in the 1914 war so it was natural that I should consult with him about my latest idea.

He was less than enthusiastic. He said that the shipping business, from which his livelihood derived, was already feeling the pinch following the Wall Street crash. When shipping started to decline, he said, the rest of the world's economy followed. There was every chance of a widespread slump which could lead to financial trouble in England. With a Labour Government in office and a Prime Minister and other ministers having strong pacifist affiliations, there would be cuts and cuts and cuts again in the Armed Forces. The Royal Air Force, which was the least popular of the three services and had least political clout, would probably lose most. This, he said, was no time to join. I might be out on my ear within eighteen months. Just at that time, moreover, there was a strong general belief that the Locarno Treaties and the more co-operative attitudes of Russia and Germany had already made Europe a more peaceful place. The popular clamour for disarmament, to which a Labour Government was especially vulnerable, was stronger than ever. However much I disliked being "the" Aviator, said Chabot, the food industry would survive in the bad times which were clearly ahead, while "an" aviator in a shrinking Air Force might be out of a job in no time.

I was in no position to contradict him on matters of world economics or British politics and I probably believed his views were sound. But what matter? I was twenty-one, fascinated by the idea of flying and utterly disgusted by everything I had learnt of, and everybody I had met in, the grocery trade. In the last month or so I had exchanged the sentimental memory of the wartime "stunts" above Stubbington for a real interest in modern flying. I read aviation magazines, watched the activities at an RAF aerodrome from behind a hedge and even once penetrated into a flying club on the pretext of finding out the cost of learning to fly. That, needless to say, was well out of my income bracket but the contact with the world of flight, the romantic instructors in their ex-RFC leather coats, the hard, pretty girls with their long cigarette holders, the rich young men boasting about their adventures, fitted perfectly with my picture of a dream world to which, if I joined the Air Force, I could acquire a key.

I put in my application for an RAF Commission and, after some bad moments when my reasons for leaving the Royal Navy provoked questions about my amenability to discipline, I was accepted. I could tear up the horrible "Aviator" leaflets, return my unused stock of ten shilling notes and hand in my notice, secure in, at least, a five-year contract in the course of which I should become, within my personal limits, a reasonably skilled pilot. Chabot, smiling in his delightfully pink and spontaneous way, was the first to wish me godspeed on my journey to the RAF Depot at Uxbridge for the initiation course.

Here were assembled twenty-five young men from varying national, social and educational backgrounds to be kitted out as officers and hopefully persuaded that the Royal Air Force was a disciplined service and not a glorified flying club. To this end we were given lectures on such subjects as the duties and responsibilities of an officer, behaviour and customs to be observed in the Officers' Mess, the organisation of the service and the ranks and functions of its personnel. The Royal Air Force had, we learnt, sprung from the loins of two most unwilling parents, the Royal Flying Corps (Army) and the Royal Naval Air Service (Navy). Each had fiercely resented being forced to give birth to what they regarded as a kind of Glamis monster which they devoutly hoped was destined only to crawl about in the lowest regions of the defence establishment, starved and ignored by all. And so it was for quite a long time.

It was the job of the Uxbridge Depot to persuade us that the founding fathers had managed to infuse the new service with some at least of the traditions of the old. They had hoped that the smartness, discipline and strict hierarchical precedence, by which so much store had been set in the past, would not be lost in the effort to created the hybrid to which the Army and Navy had contributed on a more-or-less equal basis. What in fact emerged was a new sort of drill, a peculiar uniform of a ghastly colour and queer ranks for the officers which nobody outside the service understood. The whole produced a mildly comic effect since many of the absurdities which time had hallowed in the older services could only be seen as ridiculous in the modern, highly mechanised and necessarily flexible world of aviation.

But morale and discipline of a sort there was. The rock on which the Royal Air Force was built was the passionate devotion to the art and practice of flying which inspired most of its members. Those who were more attached to the forms of service life than to the pursuit of improvement in aviation were a minority and seen by the majority as no more than an unimportant drag on the real business in hand.

At Uxbridge we had to buy our uniforms and submit them to an officer whose duty it was to see that our tailors made no deviation from the regulation patterns. Each of us was provided with a grant of fifty pounds to cover the purchase of a uniform greatcoat, uniform tunic, trousers and cap, breeches and puttees, mess kit jacket and tight trews and a pair each of service boots, shoes and mess Wellingtons. It may now seem something of a miracle that tailors managed to stay inside the grant, but then even a moderately expensive tailor took you only a few pounds over.

The Mess, as became the RAF Depot at which senior officers were often accommodated between postings or on return from overseas, was comfortable and the food good. Our quarters were sparsely furnished but perfectly adequate and a civilian batman was provided between every six officers. It cannot have been an arduous job. My attendant was an oldish character of lugubrious habit and, while obviously disapproving of new officers as a species, was equally anxious to earn his expected gratuity. Unpacking my dinner jacket he said, in a voice of positive Jeevesian gloom, "It's the leave period, sir, so we shan't be changing for dinner."

Having completed our initiation course without any major disasters we were commissioned into the Royal Air Force as Pilot Officers on Probation. This meant that for a year you were liable to instant dismissal without redress for misbehaviour or unsuitability. We learnt that the procedure was quite often used by the authorities to dispose of entrants who failed to learn to fly to the required standard. This gave us all furiously to think since, although it was obvious that some would be better than others, it had not occurred to us that anyone would be incapable of flying at all. This was a new concept and I remember that we looked at one another in some distress, slightly reminiscent of the disciples saying "Is it I?"

We arrived at RAF Station Sealand on a Saturday to find the whole place virtually shut down with most of the staff still on leave. Our course did not formally start until the Monday, so the more adventurous of us sallied forth in somebody's car to taste the delights of the night life of Liverpool, a few miles away across the Mersey.

I do not remember the whole course of the evening except that after a single drink at the Adelphi, where our dress was not up to the standards of the house and the drinks were out of our price range, we explored a series of less exalted hostelries. After closing time one of our number, a big Irishman, was provoked by a local and a fight ensued in which the police intervened. Suspicious of the Irish accent, they blamed our side for the fracas and we were hauled off to the police station as the guilty parties, charged, and told to appear at the Magistrates' Court at ten o'clock on Monday morning. In vain did we beg and implore that this was impossible, that our careers were at stake, that we were officers, although perhaps not noticeably gentlemen at the moment, and that we would guarantee to pay any fine. The police had heard all that before. The Magistrates' Court at ten o'clock it was to be.

We woke on Sunday in a much chastened mood. I, in particular, felt that as I was that much older and perhaps a little more sophisticated than the others, I should somehow have prevented us from getting into such a silly but potentially dangerous scrape. The words "On Probation" floated before my eyes. How were the authorities likely to view this as a first appearance in the capacity of an officer?

After discreet enquiries from my new batman, I ascertained that virtually the only course open to us was to see the Station Adjutant, who happened to be on duty that week-end, and make a clean breast of the whole affair. I gathered that the reputation of this officer for sympathy with the high spirits of young pupil officers was less than outstanding.

So, after a gloomily teetotal lunch, we changed our clothes and set off to No. 4, Officers' Married Quarters, an ugly villa in a row of ugly villas, and, with considerable qualms, rang the bell.

I should explain to the modern reader that it was the custom, nay the law, in the Royal Air Force of that time that officers on arrival at a new station should, within a month or so "call" on the wives of all the married officers who lived nearby. If the lady was "Not at Home" you gave two of your calling cards (die stamped, never just printed) to the maid or batman, who deposited them on the silver salver invariably displayed on the hall table.

On our distasteful business with the Adjutant we were naturally unmindful of such formalities and when, in answer to our ring, an untidy maidservant opened the door, I asked nervously to see Flight Lieutenant Ransom. The girl said in a tone of reproof that she thought Mrs Ransom might be at home and showed us into a bare, uncomfortable room containing a minimum of inelegant furniture and curtains and carpets of an almost incredible ugliness. We stood self-consciously waiting.

The Adjutant and his wife came in together. He was a tall ascetic looking man with pale eyes, a pale, rather blotchy skin and pale hair, thin and sandy. His wife was the female equivalent except that she was even more colourless and had none of his submerged aggressiveness. To our surprise they both, he in the lead, greeted us with almost effusive pleasure and enthusiasm.

"Ah ha!" he said, rubbing his thin hands together. "You're from the new entry?" We nodded glumly and I, as the agreed spokesman for the criminal classes, fumbled for an appropriate opening to my prepared speech. I had not bargained for the presence of his wife. However he pre-empted anything I might have volunteered with a flow of happily cordial welcome and I heard the lady, following his lead, similarly address one of my companions in a faint monotone.

"Excellent, how most excellent," he said, his forced smile hardly reflecting the feelings of his audience. "What a splendid start to your course. I really do congratulate you. The Uxbridge lot must have briefed you properly for once. I do appreciate good manners and by no means all the new entries lately have come up to scratch. Most of them spend their first Sunday here touring round the country or wasting their time and money in pubs. . . "

By this time we were all gasping with astonishment, not really understanding what he was talking about. We didn't have long to wait. He turned to his wife, "Don't you think, my dear, it's the height of good manners for these young officers to spend their first afternoon calling on us? It shows they understand already that a Station Adjutant is the hub on which the whole station turns, eh? Also that even for young officers the social part of service life is important, eh? Splendid, excellent, eh?"

His shabby wife said nothing beyond the vague expressions of agreement with her husband of whom she clearly stood in some awe. He continued to expatiate on the importance in the Royal Air Force of good manners and behaviour with occasional comments on how too often direct entry officers fell short of the standards set by himself and his peers.

"But," he said, "we haven't got your names. Rosie didn't bring us their cards, dear, did she?" I tried to mumble something apologetic about not having completely unpacked but nothing really came out. I was beginning to feel that the situation was completely out of hand.

When the time came that we could decently interrupt the flow of the Adjutant's dissertation, I muttered something about us not keeping him and, obviously relieved, his wife accompanied us to the front door. I saw her glance at the inevitable salver, bare of cards, as we said our goodbyes. With the door ajar she watched us start down the path but, before she could shut it I plucked up the courage to turn back.

"Have you forgotten something?" she asked.

"Er, no. I mean, yes," I stammered. "The thing is, er, please could we have a, er, a private word with Flight Lieutenant Ransom?"

The others came back to support me while Mrs Ransom withdrew and the horrid facts were related to the Adjutant. If we had hoped that our previously ecstatic reception might work in our favour, we were soon disabused of any such idea. In fact it made matters worse because the Adjutant could, with some justification, think he had been made a fool of or, worse, had made a fool of himself. Never has atmosphere changed so abruptly. The pale eyes narrowed, the pallid lips compressed into a straight line, the thin hands which had been rubbed together in pleasure were clenched in barely controlled fury. The speech which had been so affable became staccato and almost incoherent.

"What infernal cheek. Don't you know who I am? . . . my free time . . . my wife . . . pretending you were calling . . . drunken young sots . . . not fit to be officers . . . straight before the CO on Monday . . . report to my office . . ."

I ventured to remind him of the Magistrates' Court which only made him angrier than ever but eventually he calmed himself to say, "Oh, yes, alright. Go to your bloody Magistrates' Court. I hope they put you in jail where you belong . . . when you'll be chucked out of the service as you deserve. Now, GET OUT." We crept away.

However, the Air Force of 1930 was pretty easy going and, although we had a dressing down from the Station Commander, it was soon clear that our peccadillo, while not to be repeated, would not really be held against us.

The first days at Sealand were, nevertheless, profoundly disappointing. I suppose I had seen myself immediately being initiated into the arts of looping and rolling until I was quickly the equal, if not the superior, of those wartime heroes I had admired from a distance at Stubbington.

The reality was very different. We were marched to and fro, going from one department to another and being issued with a formidable mass of equipment, including a variety of manuals and a vast tome called *The King's Regulations and Air Council Instructions* complete with a formidable number of amendments which had to be incorporated in the text in our spare time. This volume laid down standards for every facet of Air Force work, recreation and discipline, including a long list of offences and the penalties they would or could incur. I was fascinated by the number of misdemeanours which might entail the offender suffering "death or such lesser punishment" as authority might prescribe. It seemed that one had handed over a good deal of personal freedom in exchange for the privilege of becoming a pilot.

After three weeks this aim still seemed tantalisingly distant. We saw the machines being manhandled out of the hangars, the engines being run and the instructors climbing into the cockpits and taking off with a roar. For ten minutes every morning the air above the aerodrome was alive with spectacular aerobatics as the first air tests of the day were carried out and we would watch with admiration and envy the skill and ease with which manoeuvres we only half understood were completed, often far lower than was permitted by the regulations which were already being instilled into us.

New pupils, however, were for the time being confined to the classrooms and various ancillary departments where we were given lectures on theory and discipline, fitted with our flying clothing and parachutes, allotted to flights and instructors, and, it seemed, lectured again until admonitions were running out of our ears. Then the weather went sour and although, a few new pupils might be taken as passengers on the air tests, there was no question of any serious flying instruction. It was very galling, especially as the ground instruction was given by indifferent lecturers who, whatever their knowledge of their subject, had in general neither the skill nor the will to pass it on.

An exception was the Senior NCO who initiated us into the workings of the Vickers and Lewis machine guns which, having done good service in the 1914 war, were still standard equipment in the RAF. These ingenious, lethal toys were obviously his passion. He had used them during the war, knew every detail of their construction and understood their vagaries, which were many. He taught us by the repetition of a descriptive patter in which he was word perfect and able exactly to synchronise speech with demonstration. It was slightly monotonous but had a curious poetry of its own and was clear even to those who were not mechanically minded, of whom I was emphatically one. Many years after I found that our armourer flight sergeant, and many hundreds before and after him, had been preserved, as if embalmed in glass, in that classic war poem of Henry Reed, *The Naming of Parts*:

Today we have naming of parts. Yesterday
We had daily cleaning. And tomorrow morning,
We shall have what to do after firing. But today,
We shall have naming of parts. Japonica
Glistens like coral in all of the neighbouring gardens,
And today we have naming of parts.
This is the lower sling swivel. And this
Is the upper sling swivel, whose use you will see,
When you are given your slings. And this is the piling swivel
Which in your case you have not got. The branches
Hold in the gardens their silent, eloquent gestures,
Which in our case we have not got.

I do not now remember that NCO's name but I have had a
Japonica in a garden of my own. The Vickers and Lewis guns
have gone the way of bows and arrows and given place to far
more fearsome weapons, but Reed's poem remains for me a
picture of the dedicated NCO to whom the service and its lethal
toys were life, but who was able to give humanity as well as
discipline and knowledge to those he instructed in the minor arts
of war.

The excitement of learning to fly at an RAF training school
was tempered by the placidity of the regime and a leisurely time
schedule. The exercises we did were carefully numbered and
standardised, and all we pupil pilots travelled along the same
path at roughly the same speed. There was fierce competition for
who would be first to achieve solo flight but the instructors, to
their credit, gave no encouragement to any such contest. They
were meticulous in their insistence that each lesson was covered
and mastered before proceeding to the next. All this was
sometimes tedious and frustrating for keen young learners but it
probably paid off. Everyone was tested by the Flight Commander
before their first solo and no instructor wanted to have a pupil
turned down through some oversight or failure in strict adherence
to the syllabus.

This test was something of an ordeal. Most of the instructors
were little older than their pupils and in my case a year or two
younger. They were experienced enough as pilots but they were
of our generation, had learnt to fly like us two or three years

earlier and, although we were awed by their manifest skills, we could hope to be of their fraternity before too long. But the Flight Commanders were a different breed. They were first world war pilots, mostly with an MC or a DFC. They had flown SE5s, Camels and Pups, and had learnt to fly on BE2Cs or RE8s without any real instruction. They had been in France in the days when the life of a pilot was on average not more than a month. They had lived through incredible nights of drinking and wenching with pretty French girls to come back at dawn to fly. We would have other experiences but we would never know the days of taking a pistol with you as a fighting weapon in the air: you just might have a lucky hit on an enemy, who was sometimes so close that you could see his face, while being careful not to shoot your own struts. Then if you did not have enough money to go out there was drinking and talking in the mess, but you did not look at the empty chairs, knowing yours might be the empty one tomorrow. You talked of girls and flying, the Hun and his machines and tactics, sometimes of the future, of the "world fit for heroes" which Lloyd George was promising.

Our Flight Commanders did not live in such a world, but it was better for them than for many of their contemporaries.

The first weeks at Sealand were enlivened by two events of considerable significance to the world of flying of which we now felt we were a small but enthusiastic part. The first happened on a Sunday morning when the aerodrome was deserted and a strange aeroplane of unusual shape circled the field and seemed to be signifying a wish to land. There was of course no radio communication available so I, as the junior pilot left in charge of the deserted flying area, shone a green light and fired green Verey cartridges to encourage the stranger who duly landed, taxied up to the hangars and switched off.

The aircraft was very different and far in advance of anything I had ever seen. It was a monoplane, rare in England then, it had a closed cockpit, streamlined wheels and a general air of modernity. Out of the cockpit staggered two men, grey with fatigue and anxiety, almost speechless but just able to mutter in broad American voices "Do you speak English?" and "Where the hell are we?" After I had reassured them on both counts they seemed to take heart and announced themselves as Harold Gatty and Wiley Post, Americans who had set out to fly round the world. Could we let them have what they called gasoline and a bit of a rest before they got going again?

Flying the Atlantic at that time, only three years after Lindbergh's flight from America to Paris, was still a considerable feat. The concept that these strangers, albeit they hadn't any idea where they were when they saw the aerodrome, had last seen dry land in America, almost a week away by the fastest boat, brought a new perspective into my ideas of flying. It also made me realise that Britain was not necessarily, as I had subconsciously assumed, in the forefront of aviation development and techniques.

Until then I had been preoccupied with the very limited aspects of flight which made up my own experience. The only aeroplanes I had seen at close range were doing the sort of things I had started to do, taking off and landing, manoeuvres in the air to test and improve skill in handling, how to deal with engine failure, that kind of thing. The notion of being in close touch with a transatlantic flight was for me something quite extraordinary, even more so to have taken a minor part in helping these two heroes on the fabulous trans-world journey which they went on to achieve.

The second event was less happy and came as a terrible blow to the RAF, to which I had already formed a loyalty, and a shattering reminder of the fragility of man's mastery of the air.

On the edges of the flying fraternity there had always been, and in fact still is, a small coterie placing faith in the future of the airship. The British had always been uneasy about German superiority in building these monsters and memories of the Zeppelin raids, which had brought a real degree of terror to London and a few other cities in what was then still "the war", were by no means dead. Now the Germans, freed in this area from the Versailles Treaty restrictions, had resuscitated their long experience in the field and had already forged ahead. The Hindenburg which was probably designed and at least part constructed long before the Versailles treaty restrictions were lifted, was operating on commercial routes. I could admire the skill and enterprise which had gone into building her, but at least some of the dislike and suspicion of Germany, which had lain dormant in me since the Peace Treaty, was stirred by jealousy of the success of the Hindenburg and a feeling that there was an element of defiance against rearmament prohibitions in her construction.

In face of what seemed then the undeniable possibility that the airship had a future in long-distance transport, the British were belatedly building two large airships, the R100 and the R101. The R101, slightly the more advanced of the two, had been entrusted to the RAF to test and operate in the first place. No one hoped more desperately than I that the she would prove a worthy rival to the German Hindenburg. Success in her maiden flight on the route to India, which it was planned that she should operate commercially, would prove that we were still in the race.

At the time there had been all too many rumours of doubts as to whether the trials and tests of the great airship had been sufficient or satisfactory. The number of RAF officers who believed in, or were concerned with, airships was very small, but nevertheless the R101 carried RAF markings and was operated by an RAF crew. The whole service felt that, willy-nilly, its reputation and prestige were staked on the R101.

As the scheduled date of departure approached, even such tyros as myself anxiously studied the reports of progress and I was not alone in heaving a great sigh of relief when I heard that the ship had left its moorings and set out on its pioneering voyage. Success would bring the prospect of untold benefits to the British Empire and to India in a spectacular improvement in communications between the sub-continent and Europe. Exaltation and pride were not stinted in the BBC's announcement that the enterprise had, in spite of less than favourable weather forecasts, started on schedule. There seemed every hope that the faith of the enthusiasts was to be rewarded.

It has only too often been the lot of my generation to hear of sudden and terrible disasters through the medium of radio or television. The crash of the R101, announced by the BBC in an emergency message only a couple of hours after the triumphant description of her departure, was the first of such sombre announcements that I remember to have heard on what was then called the wireless. It was certainly the first in which I, in common with every member of the RAF, felt a close personal interest. I have a vivid memory of the absolute gloom with which the broadcast was received in the Mess at Sealand. There was no discussion, no recrimination, no comment. Just shocked silence.

It transpired that the rumours and forebodings had been only too well justified. The wretched airship had only travelled a couple of hundred miles when, encountering a thunderstorm, it had failed to maintain enough height to clear a hill near Beauvais in France, a hill which was, in aeronautical terms, no more than a pimple. It was said and generally believed that the decision to go was taken by the Air Minister, Lord Thompson, entirely on his own responsibility. He had felt, apparently, that his reputation depended heavily on keeping to the planned date of departure since he had repeatedly given his personal assurance that the project was fully satisfactory and up to schedule. He had, consequently, been constrained to overrule technical and meteorological advice which had urged a postponement. He and his very experienced civil aviation chief, Sir Sefton Brancker, as well as most of the passengers and crew, died in a holocaust of blazing hydrogen when the great dirigible hit the hill and exploded. With them died any hopes Britain had of competing with Germany in airship construction and operation. In retrospect, this may in the long run have been just as well, but at the time the whole country, and particularly the RAF, felt it as a major disaster.

For me, and I suspect for many others, distress was sharpened by a sense of humiliation at the contrast between the total success of the German Hindenburg and the total failure of the R101.

I knew that Germany was in deep financial trouble and that there were five million unemployed there. In spite of such troubles she had achieved a definite, but still limited, place in Europe and the League of Nations. This I thought right, but I had no wish to see Germany lording it over Europe in any field, however minor. Without any real understanding of the politics of the time I had a gut feeling that the exaltation of Hindenburg as Head of State was not a good omen. For me he was an old style Junkers General, a friend of the exiled and discredited Kaiser and the epitome of the German military class. I thought the naming of the successful airship after him was nothing, more or less, than the Germany I had been brought up to loathe cocking a snook at the victors of Versailles.

I doubt if I knew the name of any other German politician. Certainly I have no recollection of any significance for me attaching to the news that in the German election of 1930 one hundred seats in the Reichstag had gone to a new party led by an Austrian named Adolf Hitler. It was the time of the heyday of the spirit of Locarno, when everyone guaranteed everyone else and Germany, almost totally disarmed, was of very secondary significance in the cosy world of collective security under the League of Nations.

I think it was the figure of the old General and his associations with the past as much as the success of the airship which bore his name that revived my suspicions and dislike of Germans. I had not the faintest premonition of war. I knew little of the League of Nations except that it had been set up by what I thought was universal approval to take care of all of that sort of thing. I loved travel and spent most of my summer leaves in France but never crossed the Rhine nor had the smallest desire to do so.

My interest in such matters, never great, vanished when, at last, we started flying.

For most people nowadays, to fly for the first time is to be huddled twelve abreast with three or four hundred others in a brightly lit compartment with small windows, bells to ring, people to talk to and a pretty hostess to bring you a drink which, if you are lucky, may be free. Even if you sit near a window you will have little impression of movement as you take off. The noise is no more than a train, the air you breathe is what you brought with you from the airport. Nevertheless, when you have walked up and down, been to the lavatory, had your drinks and lunch, fastened your seatbelt and felt a little bump as you land, you have flown. Flight is not a miracle any more, just a few hours shared with all those others in a huge hollow cigar smelling of plastic whose like is used by millions in every continent.

For us in 1930 that world was far away in the future. None of us visualised it and many of us would not see it, being already marked for sacrifice to the twin Moloch gods of war and aviation. At that time the huge majority of people even in such an advanced country as Britain had never flown or even seen an aeroplane at close quarters.

A first solo flight is, like first love, a unique experience for everyone who is fortunate to taste it and, as with first love, there is a huge psychological difference between the first experience and all the other times that follow.

No one who is not a pilot (and we are an infinitesimally small proportion of the world's inhabitants) can understand the daunting solitude of flying solo for the first time. You can be alone in a field or on a mountain or in a boat, but in each of these you are surrounded by an element, earth or water, which is familiar and will, in its way, support you. There is nowhere else the total separation from the material world that a pilot experiences when for the first time no contact or communication with another human being is even remotely possible.

If there is a radio link with the ground, as I expect is nearly always the case now, the cool measured voice of the operator or controller to some degree reinstates the umbilical cord. The pilot can ask questions, get answers, perhaps comfort. The modern aviator has many advantages, his speed is enormously greater, his engine more reliable, his instruments and navigation infinitely more accurate and trustworthy than in former times, but although his first solo will always be a memorable experience, he will never know the loneliness of the time when wheels leave the grnd and there is no one, but no one, to turn to: when no questions can be answered, no help given. You're on your own.

After elementary training and a month's leave, the course was divided into two halves for advanced training, half to fly Bristol Fighters, the others to go on to Siskins. The names were misleading since the "Bif", as it was known, was a two-seater relic of the 1914 war in which it had been a notable success, but it was now in no sense a fighter. Even by the standards of the day it was slow and clumsy but, in the interests of economy, it was retained in the service for general duties, training, army co-operation and light bombing. It was a graceful aeroplane, efficient in its time and much loved by all who flew it. The Armstrong Whitworth Siskin, already obsolescent, was the standard RAF single-seat fighter, with a dual control version which was used for our instruction.

I had been torn between a desire to become a "fighter boy" and fly the fastest machines in service, or to accept the less glamorous alternative in which you could be posted overseas. My application for the latter as being a way to see the world and get out of debt had no effect as, on return from leave, I found myself posted to the Siskin flight and therefore destined after qualifying, to serve in a fighter squadron. I accepted my fate happily enough. I was naturally bewitched by the romance which was still attached to the great names of the 1914 war: Bishop, McCudden, Richthofen, known and revered by every schoolboy, the true Knights in Shining Armour of that muddy and earthbound struggle.

The Siskin, in common with many of the RAF aircraft designed and used between the wars, was only a moderately successful type. It was by no means entirely without vice and was not really suitable for inexperienced pilots. It had quite a good rate of climb, reasonable endurance and good manoeuvrability, but it was not fast and had a way of playing tricks without warning if the speed was allowed to drop. Landing accidents were pretty common.

My contribution to this toll was two on the same day, one before lunch and one after. The first mishap occurred after the instructor who had carefully nudged me through half the course was suddenly posted away and I was having my first flight with his replacement. Whether my new mentor had an exaggerated idea of my capability or for what other reason I cannot now assess, but he and I performed the unusual feat of coming to grief together. In such case the responsibility for an accident is assigned to the instructor, irrespective of who was actually flying the aeroplane at the crucial time. The instructor's brief is that he may, in fact must, allow his pupil to make mistakes, but should take over control before the mistake can lead to trouble.

In our case he was testing me on the exercise called "Advanced Forced Landings". It was a rule, stemming from earlier times when engine failure was fairly common, that the pilot of a single-engined aeroplane had to keep an eye open below him for a field in which he was likely to be able to land if his engine failed. To exercise his pupil, an instructor after, or even during, another manoeuvre would suddenly throttle back the engine and say "Your engine has failed. Pick a field and make a landing". When my new instructor tried this out on me we were near the field in which instructors with their pupils were allowed to land. Seeing this field I went through the prescribed routine, and having done gliding turns to lose height, turned onto my final approach. Alas, I had less than adequate height to clear the hedge which guarded the field. To remedy this, I succumbed to the notorious temptation of trying to prolong the glide by lifting the nose and losing speed, with the result that we did just clear the hedge but stalled and settled in some fairly long grass with a broken undercarriage and propeller and a very sheepish look on two faces.

Although the bad flying which caused the crash was entirely mine, the instructor, as the pilot in charge, had to take the blame. When he realised, as he should have done and I did not, that we were not making it, he ought to have taken over control, put on the engine and told me I was a bloody fool. None of these things did he do. I never knew why, nor what kind of reprimand he got from his superiors but I expect it was quite severe. To his credit, he never took his humiliation, for such it must have been, out on me.

It was RAF policy that a pilot should fly again as soon as possible after an accident, so after lunch my new instructor took me up again. Giving me a check and practising various manoeuvres designed to maintain my confidence. After three-quarters of an hour or so, including several landings, I was told to go solo again. This I did and thoroughly enjoyed myself doing aerobatics, steep turns, spinning and several landings. When my time was up and I was due to come in, I suppose I was over confident after two or three good landings and I managed to make a mess of the final one. The Siskin finished up on its back, I hanging in my straps, fire engines screaming, petrol dripping. I had no excuse, it was sheer carelessness or lack of skill or both and I was desperately fearful that I might be suspended.

The Siskins we flew were notorious for doing this. It was said that this was because they were designed to carry a heavy wireless set immediately behind the cockpit and, since this was not needed in training aircraft, the weight lost by removing the bulky set was replaced by a smaller weight in the tail. If the tail started to flip upwards on a bad landing the weight in the tail produced a tendency to go on up and ultimately over so that you finished up on your back. I don't know if this was really true, but it certainly happened to me and a number of others.

I was astonished that after these two mistakes I was one of only about six of us who passed out with an assessment of "Above the Average", qualified by "Apt to be careless at times". How right.

3

Flying for Fun

The Peace Ballot

In the event I was posted to No. 41 (Fighter) Squadron at Northolt, a few miles west of London, so I forgot my passing desire for overseas adventure and resigned myself to the permanent overdraft which such a proximity to the bright lights would entail.

My life as a young officer pilot in a fighter squadron at the time was about as pleasant as I could wish. I was being paid and kept for the sole purpose of doing what for me was the most exciting thing in the world, flying a fast and highly manoeuvrable aeroplane.

Service life brought some small constrictions on freedom. You had to wear a uniform, appear punctually at certain times, obey sometimes tiresome orders given by authorities for whom your respect was by no means absolute. But these were minor discomforts, minor irritations, compared with the license to venture alone, almost at will, into the glorious freedom of the air. This freedom was and is common to all who taste the joy of flying, but to none, I think, has the joy been given in such full measure as to those who were lucky enough to fly the last of the open-cockpit fighters.

Humans have always rather enviously associated birds with the idea of freedom. "Free as a bird", we say. The quarrelling sparrows in a suburban garden cock a snook at the garden's owner. For all his prosperity he is tied there by his mortgage, his job, his children, while the birds chase one another pointlessly and light-heartedly over his flowerbeds and round his chimney pots, nibbling his lettuces and doing their droppings on his spotless patio. Their silly chirruping is the triumph of their freedom over his bondage to the 8.15.

Even more striking is the lordly, elegant freedom of the swallows and their ilk, curvetting high when the weather is fine, swooping low with alarming turns round trees and buildings when their insect prey is hugging the earth. Sparrows as well as men may envy the swallows their freedom to respond to the warning of the damp, cool autumn evenings which call them to the South where the days are still long and lazy and there are no frosts or snow.

Many poets, good and bad, have sung the message of the freedom enjoyed by the birds, but their verses have seldom probed the essence of this freedom which is surely contained in their unique ability to move without constraint in three dimensions. They can turn and wheel, climb and swoop with a natural ease which no earthbound creature, not the bounding antelope nor the silent, sinuous serpent, least of all the clumsy two-legged human, can begin to rival.

No. 41 Squadron was equipped with Armstrong Whitworth Siskins, the type I had trained on at Sealand, but there was no comparison between the tired old hacks of the Training School and the polished beauties of a front-line squadron. With real Vickers guns in the cockpit and a radio telephone set, which occasionally worked, all were resplendent in the squadron livery, a wide scarlet stripe along each side of the fuselage and across the upper wing. The Squadron crest, a red cross of Lorraine under the Roman figures XLI, was emblazoned on the tailplane. I little knew then what great significance that cross was to acquire through General de Gaulle selecting it as the symbol of Free France in the coming war, of which I had not the slightest inkling. I only knew that cross as the badge of the little town of St Omer in Normandy which had awarded the right to wear its crest to No. 41 Squadron who had used their aerodrome to fly against the Germans in the first world war.

On reporting to 41 Squadron I was told that an almost brand new Siskin, J8830, was to be virtually my own personal property. It would be maintained with care and pride by a ground crew assigned solely to my aircraft which would be flown only by myself and an NCO pilot. With the fitter and rigger I would discuss every quirk of her flying habits, every blip of the Armstrong Siddeley Jaguar engine. It was as if an impecunious hunting man were suddenly presented with the horse of his dreams after trailing the field for years on hireling hacks. The richest of civil flyers could not have procured even half an hour's flying in a machine with the horsepower, speed and aerobatic capability of that into which I could climb at will every morning after breakfast.

Twelve years had then passed since the Peace Treaty with Germany. Apart from some rather distasteful behaviour by Japan in the Far East, which for the average English person might just as well have been another planet, it is little exaggeration to say that the idea of war had disappeared from most people's minds. The League of Nations, heavily impregnated with the aura of peace, was believed to be perfectly capable of dealing with such minor disputes as might arise between its members. That Germany had been elected to be a member with a permanent seat on the Council as befitted a great power seemed to ensure that any further grievances arising from the Treaty of Versailles could and would be ironed out within the elaborate machinery of Geneva. In conformity with these beliefs, the British Government had instructed all its agencies that they were to operate on the absolute assumption that there would be no war for ten years, a timescale which, without any real rationale, was automatically renewed each year.

Mr Winston Churchill, Chancellor of the Exchequer until three years before, had been adamant that his colleagues at the service ministries applied this rule with the utmost rigidity to their estimates of the requirements of defence. In 1932 the Royal Air Force had for a number of years been operating on a very short financial leash indeed.

At the time I knew little of such matters and hardly even noticed the main effects, which were that we had no really up-to-date aircraft and that genuine training for war, as even the most remote possibility, hardly entered into the activities of a first-line fighter squadron. All I cared about was the marvellous feeling of this splendid machine responding to the controls, turning vertically, rolling on the axis, looping, spinning and flying inverted which even the birds could not do. It was perhaps not coincidence that many of this happy generation of fighters bore the names of birds: Gamecock, Grebe, Flycatcher, Siskin. The Flycatcher, a Fleet Air Arm fighter smaller than the Siskin but with the same powerful engine, was a great favourite with the public at the annual RAF display at Hendon. Six of them would fly in a closed circle above the aerodrome, each breaking off in turn to dive almost vertically and, engine roaring, drop a smoke bomb on a target marked out on the grass in the middle of the field. The public loved it, little knowing what terror that same manoeuvre was destined to bring to Spaniards, Poles, French and the bedraggled remains of our own army at Dunkirk when used in deadly earnest by the Luftwaffe.

There were no "bird" names for British fighters after the Siskin, and as the halcyon times faded in the face of events, that aircraft's successors, the last of the open-cockpit biplane fighters, had more vindictive titles: Bulldog, Fury, Demon, Gauntlet. But those who flew them still knew the wonder of flying with the rush of air on their cheeks, tugging at your goggles if you leant out, whistling louder than the engine if you throttled back. We did not know the thrills and misadventures of the pioneers, their engine failures and the dangers of living as they did, on the edge of the unknown. In comparative safety we reaped where they had sown and could do a thousand things they never dreamed of. The main thing for us was that it was all great FUN.

The training of pilots in the fighter squadron of those times was pretty much a Do-It-Yourself exercise. There was a little, a very little, desultory ground instruction in technicalities and a half-hearted commitment to minor administrative duties. But most young pilots were determined to fly as much and as often as they could and that keenness was really the beginning and end of their Air Force existence.

The Siskin was one of the first RAF fighters to be fitted as standard with a Radio Telephony set and many hours were spent testing and trying to get results out of this rudimentary equipment. There was no question then of any ground control of movements of aircraft which was just as well since our R/T sets spent much more time producing the oddest selections of whistles, catcalls and distorted intermittent buzzing than in conveying the human voice. We would try endlessly to "raise" our ground station from distances of ten or fifteen miles, and to have any sustained communication if you were twenty miles or more from the aerodrome was an event indeed. Landings and taking off in daylight were done entirely at the discretion and on the responsibility of the individual pilot, as were all his manoeuvres in the air.

I think this partly accounted for the almost obsessional belief that proper flying was done entirely by the feel of the controls and knowledge of the aeroplane and not by reference to the readings of instruments. The instruments of the time were simple but, although they were accurate enough, it was a matter of pride to use them as little as possible. You were expected to be able to maintain the best gliding and climbing speeds without so much as a glance at the airspeed indicator. Your turns should be correct, that is without sideslip or involuntary change of altitude, entirely by feel and by keeping the nose on the horizon. The rationale of this stemmed back partly to the patrols and dogfights of the first war, when the constant lookout for enemy aircraft could not be interrupted even for seconds by looking in the cockpit, and partly because our aircraft did not have very good all round vision and it was necessary to keep watch continuously against the danger of collision. The system made for elegant flying in reasonable visibility and was a safety factor in the low flying which was our only real way of coping with bad weather. It did, however, store up troubles for pilots, of whom I was one, who would later be confronted with the transition from slow biplanes where "feel" was natural, to faster monoplanes with different characteristics, and from flying by visual points of reference, the horizon, landmarks and lights, to the very different conditions of flying in war.

A considerable part of any time in the air left over from improving flying skill and wrestling with the R/T was spent in formation flying. There was a lot of boredom and frustration in our often unsuccessful efforts to make radio contact with the ground station, but at least that work had a small place in the development of radio communication which has played such an immense part in the progress of flying to its present standards, military and commercial. The hours spent in the perfection of formation flying had, by contrast, absolutely no practical value but were a source of never-ending pleasure. You started by joining up in the air with your leader, keeping a wingspan away for safety. When you had mastered the gentle adjustments of throttle and control movements necessary to stay in the same place relative to him, you gradually learnt to fly closer until your wingtip overlapped that of the leader with your cockpit just in front of his tailplane. In such tight formations we spent many happy hours of quite hard work because, although you might think that two exactly similar aeroplanes would tend to stay put in relation to one another, in fact there was a constant need for small adjustments. It was vitally necessary to keep position accurately if you were near an aerodrome occupied by another squadron. To permit a "married man's gap", an appreciable space between aircraft, was a stigma indeed.

As you became competent in this curious art, you progressed to the stage of taking off and landing in formation. As the grass aerodromes, although reasonably flat, were by no means billiard tables, these exercises could be somewhat hair-raising as you bumped along the ground trying to keep up with but not to overrun the leader. The Siskin had no wheelbrakes so control on the ground was less than absolute.

A good formation was regarded as the hallmark of a good squadron and many hours were spent in perfecting this elegant but utterly useless concept. The absolute stability which a good squadron formation could preserve, with an impeccably equal distance between each aeroplane and between each of the three flights, gave a totally unjustified impression that here was air power at its height. It was, in fact, simply display flying and bore no relation whatever to the function of fighters in a real war.

Soon after I joined No. 41 Squadron we were re-equipped with the new standard fighter which was supposed to bring British air defences up to date. In fact the Bristol Bulldog had little performance advantage over the Siskin. It was only marginally faster, had a better rate of climb and higher ceiling but was less manoeuvrable and had a wider turning circle. The later models were the first RAF fighters to have brakes, which was an enormous advantage, but the earlier mark, with which we were first equipped, had a disconcerting tendency to "dip" a wing when not travelling directly into the wind after landing and without brakes the tendency, once started, was difficult to check. The Bulldog never became one of those aircraft which have occupied a special place in the affections of the pilots.

"Birds and fools fly" went the RFC saying in the 1914 war, "but only fools fly by night". Now that flying at night in good or bad weather is regarded by pilots, passengers and controllers as no more hazardous or difficult than flying by day, it is odd to remember the time when night and day flying were seen as two quite separate arts. In the time when engine failure was always just round the corner the old saw wasn't all that far out, and although by the time I joined 41 Squadron night flying was an integral part of life, it was still unpopular and only carried out by quite experienced pilots. There was no dual instruction nor much theoretical study of the subject but fighter pilots had to be competent in the art. Within that directive most squadrons did as little as was reasonably possible and it was notorious that a good deal of that was carried out by moonlight when conditions differed very little from daylight.

Nearly all Squadron Commanders and a good many Flight Commanders were married men past their flying prime with little stomach for giving up their leisure to setting an example by exchanging their comfortable hearths for a draughty cockpit on a cold, dark night. Since the chances of seeing, let alone intercepting, another aircraft at night were virtually nil, the whole subject of night flying was regarded as a bore, interfering with free time and posing some extra risk to aeroplanes and pilots with little to show for it.

On grass aerodromes night flying was done from a flare path, an expression now forgotten except as the title of a Terence Rattigan play. The flare path consisted of a "T" with five large "Money" flares as the stem, the first two fifty yards apart and the rest at hundred yard intervals. Two more flares provided the cross for the "T". There was one other flare which marked the boundary of the field straight ahead and there were red lights on all hangars and high buildings or masts and a large red beacon which flashed the identification letters of the aerodrome in Morse Code.

A "Money" flare had a core of asbestos-based material soaked in paraffin which gave a flame two or three feet in height but only lit the ground for a yard or two around. The first rule which you had to assimilate was that there was no intent to light up the aerodrome. You were to take off and land by using the line of the flares and on no account to try to judge your height by looking for the ground. This was quite a hard lesson to take in, but you soon learnt the sense of it.

Part of the curious mystique which separated night from day flying was the convention which forbade the use of the engine in normal approaches and landings on the aerodrome by day. To be caught "rumbling", i.e. having to use the engine to reach the desired position on the field, was regarded as evidence of lack of skill and many have resulted in the accidents caused through a pilot's unwillingness to be caught in this harmless practice. At night, however, it was accepted that the method of approach and landing by the exact judgement of your glide was not practical. So the method recommended was, as is universal now, to use the engine to maintain control of speed and height and "feel" your way on to the ground. The glide path indicator had not been invented so you had to use the change of angle in the line of flares as the guide to your approach. This resulted in a "wheel" landing as opposed to the classical "three point" which all then aspired to by day. By night the inflexible rule against using your instruments as a primary guide to flying was by no means forgotten but it was slightly relaxed.

There was a modicum of control from the ground in that permission to take off and land had to be obtained. This was given or denied by the duty officer standing at the first flare who would flash the appropriate identification letter by red or green light. Our radio telephony was not reliable enough to be of the slightest use for such a function.

When you found yourself on the night flying detail for the first time the flare path would be laid out half an hour or so early and the tyro would taxi out in broad daylight and do a circuit and landing trying his best to use the "night" technique of watching the flares and not looking for the ground. As the light faded there would be a couple of "dusk" landings and then, when you taxied round for the next take off you would find, with a slightly sinking heart, that it was actually dark and you were night flying for real.

As soon as you had gained a reasonable height and settled down, there was no problem in ordinary flying. From Northolt, the ground to the East was a maze of lights and, after a few sorties, you got to know landmarks quite different from those you used by day, chiefly the few "arterial" roads lit up with the, then rare, fluorescent lighting, the dark blobs of the reservoirs near Staines and the red obstruction light on the Harrow gasometer. From any of these you got to know the approximate course to fly for home. There was no other form of navigation or knowing where you were. You soon became confident enough to do aerobatics, since on a good night, and it was only accidental if we flew on anything else, there is often a clearer horizon than there is by day.

The elementary navigation exercises we did at night entailed flying over what seemed to us quite a distance of unlit country where there was no possible check on your position. The shape of towns, as seen by their lights, was often very different from the way they appeared on the map and no other form of map reading was possible, nor did we have any navigational aids. The relief on seeing a welcoming beacon showing that you were near the aerodrome for which you were bound was considerable although in modern terms the distances we covered were insignificant, a hundred miles each way at most.

Flying was at this time the central thing in my life but that was not to say that there were not other interests; girls and sport, in particular cricket, golf and squash. I wasn't particularly virtuous and I managed to have plenty of "cakes and ale".

My elder brother and I had been great friends in adolescence and early manhood and now, on my posting to Northolt, our paths converged again. He had made a rich marriage and, being blessed with outstanding good looks and immense charm, he was already a well-known figure on racecourses and in the clubs and night spots of London which went merrily on their way, oblivious of the depression and of the dreadful unemployment figures.

In company with Jack, I pursued two parallel lines of gaiety, one based on his married life, the other harking back to bachelor days when he had been *persona grata* with the famous Mrs Meyrick and her pretty daughters at the 43 club in Gerrard Street. The place of the 43 in the hierarchy of London night spots had been taken by the Bag of Nails just up the road, usually called the Bag o' Nuts. This was run by "Milly", a splendid character who might have been the model for John Steinbeck's *Dora of the Bear Flag in Cannery Row*. She, too, had a very soft spot for Jack and would give him special treatment and endless credit.

Most night clubs in those days were faintly raffish because of the licensing laws which forbade the sale of drink after eleven o'clock. We often went to the Bag o' Nuts, raffish, to Murrays, on the borderline and in our more respectable moments to the Embassy, graced often by the Prince of Wales, or the Kitkat. I preferred the last which had marvellous cabarets with stars like dear huge Sophie Tucker ("nobody loves a fat girl but oh! how a fat girl can love") and a succession of American big bands: Paul Whiteman, Ted Lewis and the rest.

When we got in late, which was often, I would spend two or three hours in one of the Turkish baths in Jermyn Street and go back to Northolt on a train which got me there in time, with the help of a very efficient batman, to have a bath, get into uniform, have breakfast and be on parade at half-past eight with seconds to spare. Sometimes I would make my way back in the small hours in Jack's large two-seater Chrysler, an object of admiration and envy as it stood outside the mess among the assorted medley of less distinguished vehicles common amongst young Air Force officers. On those days I had to take Jack's car back to London which was apt to mean another night of the same.

I was naturally thrown much in the company of the "best friend" of Jack's wife, an outstandingly amusing and attractive girl, like me pretty well penniless, although she had rich and distinguished relations. Competitors for her favours included the heir to a rich and well-known peer, a famous and very amusing actor and a promising young politician who, before his marriage, had been a drinking companion of Winston Churchill and F.E. Smith. She and I often made a foursome with my brother and his wife, but she also seemed to enjoy the relatively cheap amusements which were all that I could offer when we were *à deux*.

In the South of France, where we went together for August, she and I stayed at a small hotel in Juan les Pins, then a village infested with mosquitoes. We alternated between drinking Pernod in cheap cafes and joining up with my brother and his party at the Carlton in Cannes and going in their motor boat for bathing picnics between the Isles des Lerins where the Mediterranean was still translucent and unpolluted. After lunch Jack and I would quite often do a "Mad Dogs and Englishmen" and play tennis in the heat of the day, when the courts behind the Carlton were always empty and available.

Most prolonged courtships have their ups and downs and mine was no exception. Although Joan's parents were unenthusiastic, they were not in a situation to exercise any dominant influence and we were duly married with the usual formalities at St. Paul's, Knightsbridge in the presence of our friends, relations and my brother officers. It was the excuse for Easter in Paris and many splendid parties.

By the spring of 1935 my new wife and I had been happily installed for nearly a year in our comfortable little suburban house not far from the aerodrome at Northolt. There was plenty of local fun and we could also frequent our old London haunts and friends. I had played a good deal of squash that winter and managed to be runner up to the RAF champion as well as playing in the Bath Club Cup competition and in the Amateur Championship.

Joan and I were so fully occupied with our own amusements that the affairs of the great world had relatively little impact on our easy and pleasant life. The confusion which followed each inconclusive election in the Weimar Republic affected us not at all. For us the Nazis were just another political party, perhaps somewhat suspect, but that was mostly because the word Socialist appeared in their full title. Like many Englishmen I had a sneaking feeling that some parts of the Treaty of Versailles were a bit vindictive and that the French, much as I enjoyed rollicking and cheap drinking in their country, didn't always play fair. An uncle of my wife's who was big in the City of London was known to approve of Hitler, as did the Prince of Wales and plenty of others. Who was I to question such opinions when I knew nothing of Germany except my own prejudices?

Although I never lost the anti-German bias which I had acquired as a small but fairly pugnacious boy, I was now inclined to distrust this gut feeling as being just an emotion left over from the past. With the Germans in the League of Nations it seemed time to suppress such irrational feelings.

We took the *The Times* although we read little of it except the cricket, racing and the book and theatre reviews. In spite of not being very news-conscious, some disquiet about events in Germany had been stirred in me by talk with a friend of my mother's. Returned from a visit to Cologne, she told us that things there were much improved, there was a confident feel in the air and visible signs of prosperity burgeoning. But undercurrents made her uneasy. She had been in Germany at the time of President Hindenburg's death. She believed the old General had been genuinely mourned and she was sure that many Germans would feel lost without the President who had been at least a symbol of the old virtues of integrity and legality.

Her German friends, who welcomed the new spirit of hope which Hitler had undoubtedly kindled, had been unwilling to discuss the unseemly speed with which the *Führer*, as Hitler was now called, had subsumed the powers of the President's office into his own. Without understanding the legal complexities, his action seemed to me to be strange and even a little sinister, but a prosperous Germany was surely in the interests of everyone and, if Hitler could produce it, maybe he had some elixir to which the rest of the world might well pay attention.

One winter evening early in 1935 I had been on night flying detail. It had been cold and uncomfortable at sixteen thousand feet with poor visibility and it was a relief to be finished and home for a drink and a snack by our cheerful drawing room fire. It was small and suburban but Joan had made it very comfortable and civilised. She didn't much like my flying and especially night flying, but we didn't talk about that and when we had settled down with our whisky she made an announcement.

"While you were out," she said, "I had a visitor. A man."

"Tut, tut," I said, "and who was this man?"

"I don't know exactly," she said. "I called him Mr Guppy."

I laughed. We had lately been amused at a drawing by "Phiz" in an old copy of Dickens' *Bleak House* which showed a pretentiously dressed young man being ushered by a powdered footman into the presence of Sir Leicester and Lady Dedlock. The picture was perfectly balanced between caricature and reality and the caption ran "The Young Man of the Name of Guppy". You could almost hear the contempt in the footman's voice as he announced the nervous but determined visitor.

"Why Mr Guppy?" I asked. "I hope you haven't got a terrible secret like Lady Dedlock?"

"Not really," said my wife. "He just was Mr Guppy in modern dress, if you can imagine that. Anyway, he brought these," and she handed me a bundle of papers.

The papers Mr Guppy had left were leaflets and voting forms for an enterprise which had already achieved some fame as the "Peace Ballot". Sponsored by the League of Nations Union, the idea of this was to find out and publicise the degree of support in the country for the objects of the League. At a time when there were no professional opinion polls this was a considerable undertaking since, if the results were to be at all convincing, they would have to be based on a very large number of completed ballot papers. In good English fashion the whole thing was done on a shoestring but, since the enterprise was strongly supported by the Labour and Liberal parties and by religious bodies, Peace Societies and Women's Organisations, most people in England were aware of the project.

After breakfast I asked my wife whether she had looked at the papers.

"Not really," she said. "I thought we might do it together as you don't have to go to work after night flying." And then added, "Only, of course, if you think we should do it?"

I suppose that our family backgrounds with naval and military traditions and my own situation as an RAF officer had made us both suspicious of the current of rather half-baked pacifism which was flowing so strongly in England at the time.

Our first instinct as we looked at Mr Guppy's literature was that this might be a trick designed to sap what was left in the country of patriotism and national pride. The armed services were not popular, money was short and every penny spent on defence was grudged. "Peace" organisations, headed by the Labour and Liberal parties, were doing all they could to reduce the size of the armed forces. We could hardly have been expected to greet Mr Guppy's offering with spontaneous enthusiasm.

Our first impression of the five questions which constituted the ballot was that they were designed to stir the emotions rather than to stimulate real thought about difficult issues. They were, in modern parlance, "loaded". It seemed to us that the intention was that you earned brownie points for each question to which you answered "Yes" but if you gave a flicker of a "No" to any of them, you would be ranging yourself on the side of what pacifist campaigners were dubbing as "warmongers". More than fifty years on I do not find that judgement to have been far out.

This kind of thing was somewhat foreign to our way of life which could only be described as basically frivolous. We took little thought for the morrow nor did we devote much time to considering high political matters. We went to "serious" plays, read "good" books, loved ballet and the theatre. We often discussed subjects far removed from flying or our sporting and social interests, but the keys to the political world were not, and never had been, in our pockets. With little or no contact with that world we did not feel constrained or competent to form hard judgements on all, or even any, of the burning issues reported daily in the newspapers and on the wireless.

Discarding our prejudices as best we could, we agreed that it would be interesting to see what our separate answers to the questions posed would turn out to be. Without discussion we would each write down our answers and then talk about them. It was rather like playing consequences.

The Questions were substantially these:

1. Should Britain remain a member of the League of Nations?
2. Do you favour an all-round reduction of armaments by international agreement?
3. Do you favour the abolition of naval and military aircraft by international agreement?
4. Do you believe the private manufacture of arms should be abolished?
5. Do you believe that if one nation attacks another, the other nations should combine to compel it to stop by (a) economic and non-military measures, and (b) if necessary by military measures?

We both answered "yes" to the first question. The League had been around as a fact of life since we were children. As we saw it, the world had decided after the 1914 war that through the League a repetition of that disaster could be avoided. It seemed reasonable that, given a forum agreeable to everyone, the nations could talk things out instead of fighting. That policy seemed to have been, in theory at least, established. It was unthinkable that Britain, the leading nation in world politics, should not continue to support the League.

"What about America?" asked Joan. "Why isn't she in the League?"

I didn't know the answer to that, but I did know that Japan had left the League in a huff and that Germany had lately renounced her newly won membership because the disarmament conference had failed. With three big powers outside, it was pretty clear that if Britain left, the League would be stone dead, and surely no one wanted that.

On the second question about reduction of armaments we both gave an affirmative reply, although I was doubtful about anything actually getting done. We agreed that the words "by international agreement" were important.

When we came to question three about the abolition of naval and military aircraft, Joan said she hadn't an answer. She didn't know what to think. I believed the suggestion to be impossible and I was sure the British Government would be unwilling to give up the use of aircraft as a relatively cheap option for control in India and the Middle East. "And anyway" I said, "Do you want to do me out of a job?" I remember Joan saying seriously that she would be much happier if I had another job anyway. I suppose I hadn't realised that she worried about my flying and we didn't pursue the subject.

On the fourth issue we both felt that it was "pie in the sky" but that a "yes" answer would do no harm. It was widely believed in England that the infamous Krupps firm was urging German rearmament and already making large sums thereby.

The fifth question was divided into two parts which were, in effect, two different questions, and here came the nub of the whole exercise. Neither of us had any idea of how relevant the problems stated in these questions were to be to ourselves, to Great Britain and to the League of Nations in the very near future, nor of how they were to dominate the world scene and our own lives.

No real discussion was needed to endorse the idea that the League should try to stop an aggressor by universal economic action. This we saw as the basis of the ideals which had prompted the formation of the League. The second part of the question, whether "other nations" should take military action against an aggressor was clearly much more debatable.

"If we say yes to that," said Joan, who was nobody's fool in such matters, "it would mean that you might have to go and fight, and possibly get killed fighting, for the League of Nations in some place which wasn't anything to do with England at all?"

I agreed that you might put it like that.

"Well?" she asked.

I replied to the effect that the answer must be "yes" although on the face of it that clause wasn't likely to be invoked. It seemed clear that no nation, except perhaps the United States, could survive, let alone continue a war, for more than a few months if all the countries of the world stopped all trade with it. At that time most people thought that "sanctions" really meant the stoppage by all nations of all trade, all dealings of any sort, with the delinquent. No nation could live with that.

So, I suggested, there should in practice be no need for military action, but if the threat were not available there would be backsliding. If economic action was to work I thought it would be necessary to have the real possibility of military action in the background.

"So we should say yes to both questions?" asked Joan.

"Provided we mean yes," I said.

"And do we?"

"I think we do," I said. "If we don't, we're back to square one. Business as usual means wars as usual and that's what the League was set up to stop."

In spite of what now seems my naivety in these matters, I know I realised that in practice action by the League of Nations meant action by Britain, who was its undisputed leader. I believed that, as long as Britain made clear what she was prepared to do, other nations would follow. As for those outside the League, I didn't really understand why America wasn't in since the League had been President Wilson's brainchild, but I had faith that she was imbued with the same ideals and traditions as ourselves and would surely in emergency not thwart the League by supporting an evil-doer.

I knew little or nothing about Japan or her actions in Manchuria. I had a faintly friendly feeling for our first war allies and a groundless faith that they would never do anything really horrid. I could not lose my ingrained distrust and dislike of Germany, but it simply did not occur to me that our lately defeated foe, almost totally disarmed under the Versailles Treaty, could be a major military factor in a world where all talk was of disarmament and peace.

So Joan and I signed our ballot papers with a "Yes" reply to four out of five of the questions, and we did so in the full knowledge that we were recommending that I and my contemporaries should be involved in some kind of demonstration of armed force if the League of Nations was to function as the guardian of peace. Further, I accepted that Britain would have to lead the League of Nations in war against any nation which explicitly transgressed the principles of the League. I knew that I would be personally involved in any such war. I thought that if Great Britain made it clear that she would exert her very considerable economic strength against an aggressor and, in the last resort, commit her armed forces against him, there would be no war. We learnt in the following summer that the mildly idealistic and increasingly pacifist British public, had supported the "Peace" ballot in unexpectedly large numbers, presumably having thought along much the same lines as we had.

With hindsight this kind of thought may seem to have been little short of absurd. That is not to say that what we hoped and expected of the League of Nations was impossible. It is, however, to accept that the impediments were far greater than we realised and the determination to overcome them very much less.

I suppose I knew in the New Year of 1935 that there was uneasiness about affairs in Europe, but I think that, like many others, I had confidence that Britain was still "top nation" and would be able to see that the League sorted out any real troubles. It was hard to think very highly of our Government. Poor Ramsay Macdonald, still shakily Prime Minister, often came to Northolt. He would be flown in an open cockpit Fairey IIIF of the Communications Squadron to his homely cottage at

Lossiemouth where he could find for a day or two the peace denied him in his ramshackle political life. He cut an incongruous figure, old and frail, in his borrowed flying kit, goggles and helmet and, as one tucked him into the uncomfortable cockpit, it was clear that, fortunately, he had no idea of the hazards of his journey or how crude were the navigational aids on which his pilot relied. But although it was not difficult to respect the enterprise which made him choose this swift but uncomfortable mode of travel, the idea that our affairs were in the hands of this clearly decrepit old gentleman was far from reassuring.

The spring and summer of 1935 were halcyon times for us. There was cricket, squash, ballet and plays in London. We went to the Derby and backed the winner, and to a couple of days at Ascot where we backed some losers. We were often rather lucky at some illegal roulette parties conducted at various Kensington addresses by a certain Mr Edge who seemed to like us being there with his much richer clientele.

Having decided we could not afford our usual expedition to the South of France in August we were persuaded by some friends to take our car and meet them at a totally unknown seaside village on the Spanish Mediterranean coast where there would be empty beaches, lovely swimming, cheap wine and no one else there. I found the fare from somewhere and booked our small car on the Dover ferry to leave a couple of days after the end of the Air Exercises which were the culmination of the "training" season. These always took place at the end of July so that everyone could have leave in August.

That year the squadron operated in the exercises from a large field which subsequently became the aerodrome of Wyton but was then without any buildings or facilities. I was in charge of the advance party which pitched the tents and made the arrangements for the squadron to arrive a couple of days later. I necessarily had my car because I had to visit the local town to get supplies, arrange deliveries, liaise with the Post Office about communications and do a host of other duties for which I had to be mobile.

On the last day of the exercises, which had up to then been pretty futile, the squadron was ordered to the state of readiness which entailed nine aircraft standing on the aerodrome with engines stopped. When the order to take off came, all started up and the CO, who led the squadron from the centre of the leading flight, opened his throttle for take off, everyone else following in tight formation. I was flying as No. 2, on the right of the leader. Just as his wheels were leaving the ground, and mine, just behind, were doing the same, his machine lost speed and failed to rise. The rest of the squadron continued to climb and completed the exercise, flying all the while in tight formation. It was hardly surprising that, after an hour or so of patrolling, we returned to base having seen nothing of the "enemy" in spite of beautiful weather and almost unlimited visibility.

When I taxied in my ground crew, running out to meet me, seemed inordinately amused. I was glad to see them laugh because it meant that the Squadron Leader, who was an immensely likeable character, had not been hurt in the crash which must have followed his engine failure on take-off.

Levering myself out of the cockpit I asked what the hell the great joke was. They pointed to the far side of the field where our tents were pitched, well dispersed in mock war conditions. There, close by a tent, was the tail of an aircraft pointing skywards. It had obviously been unable to stop, had hit some obstruction with the undercarriage and finished up with its nose in the ground. The Rolls Royce engine of the Demon was well above the level of the pilot and if the aircraft were suddenly stopped the nose, with the heavy engine, naturally tended to drop very sharply. This was clearly what had happened. What I did not know, although the ground crew did, was that the obstruction which had stopped the aircraft was my poor little car, which had been crushed out of all recognition by something like a ton of metal descending on it at speed. I had to smile because it was done with such complete and grotesque accuracy that the big engine had gone straight through the roof. There was no recognisable car to be seen.

My first thought, after I had made sure that the Squadron Leader was not hurt, was that the insurance might not pay up quickly since the responsible party was the Government who could be trusted to obstruct any action for months rather than weeks. Telephoning from the single line on the camp wasn't easy and I had plenty to do in getting the squadron packed up for the return to Northolt. I saw no alternative to kissing goodbye to our reservation on the cross channel ferry in three days time and, instead of sunning ourselves on a beach in Spain, spending our leave at home arguing with the insurance and His Majesty's Government in an effort to retrieve something from the wrecking of my car. There could hardly have been a more depressing prospect.

However, after a single telephone call to the insurance brokers I took their advice to "leave it to us", and found myself in three days time with a brand new car, licensed and insured, with continental papers and the same ferry reservation I had made for the old one. We left for Spain on the day we had intended. That was in 1935.

In Spain, which was then undergoing an experiment in left wing "democracy", we were light-hearted tourists without a smattering of the language, but even so we had been conscious of an underlying sense of unease. When we got back to England, however, we soon realised that the international atmosphere had radically changed. It was as if Europe had been a pot quietly heating up on a slow fire, and now the first signs of boiling were showing.

The build-up of Italian troops on the borders of Abyssinia (now called Ethiopia) had become too great to be ignored, although in England this was mostly dismissed as a storm in a teacup. The argument ran that if a sophisticated European power with an ambitious government wanted to join the ranks of those nations who, with Britain in the lead, had carved up Africa in the nineteenth century, who were we to say that was a crime? The Italian talent for civilising would soon outstrip, for instance, the efforts of the impoverished Portuguese who "owned" large chunks of Africa. Abyssinia, from being the most backward of

African territories, might become one of the more advanced. It could be seen as being to the advantage of everyone that Italy should go ahead and haul the Abyssinians into the twentieth century. Some kind of fudge could surely be arranged to quieten down the talking shop at Geneva.

This, I could see, was one side of the coin. Soon enough I began to see the other. Like it or not, Abyssinia was a full member of the League of Nations and had asked that body for arbitration which Italy had refused. It was irrelevant that Italy had sponsored Abyssinian membership of the League while Britain had opposed it on the ground that the country was too backward to warrant a place. What was only too apparent was that a member of the League had deliberately and openly deployed strong modern forces in such a way as to indicate willingness to go to war against another member in order to achieve the domination of her victim. Abyssinia had asked for arbitration, soon she would ask for protection. And then what? The League's principle was that its members would "stop" an aggressor by economic measures and, "if necessary" by military.

It still seemed to me that, if the determination of the League's members was made clear, and that meant in the first place Britain's determination, not even the strongest country could or would defy the world. And Italy was by no means the strongest country. But what of Britain's determination? In the tranquil, peace-loving Britain of 1935 there was no widespread detestation of the dictators. The Prince of Wales and Winston Churchill were said to admire them and my wife's uncle, a director of the Bank of England, was a friend of Ribbentrop, Hitler's ambassador in London. I think I suspected that continental peoples were not very good at democracy anyway. It had never taken root east of the Rhine except perhaps in Czechoslovakia. Many in England believed that if the queer Continentals preferred their affairs to be run by dictators, that was their business. It was common to say that we had more affinity with the Germans than with the French and Mussolini had made the trains run on time so he couldn't be so bad. All the nonsense about Abyssinia and strutting about in black breeches and high boots was a bit of a joke. England could sleep in peace. But I didn't like the bit about affinity with the Germans. I had schooled myself not to hate them any more but that hadn't made me like them one bit.

I thought of our signatures on the Peace Ballot form less than a year before when Joan and I had both stated that we supported the League and its policies. Something like a quarter of all British people had signed ballot forms and an overwhelming proportion, like us, had voted in support of the League. To have got this number of signatures was a huge achievement by the promoters of the ballot, but even more extraordinary was the solidity of public opinion. It now seemed possible that the resolve of the signatories, and particularly that of the British Government which, in democratic theory was supposed to give effect to the wishes of the British people, might be tested in earnest.

Back in England at the beginning of September after what had been a dream of a holiday in the Spain of 1935 we had little time to cogitate on these matters. We had hardly settled down in our little house before the order came that No. 41 Squadron, in company with most of the other fighter squadrons, were to crate their aircraft and all available personnel were to be kitted and prepared to go overseas forthwith. Those not available for health or other reasons would be replaced and the squadron brought up to full wartime strength.

The many private and duty arrangements I had to make more than occupied my time for a pretty frenzied fortnight. One of our flight commanders was not available to go so I, as the senior Flying Officer, had to take over his Flight. There was a plethora of tasks, many small but all apparently essential. The kitting of airmen and checking of records, the packing of documents, instruction books and papers, the decision to abandon our little house and put the furniture in store, my wife being unwilling to live there alone, trying to find time to see friends and relations, all consumed the precious days, hours and even minutes. Service people were supposed to be prepared for this sort of upset but we certainly weren't. Joan and I realised that this was no ordinary watershed in our lives, and that things for us would never get back to the stable and easy-going existence we had known for the first eighteen months of our married life.

Italy's preparations were proceeding apace and the international situation deteriorated by the day. The squadron's departure date was advanced and we heard that the Home Fleet was reinforcing Gibraltar. There was no mention of any other nation making any move and it seemed that Britain alone was putting pressure on the Italians in the name of the League of Nations. The growlings of the Italian dictator, Mussolini, proclaiming the injustices and indignities perpetrated on helpless Italians by the brutal Abyssinians, grew louder and his threats to make war on anyone who tried to thwart him more persistent. The Abyssinian representative at Geneva implored the League to help, arbitrate, inspect, anything. Talking continued. An added complication was that Joan had never really driven a car and in what very little spare time we had I had to teach her. She managed, but it was a bit wobbly.

On departure day we still did not know our destination but, as we had tropical kit, it was clearly somewhere in the Mediterranean or Middle East. In company with another recently married officer and at the urgent wishes of our wives, we made a pact that, as soon as we knew our destination, the two girls would take the first boat and join us.

We were to leave by special train in the early afternoon and the officers of the Station Headquarters at Northolt and of No. 24 Communications Squadron gave a farewell luncheon party for No. 41 Squadron officers and their wives in the Northolt Mess. For many of us it was a sad occasion. Joan and I were being separated for the first time since our marriage, and a good deal of the mess champagne was consumed. Somehow we managed to join the squadron on the parade ground, standing unsteadily at ease while the Station Commander, Wing Commander Keith Park, later a famous Group Commander in the Battle of Britain, wished us farewell. Then we marched, if our unsteady progress could be called that, to the railway station a mile away. The band played the Royal Air Force March and the troops joined in with the irreverent version:

We-ee-ee are Fred Karno's Air Force,
No – o bloody use are we-ee . . .

The girls came behind in cars and joined us on the platform where, with stiff upper lips, we took our leave. It was a curious departure, not dramatic like going to a proper war, but disturbing because of the uncertainty. Most of the girls cried a little and the drink soon died out of us as the train drew off round a bend and the platform was lost to sight.

The train had stopped so often during the night that it took me a little time to realise that a halt just after dawn might be the final one. Pulling up a blind, I recognised the familiar shape of the Liver building towering over the turgid stream of Mersey. The train puffed and blowed and shunted along gloomy nineteenth-century dockside tracks until we finally came to rest, and the order to de-train and fall in by flights was given by the squadron Warrant Officer, immaculate as ever, marching along the quay below the train.

The *SS Cameronia* of the Anchor Line was waiting alongside with steam up. She was an Atlantic liner, not comparable to the great Cunarders or the *île de France*, but she was a fine ship. Built at Greenock, she had been designed for, and had always been used on, the northerly transatlantic run from Glasgow or Liverpool to and from Quebec. In normal service she gave a standard of considerable comfort for first class passengers and had adequate accommodation for a large number of third class and emigrant traffic. Because of the urgency with which the Government had chartered her, there had been no time to make any modifications to fit her for the job she was now to undertake as a trooper.

The quayside, with its greasy uneven cobbles, criss-crossed by railway lines, was not the ideal place to parade. After the night in the train, officers and troops alike were somewhat more bedraggled than at our departure from Northolt, even if everyone was a good deal more sober. For many of us, certainly for me, that sobriety was increased by the confrontation with reality imposed by the great black side of the ship which towered above us while we waited for the order to embark. All the bustle and business of packing up and preparation, the sadness of being pushed unceremoniously out of our first happy little house, the endless detail of what was to go where and who was to do what, had conspired to obscure what was, in this moment of waiting, suddenly apparent. I did not yet know exactly where the *Cameronia* would be taking us, but clearly it would be somewhere close enough to the Italian armed forces to mix with them should the League of Nations require it. War, and the implications of war to front-line units of the Royal Air Force, became all too real.

For some reason the despatch of a very large proportion of Britain's small Air Force towards the possible zone of operations against Mussolini's adventure in Abyssinia was not, and I think has never been, publicised. Mr Anthony Eden, a popular figure both in England and at the League of Nations Headquarters in Geneva where he had Governmental responsibility under Sir Samuel Hoare, had spent much of the summer rallying British and international opinion in favour of the exercise of "sanctions" against an aggressor who violated his undertakings under the League's Covenant. In September the British Foreign Secretary, not normally the most inspiring of figures, had made a speech of considerable passion at Geneva, pledging that Britain, the acknowledged leader of the League's many nations, would stand by her commitments to the full. That meant economic action against an aggressor, backed up if necessary by military measures. It was what the Peace Ballot had envisaged and it fulfilled the highest hopes of those who supported the League and the notion of Collective Security. British warships had been despatched to the Mediterranean and we were parading in the drizzle on the quay at Birkenhead, our aircraft already on the way to an unknown destination.

Now that few of us travel by sea, most people have not known the curious excitement generated by a great ship tied up at the quayside, engines running, dirty liquids gushing from various pipes, some noise and vibration from below, plenty of activity on her decks, gangways in position. I have never been, nor wanted to be, a seafaring man but I can understand that a ship can have a near human personality. When she is straining to leave her unnatural captivity in harbour, tugs fussing around ready to ease her way seawards, there is something about her akin to a live thing with desires and impulses in contact with those who sail in her.

As the *Cameronia* passed the coast of Cornwall, she was met by a pinnace which was presumably bringing orders and Intelligence about our mission. We were told the boat would take letters for home and since, in spite of the secrecy and drawn blinds of our departure, there were apparently now no security inhibitions I was able to write to Joan that our destination was Aden. That seemed, as far as I could tell, a not particularly dangerous location, so I suggested in my letter that she book a ticket by the next mailboat to Aden of which I knew nothing except that school geography had described it as a coaling station for the then coal-fired ships of the Royal Navy and the huge British merchant marine.

The *Cameronia's* first stop was at Gibraltar where we arrived at night, refuelled and left without setting foot on shore. It was then that I began to lose the curious sense of unreality which had lain over me ever since the order that the squadron was to go overseas. All through the time of preparation, of packing up our little house, of acquiring tropical kit, of hectic farewell parties and the nightmarish train journey to Birkenhead, I had had a dreamlike feeling that it wasn't really happening to me but that I was watching it all happen to someone else. In the great harbour under the dim shadow of the rock you were conscious, even in the dark, of the reinforcement of British power, with the blacked out shapes of battle cruisers, battleships, aircraft carriers and destroyers all with steam up. What had seemed a flight of imagination suddenly became reality. We, the British forces with those magnificent toys we had been given to play with in peacetime, were not playboys any more. We had become pieces on the international chessboard, units of pressure, to be moved, deployed, perhaps ordered to fight, our lives at the disposal of players who did not know that we, as individuals, existed. It was still dark when we slipped out of Gibraltar and set course into the first faint signs of dawn.

At Malta, where two squadrons equipped with Bulldogs disembarked, the *Cameronia* stayed longer, although no one was allowed ashore except those disembarking who included a few, very few, anti-aircraft artillerymen.

Between them these small forces were to provide the defence of the island against possible attack. I had been to Malta before and expected to see the usual formidable array of the Mediterranean Fleet, spick-and-span in the sunshine against the warm brown stone of the walls of the immense harbour, one of the more splendid sights of Britain's imperial glory. Now there was not a single warship to be seen; not a white ensign flew.

As the lighters bore our comrades to the shore, the *Cameronia* wasted not a minute in making for the open sea, and it was impossible not to feel that the tension on board was noticeably greater. The empty harbour and the all-too-small contingent we had left there reminded everyone that the island was only a hundred miles from Italian territory where large numbers of men, aircraft and ships were available, and, according to Mussolini's fiery speeches, only too ready to fight to the death against anyone who dared to thwart the ambitions of their beloved *Duce*. It was an extraordinary reversal that the great British Empire was likely to find it impossible to defend its main base in the Mediterranean, an area where British sea power had been supreme since the days of Nelson. But who, knowing what happened a few years later at Pearl Harbour, would say that their Lordships of the Admiralty were wrong in deciding to evacuate?

The airmen of my Flight were accommodated with hundreds of others in the cabins designed for emigrants and third class passengers. By service standards they were by no means uncomfortable; certainly, as the "old sweats' never tired of telling them, they were far better off than they would have been in one of the ancient and overcrowded RAF troopers. A general feeling of cheerfulness and adventure pervaded these quarters, fostered by the senior NCOs, most of whom had done tours abroad before. They took great pleasure in telling the first-timers how lucky they were to be travelling in accommodation designed, they untruthfully said, for the Vanderbilts and the Prince of Wales and such.

In the Officers' quarters, which comprised the whole of the accommodation used by the first class transatlantic passengers, I found many friends and acquaintances from other squadrons. It was soon apparent that virtually the whole strength of Fighting Area, the rather odd name then applied to the fighter element of the Air Defence of Great Britain, was collected on board the *Cameronia*. The only exceptions were the three short range "interceptor" squadrons equipped with the new "Hawker Fury", a beautiful, fast and very manoeuvrable aeroplane but totally useless operationally because of its very short range. Three or four other fighter squadrons had given up their equipment and personnel to bring those on the *Cameronia* up to full strength. With the German Luftwaffe growing steadily more significant, the Air Staff must have had some uneasy moments as virtually their whole effective fighter strength sailed away to foreign parts.

If the evacuation of Malta by the Navy had shaken my faith in British control of the Mediterranean, a good deal of my confidence revived as we reached the crucial area to the east. At Alexandria, where we disembarked two more squadrons, it was not possible from our berth in the outer harbour to assess the full naval strength assembled there. But within our view there were battleships, an aircraft carrier, cruisers and destroyers and the busy traffic of boats and pinnaces was enough to suggest that a really formidable force was in readiness.

Even more impressive and reassuring was the experience, as the *Cameronia* made for the Suez Canal, of passing within a few hundred yards of the sixteen-inch guns of the British battleship *Queen Elizabeth*, enormous, graceful and menacing as she lay at anchor outside the entrance to Port Said harbour. Every Italian trooper and freighter passing through the Suez canal en route for the build-up of forces at the port of Massawa in the Italian colony of Eritrea which effectively separated Abyssinia from the Red Sea, had to pass under the guns of the QE, as she was universally known. She was the current guardship, reminding all who passed that British sea power would be at the disposal of the League of Nations should it decide to frustrate the Italian intent to colonise Abyssinia.

That such a warning should be totally disregarded by Mussolini seemed to me at the time to verge on madness. Admittedly there was a convention, to which Britain subscribed, which laid down that the Suez Canal was open to all vessels of all nations in peace or war, but that there was nothing to prevent a nation or alliance from intercepting ships approaching the bottleneck of the entrance or from pouncing on any who emerged from the Canal at Suez. This was my first introduction to large-scale strategy in practice; but to me it was clear that the greater the store of the huge variety of necessaries for modern war that the Italians might have assembled for the quarter of a million men supposed to be ready on the Abyssinian border, the greater was the hostage given to fortune. The plight of this large body of men, if their lifeline through the Canal were cut, would be grim indeed. And grim indeed, I thought, would be the retribution which would fall on the maniac who, in his search for glory, had put them there. Would he have had second thoughts, I wondered, if he himself had passed under the guns of *HMS Queen Elizabeth*?

It happened that the ship immediately preceding us in the passage of the Canal was an Italian trooper of about our own size, and she was anchored in the Great Bitter Lake awaiting her turn to enter the southern section of the Canal when we emerged from the northern end. We anchored alongside and very close to her, and it soon became obvious that something was afoot on board the Italian ship. As we watched, what I took to be the complete complement of uniformed soldiers aboard were seen to be massing on deck, facing us across less than a hundred yards of water. It seemed unbelievable that so many men could have been crammed into a ship of her size, but more and more appeared, packed shoulder to shoulder, until the vessel took on an appreciable list in our direction. Meanwhile our own troops, scenting fun, had assembled in some force on the foredeck and many of our officers were also watching to see what was going to transpire.

We soon knew. At a prearranged signal a thousand or more clear Italian voices broke into the not uninspiring strains of the Fascist anthem, well-known as a dance tune in England. We listened enthralled to a second rendering, even better orchestrated, impeccably tuneful as it wafted over the still water of the lake. I reflected that there was really no suitable British riposte. To have launched into *Rule Britannia* would have seemed to be overreacting towards a nation which we in no way regarded as our equal. However they hadn't finished. The last strains of the anthem were just dying away across the water when every arm of the crowd massed so tightly on deck was simultaneously raised in the threatening Fascist-salute, accompanied by co-ordinated cries of "DUCE, DUCE, DUCE, DUCE", shouted with such fervour that the whole ship seemed to rock in time with the staccato yells.

This, of course, was too much for the troops on our foredeck who had the answer in a trice. They burst into shouts of laughter and cheers and then followed up with an answering chorus of "DOOCHAY, DOOCHAY, DOOCHAY, DOOCHAY" and more cheers and roars of laughter. For the first moment or two I suspect that some of the Italians thought they were getting some unofficial British support for their leader and their enterprise, but after a time the roars of laughter and intermittent yells of mirth and cheering from the *Cameronia* produced a bewildered and uneasy silence on the Italian side which lasted until their ship weighed anchor and resumed her voyage.

4

Flying for the League

Mussolini Against the World

Much as the comfort, even near-luxury, of the *Cameronia* had been appreciated in the relative cool of the Mediterranean, going through the canal and the Red Sea we were reminded that the ship was fully equipped to protect her passengers from the arctic gales of the Northern Atlantic but totally unready to cope with 100 degrees Fahrenheit in the Middle East. She had not a single fan and, since the wind blew from dead astern at the exact speed of the ship, there was not a breath of movement in the torrid, humid air we lived in. The lower decks were a furnace and most of the troops got what sleep they could on deck.

After two squadrons had disembarked at Port Sudan on the Red Sea, only ourselves and a light bomber squadron, No. 12, remained on board. The heat got steadily worse until we were clear of the Red Sea and turned eastward along the Arabian coast. The ship's Officers, who at first had been inclined to compare the drinking habits of young RAF Officers somewhat unfavourably with those of their normal complement of first class transatlantic passengers, had in the end entered into the spirit of our enterprise and, on the night before we reached our destination, they gave us a most splendid dinner. Their cuisine on its mettle was excellent and needless to say we stretched the contents of the ship's wine cellar to the limit.

I think the ship's officers had come to share with most of us a certain pride in being a part of what then seemed likely to be a uniquely historic enterprise. That feeling had undoubtedly been stimulated by the British Foreign Secretary's speech to the League of Nations which one of the rather unsteady after dinner speakers quoted. The gist of his declaration had appeared on all the ship's notice boards and had certainly played a part in provoking an unexpected camaraderie between two very different sets of people. The feelings that prompted the toasts we drank and the songs we sang on the night before disembarkation sprang from a deeper root than the alcohol we consumed or the high spirits natural to the end of a voyage.

Sir Samuel Hoare's words still evoke for me the ghost of the enthusiasm which I and many others felt in the short-lived euphoria of the few days when it seemed that Britain intended to lead the world into a new and permanent regime of peace through collective security. Here is a part of what he said:

> The ideas enshrined in the Covenant and in particular the aspiration to establish the rule of law in international affairs have become part of our national conscience. It is to the principles of the League and not to any particular manifestation that the British nation has demonstrated its adherence. In conformity with its precise and explicit obligations the League stands, and my country stands with it, for steady and collective resistance to all acts of unprovoked aggression.

This resolve was only too soon to be tested by a reality far removed from the comfortable ante-rooms of Geneva. The Italian dictator's immediate reaction had been one of brassy defiance, promising war against any nation which stood in his path. This was very soon followed by the order for general mobilisation in Italy.

When we disembarked at Aden, nursing our hangovers as best we could, it was still not at all clear what the outcome would be. Many of our number couldn't have cared less as they writhed and strained in their first experience of "Gyppy Tummy", that fearsome form of diarrhoea which attacks the Westerner when first exposed to Near-Eastern habits, water, food and weather. I was lucky enough to be immune but, when most of us had recovered and our aircraft had been uncrated and assembled and were ready to fly, it did seem to me that some kind of war was not very far away.

The squadron had an immediate setback in that, within days of the first flights we made from the sand aerodrome at Khormaksar, just outside Aden, the tail units of our Hawker Demons, designed for use in England, totally failed to cope with the high humidity and salt content of the local atmosphere and rapidly became dangerously corroded. The whole squadron was grounded. Serious as this was, one could not help surreptitiously smiling that the considerable efficiency with which the whole operation of our move had been conducted was, temporarily at least, frustrated by this one small lack of foresight. Luckily, whatever was needed to remedy the fault was soon available and we were flying again within a few days.

More serious for me was that I had a cable from Joan which showed that she had left England in a P&O mailboat which was already well into the Mediterranean. The whole of that sea was likely to be infested by the considerable Italian submarine fleet ready to pounce on British merchantmen if it came to war.

The enterprise of bringing her to Aden which had seemed such a gay and splendid way of outwitting fate, now began to look more like a rather hare-brained scheme exposing her to considerable and unnecessary risk. I began to think I ought to have modified our plan to allow for a sudden deterioration in the situation such as had occurred in the three weeks since I had left England. Too late now.

I wondered whether England was, as was historically usual, going into a war without proper understanding of what it meant. Particularly whether we were again underrating the submarine. I thought of the three old cruisers patrolling outside Emden without a destroyer escort. And the *QE* lying at anchor outside Port Said with no apparent protection from underwater attack. And, for that matter, our unarmed merchant ship which had carried virtually the whole effective strength of trained British fighter pilots unescorted through what Mussolini often trumpeted as *"mare nostrum"*. Somebody would have had a pretty red face if we'd been torpedoed. I wasn't at all happy about Joan on the P&O mailboat and I felt it was my fault.

Serious as this was, however, it had its funny side since the RAF had just issued orders for the evacuation of all British service wives and children from Aden. They would be leaving at the precise time that my wife and her companion were due to arrive. The order to leave applied to "authorised" dependants, who were living in Aden in Government quarters and over whom, of course, the authorities had control. There was virtually no unofficial accommodation in Aden and nobody had thought of any "unauthorised" person being so stupid as to come at his or her own expense to stay in that very uncomfortable, hot, steamy and generally Godforsaken outpost of Empire. All I could do was to book a room at the somewhat primitive Crescent Hotel, the only one in Aden, and, with a certain amount of foreboding, await developments.

Confronted with the imminent possibility of war, I naturally began to give more serious thought to the situation into which I had been drawn. I was perfectly conscious that British pre-eminence in the world was not unstained with deeds quite comparable with what the Italians were planning. But those deeds had been done when force was the acknowledged currency of international affairs. Now, as the Foreign Secretary had made clear in his speech, the world was engaged in a monumental effort to turn that page in history. On the new *page blanche* would be written no more tales of battles and conquests with treaties imposed by the victors. Instead, disputes would be settled by legally binding decisions peacefully achieved by negotiation or arbitration, achieved in the calm atmosphere of Geneva, where disinterested nations would see fair play. If there now had to be one last battle to establish this new system, and if it was the luck of my generation to be involved in that battle, it would be worthwhile. Our sacrifice would have been far more effective, our fight far more the "good fight", than had been any fought for country, people or religion in the past. I was no moralist but I firmly believed at that time that what the League of Nations seemed to want to do was right, and I was fully aware that without Britain in the lead the League would do nothing. It was rather exciting to be at the cutting edge of an idea which would, if it succeeded, change the world's destiny as no idea, philosophy or religion had ever done before.

It is easy now to see that the interplay of conflicting forces, political, military and economic, was too complex to allow such a straightforward solution as was then envisaged by simple people like me. I suppose I was dimly aware of the power and activity of some of these forces. American oil interests might object to interference with their freedom to trade. France, torn between fear of Communism on the one hand and fear of Germany on the other, desperately hoped to retain Italy as an ally and was surreptitiously sabotaging all attempts to make the Covenant of the League work effectively against Italy. British Conservatives had been worried that the tide of pacifism and unwillingness to pay for rearmament might overwhelm them at an impending General Election. But yet, these seemed small obstacles compared with the prize to be won. British public opinion seemed to be wholeheartedly in favour of the League and all British political parties professed support for the Covenant as a main plank of their appeals to the electorate, Labour irrationally combining this with a commitment to further reductions in British forces already dangerously weak.

As to the dangers the League and its members were courting, on any rational estimate it seemed unlikely that Mussolini would risk a final confrontation with the League. He had given a terrifyingly vulnerable hostage to fortune in placing a quarter of a million men on the borders of Abyssinia, two thousand miles from their home base, without control of their lines of supply and against the hostility of the whole world.

The Italian fleet and Italian air power were, on paper, formidable but not formidable enough to control the Mediterranean as far as Port Said in the face of the combined British and French fleets. And even supposing some Italian supply ships reached and passed through the Suez Canal, there was no substantial Italian naval force in the Red Sea to protect them on the passage to Massawa. In theory at least, it would not only be the British and French who would thwart Italian designs, it would be three-quarters of the world, united behind the League of Nations. So awful did the risk to the Italian forces in Eritrea seem to me that the declaration of war came as a shock. Until then the steps to war had, in an era when so much talk and effort was for peace, seemed unreal, shadow-boxing. Mussolini, although he commanded some respect in English upper class circles, (he made the trains run on time), was something of a figure of fun with his posturing and bragging, his pretence that his legions were the heirs of Caesar's, his endless speeches and threats. The Italians had no great military reputation as a result of the 1914 war and, while their technical and engineering achievements were widely admired, it was simply not possible to see them as world conquerors.

But here was war as a fact. Italian forces were advancing into Abyssinia, the bombs were falling, the tanks were rolling, confident bulletins from the front competed for space in the newspapers with heroic proclamations from the Duce. At Geneva the talks continued and a first feeble set of unmeaningful sanctions against the aggressor was reluctantly agreed. Italian supply ships continued to sail in safety to the single base at Massawa.

I took part in the conference at which my squadron's war plan was disclosed and discussed in detail. It was a clear example, conforming to much British military history, of staffs in peacetime, dazzled by having blundered through to ultimate success in a previous war, being totally divorced from reality in the war they now faced. I suppose I had already known that this was likely from the extraordinary and quite unpractical plans for attacks on enemy formations which fighter squadrons had been supposed to practice. These had entailed flying in the clumsy squadron formation I have already described until fairly close to the "enemy" and then breaking up to attack in sequence and from different angles in the most complex manner which could not possibly be achieved against even the most feeble opposition. This was all good fun in exercises over Britain with a friendly "target" flying according to plan, but to imagine that such tactics had any relevance in the face of a real enemy, even an Italian enemy, was living in cloud-cuckoo-land indeed.

In our case, as it seemed unlikely that the Italians would spare bombers to attack the unpromising target of Aden when their primary task was to reduce the undefended territory of Abyssinia, our Staff Officers had had further thoughts about our employment. These were inspired by the unquenchable spirit of "the offensive". There was to be no defeatist, defensive strategy. So we, with our fairly short-range fighters, were to carry the war to the enemy and attack the Italians in their lair.

The trouble about this was that the only lair of any import, Massawa, the base and port in Eritrea on which the Italian campaign depended, was out of our operational range. Undaunted, the Staff fixed on the minor port of Assab in Italian Somaliland as a suitable target. Assab had a good natural harbour but virtually no facilities. Its communications with Abyssinia were abysmal, no more than tracks, and, not surprisingly, photographs showed that the Italians were not planning to mount any attack from this quarter since they had deployed no forces whatever in Assab. Nevertheless, it was assigned to No. 41 Squadron as our primary target.

For the fighters of the time, ground attack was a secondary role, in which the two first war Vickers guns firing directly forward through the propeller would be used. In our two seater Demons we also carried a single Lewis gun in the rear cockpit but the rate of fire from this archaic mechanism was so slow that the chances of it doing any damage except to one's own tailplane were remote in the extreme. With these weapons we could, as in the first war, attack troops on the march or aircraft on the ground but such targets had to be bunched up fairly close together for ground strafing to be at all effective.

As further weapons for this role we could, and would, for our monumental attack on the unsuspecting natives of Assab, carry a quota of eight small bombs, four on a rack on each wing. These were released by the pilot who aimed by diving his aircraft at the target. This method, so effectively used by the German Stukas in World War II, depended for real results on some form of air brake so that the aircraft could dive steeply and aim accurately without picking up uncontrollable speed, but this refinement had not been thought of in England. We had to start our attack too low and do too shallow a dive to get any real results. The real joke, however, was that the bombs we were to carry were designed for anti-personnel use in Europe, heavy cased so that when dropped on a road or tarmac they exploded as shrapnel, bits flying out in all directions. Dropped in soft sand most of the explosive effect and the metal bits would be absorbed by the sand. Assab was entirely sandy, there were no aircraft there nor any appreciable troop concentrations. I found it difficult to be enthusiastic about the contribution I was to make to the establishment of the principle of collective security and the punishment of an offender against the Covenant of the League of Nations.

At this stage the P&O mailboat *Malaga* arrived in Aden harbour. Most of the "authorised" service wives had already left for England, but a sprinkling who had preferred to make for friends or relations in India were embarking on the *Malaga* as my wife and another young RAF wife who had undertaken the trip with her appeared on the primitive quay at Steamer Point. I had some qualms about how the authorities would react but fortunately the Resident, the senior Indian Civil Service Officer responsible for the Aden Protectorate, and the Air Officer Commanding (later Lord Portal, leader of the RAF in the Second World War), both had enough sympathy with young love and enterprise to wink at our having outwitted official intentions. So I took a room at the Crescent Hotel, a hostelry whose lack of elementary comforts belied its rather elegant exterior. Its electric light was erratic and dim and the current was so feeble that it would not support a single fan. The only mitigation of the damp and oppressive heat was by a primitive sheet of fabric at ceiling height which, when the punkah wallah pulled a cord, flapped in a desultory way and faintly disturbed the thick and smelly atmosphere. The "boys" who were supposed to perform this duty all had a remarkable capacity for sleeping standing up and only actually operated when woken by one of the residents. This would galvanise them into giving two or three pulls before they reverted to their normal state of upright unconsciousness.

The bedrooms were furnished with two truckle beds and precious little else except a po, necessary since the lavatories were not particularly reliable and "Gyppy Tummy" was endemic among new arrivals. The food was curried chicken, eggs or dogfish for lunch and dogfish, eggs or chicken in curry sauce for supper. Breakfast, in a temperature approaching 100 degrees, was invariably fried leathery bacon with two of the local pigeon-sized eggs. However, we had not come to Aden to seek comfort or an easy life. My wife of eighteen months had, with immense enterprise and against quite a lot of opposition, come to be with me. I saw myself as a humble member of a crusade which would change the world. Her support was a huge reinforcement to my resolve and enthusiasm for our enterprise.

The meeting of the League of Nations to consider the Italian attack on Abyssinia was commendably prompt, as was its condemnation of the Italian aggression. At the same meeting the decision was made that members of the League should apply "sanctions" in conformity with their undertakings under the Covenant. Instead, however, of voting that member countries should put into force the draconian measures envisaged in the Covenant, which would have entailed the severance of almost all social, financial and commercial intercourse with the offender, a committee was appointed to decide "urgently" what goods, materials and services were to be denied. On the surface it may have appeared that by taking this route Italian military potential could be thwarted without undue hardship to the civilian population.

Alas, here lurked the canker which could and did destroy the whole enterprise into which Mr Anthony Eden, reinforced by millions of Peace Ballot signatures, was trying to lead his country and the world. There was to be a committee.

Inexperienced as I was in international affairs, my heart sank. There was to be a committee. No-one, not even such a tyro as myself, could be deceived by the inclusion of the word "urgently" in the resolution. Chalk and cheese, oil and water, Italian and Abyssinian, were not further apart than urgency and a committee. No. 41 Squadron's state of readiness for war was relaxed but not abandoned.

For those who genuinely sought to stop Mussolini there was hope in the newspaper reports that Italian progress into the hinterland was painfully slow and that the Abyssinian warriors, in spite of their primeval equipment, were putting up a stout resistance. The Italian Air Force ranged at will but its targets were scattered and air could not be a winning factor while the ground forces were held at bay. At our unhealthy, dispersed site in the desert, (our living quarters had been sited directly downwind of the town rubbish dump and the fly population was horrific), our guns were still loaded and our little bombs ready. We waited while the world waited for word from Geneva. The Italian troopers, supply ships and tankers continued to pass under the guns of the British guard ship anchored outside Port Said.

When the list of goods and services to be denied to the aggressor emerged from the committee at Geneva it was clear to the most amateur observer that the idea was to avoid a clash between Italy and the chief members of the League. Much of what was listed was material useful, some of it essential, to a country at war. But most of it was likely to have been stockpiled and, taking into account the inevitable leakages of clandestine supplies through devious channels, it was pretty certain that Mussolini would be able to present the world with a *fait accompli* of the conquest of Abyssinia long before these feeble sanctions began to bite. In my head ran the old saw:

> We do not fear the Hottentot,
> We have the Maxim Gun and he has not.

The Italians, with aircraft, big guns and mustard gas were not likely to fear the Abyssinians who had some ancient rifles and a large supply of spears.

If, and more likely when, the Italians had won their war it was highly improbable that the League's resolve to punish the victor would be any greater than had been its determination to prevent the war. One word alone was on the lips and in the hearts of everyone who still believed the League had the duty to take the steps laid down in its Covenant to prevent war – "Oil".

Even in 1935, war by advanced nations depended entirely on a plentiful supply of oil. Tanks, aircraft, troop-carrying vehicles ran on oil. Supplies of every kind had to be brought by lorries needing oil. If oil ran short an invasion force not only could not function, it might easily starve.

In practical terms, only by denying oil to Italy and her forces attacking Abyssinia could the League bring the affair to a head and the Italians to a halt. It was said that Russia and Rumania, both members of the League and main suppliers of oil to Italy, had agreed to withhold shipments "if everyone else did". There would be complications. Supplies to Germany and to Switzerland, who felt that sanctions threatened her cherished neutrality, would have to be rationed. The attitude of the United States, then the world's largest oil exporter and a non-member of the League, would have to stiffen from the somewhat equivocal policy of "benevolence" which she had declared towards the project of stopping Italy's aggression.

The ramifications of the oil trade, largely in American hands, were then, as now, complicated beyond the comprehension of outsiders, but being so close to the scene of action fostered a possibly over simplified clarity of vision.

It seemed to me not at all impossible that if the British and French insisted that the League included oil in its list of denials, and the British and French Navies moved to implement that decision by preventing oil tankers from reaching Massawa, the Italian dictator would be faced with the choice of either making good his boasts that he would fight anyone who stood in his way or of giving in to the League's demand that he withdraw.

There would be leakages and evasions of stepped-up sanctions. There would be hard cases: Antonio's who had put their all at risk in ventures to Italy, to whom the League of Nations would seem not as the saviour of the world but as Shylock demanding his pound of flesh. But these would be the exceptions to the grand rule that the world was determined that war could and would be stopped by collective action. If the Italian forces operating into Abyssinia from Massawa were deprived of a plentiful supply of oil their situation would be untenable within a week.

If ever there was a case of now or never this was it. Nearly a quarter of a million of the best Italian troops with all their modern equipment were two thousand miles from their home base and dependent entirely upon a precarious lifeline through the Suez Canal. I doubted whether ever in the history of warfare had an army been placed in a position of such suicidal danger.

Mussolini's only hope would be to fight a naval war against Britain in the Mediterranean and, even given that the Italian navy had modern ships and equipment, surely there could only be one result of that.

It required two words from Geneva to bring about the collapse of Mussolini's mad, vainglorious enterprise – "No Oil". In the sweaty, unhealthy desert outside Aden, news was erratic and the sense of being out of the world but in the epicentre of its troubles was strong. There had been a General Election in Britain in November, from which the Conservatives had emerged with an overwhelming victory, and it seemed that their election promises of support for the League would ensure that the two words "No Oil" would now emerge from the Sanctions Committee.

It is perhaps hard for the modern reader to realise the absolute pre-eminence of Britain in the League of Nations of 1935, but it is probably true to say that with British support an important policy had a ninety per cent chance of adoption, whereas any proposal opposed by Britain was virtually sure to fail. Now, reinforced by such a strong mandate from the country, seemed the time of all times when the new British Government could lean hard on the doubters and unite the world against the aggressor.

Naive as I was, I saw things in black and white. Britain and France were both Mediterranean powers, both Red Sea powers, both Middle East powers. They were surely strong enough to bend Italy to their will and, in the name of the League, prevent her from wrongdoing if they so wished.

There were two facts which I did not then grasp. One was that Britain and France had signed an accord with Italy at Stresa which made Italy potentially their ally against Germany, whose growing strength was alarming France. The French, and some factions in Britain, were desperately anxious to preserve and even strengthen the accord with Italy. Henry of Navarre said that Paris was worth a Mass; some in Britain and most in France were saying, with equal cynicism, that an Italian ally was worth the League of Nations and its Covenant.

Secondly, British strategists placed no faith in French support for warlike action against Italy. The British naval staff believed that, after a series of economy drives, British forces were in no condition to fight alone in the Mediterranean. The Navy would win in the end but it might lose more ships than could be afforded. If the Navy, on whom as Charles II said, "under the Providence of God the safety, honour and welfare of this realm do chiefly attend", was unsure of its ability to perform its basic tasks, it would have needed a great deal of nerve on the part of politicians to put principle before safety and go ahead. Such politicians were not available in either England or France.

While the Italian attack developed we waited in the dessert in readiness to undertake our pointless raid on Assab if there was war with Italy. After a day or two, in which we had been prepared to take off at a moment's notice, day or night, it became clear that the League's action was not likely to impede Italian designs in the slightest degree. Tension relaxed and our states of readiness began to vary. The variations seemed to accord more with inexplicable whims of the Staff than with any realities of what was happening either beyond the Red Sea or in the corridors of Geneva.

But realities? What did we, young and inexperienced as we were, know of realities? The 1914 war was not even a memory to most of our pilots. Even those who, like myself, had been alive at the time, knew nothing of the strategy or the fighting. We remembered queues and casualty lists, bad food and hatred of Germany and, in my own case, the loss of my father.

I had believed so absolutely in the fiction of the war to end war that, in spite of the books I had read and the films I had seen, it was impossible for me to comprehend the reality of war.

And here we were being confronted with a new breed of war. In the war which seemed to be facing us there was no contradiction of the famous resolution of the Oxford Union that under no circumstances would its members fight for King and Country. We would not be fighting for King and Country. There was no British interest in Abyssinia. If there had been, the cynics said, we'd have been there long ago. If war came we should be fighting not for King and Country but for a principle, the principle that war was no longer an acceptable method of settling disputes or extending national territories. Another war to end war.

Maybe. For the timebeing we lived in a state of modified readiness and extreme boredom. Days off were rare and for most of the squadron not exactly thrilling with nowhere to go but the empty dustiness of Aden. Cricket, hockey, football and even golf were possible on various improvised pitches, and for me, of course, these days meant I could see and, occasionally, stay a night with my wife. But the odious climate, too much cheap liquor and a hundred other men always buzzing around, since there were virtually no other women on the peninsula, made even these brief sorties less than halcyon. Joan filled in her time playing bridge and having drinks with a shifting population of journalists who were, like everyone else, waiting for something to happen. The gifted semi-amateurs, Evelyn Waugh and Patrick Balfour, came and went. The professionals, who were fully accustomed to killing time and spoiling their livers at their employers' expense, stayed in Aden on the chance that a story would break,

Out at the desert landing ground we tried to keep the troops happy and the aircraft serviceable and ready for action. We flew little, not wanting to use up flying hours which might be needed. Inevitably, for those of us who were so inclined, there was much time for talk and discussion of our predicament and how we, the veriest amateurs of strategy and politics, saw our present and the world's future.

Even to me, ignorant as I was, it looked as if Britain, perhaps constrained by France, had led the League into selecting such sanctions as would least interfere with Italian plans. The boasting at Geneva that significant steps were afoot did more to raise Italian morale in defying the world than it did in impeding the war effort in Abyssinia.

In discussions our group was usually divided into two factions. The first comprised those who said it was not for Britain to act as the world's policeman, incurring losses of men and material which bore no relation to real British interests. The other opinion, which I found myself supporting, was that all crusades needed a leader and an inspiration. We were embarked on a crusade which might have extraordinary results in establishing the authority of the League, once and for all, as the arbiter of war and peace. No leader was credible except Britain, and if Britain threw down the torch it would be extinguished, perhaps for ever. In the damp, unhealthy heat in which we lived with the everlasting hot wind endlessly blowing the flies into our tents to crawl viciously over our sweaty limbs and get into our eyes, our mouths and our food, tempers were easily frayed. I often found it paid to wind up the argument with the banal statement that we had signed on to do a job even if we hadn't foreseen it would be this one.

Tension again mounted as the days passed and time was running out for the League to declare its next and decisive step. No one had any doubt what that step had to be. If it did not include sanctions on oil it would be as meaningless as the existing prohibitions. Russia and Romania, main sources of oil for Italy, seemed to be precariously on board. What then of America, non-member of the League, arbiter of the world's oil supplies? If she refused to deny oil to Italy, no one would contemplate the awfulness of trying to force her into agreement. All depended on America's President, Franklin Roosevelt, three years into his huge effort to pull his country out of the deepest depression ever known. Complications in foreign affairs were low on his priorities. With guns loaded, and our little bombs at the ready we waited in the damp, unhealthy heat with the hot, salty wind blowing the inexhaustible supply of flies into our tents.

Britain was the only country which had made any attemptf to intimidate Mussolini by the classic method of troop movements. Chief among these, of course, was the reinforcement of the Mediterranean Fleet which, although one heard later of reservations by the Admirals, could almost certainly have brought the whole enterprise to a halt.

One of the more curious threats to Mussolini, with his modern machinery, poison gas and aircraft, was the arrival in Aden of a body of Punjabi cavalry sent from India and stationed, with their horses, in the old town. I do not know whether they would have had a useful function in Abyssinia, but my wife and I were fortunate to make friends with some of their British officers. We had no experience of the sub-continent or its tiny British garrison but I have vivid memories of the wonderful friendship and discipline that sustained the hierarchical world of that regiment. They had acquired a tradition of bagpipes and I can still hear echoes in my mind of their beating retreat in the dusty arena of the Crater. The standard of their drill and playing would have challenged their Scottish highland brethren as they marched off in the dusk to the sad lament of *The Barren Rocks of Aden* with the great rock itself brooding over us all and the kites keeping their endless vigil over the Towers of Silence above us.

Our friends were pleased to have their horses exercised and on my days off Joan and I would ride for miles along the seemingly endless beach of firm sand. Our progress seldom disturbed the thousands of pink flamingos who stood in the shallow water, as still and orderly as guardsmen on parade, waiting, waiting. Just occasionally something, a whinny or a warning cry from one of us to avoid a rock, would startle some of the lovely birds and forty or fifty would take to the air, their flight clumsy, slow and seemingly precarious in its first stages. When they had gained speed and tucked their long legs away somewhere in their bright pink feathers they became masters of their new element and flew, confident and beautiful, in an immaculate formation no RAF squadron could have matched.

When, baulked by a dry Wadi with steeply perilous sides which we did not care to risk descending, we turned for home and gave the horses their heads, the flamingos would still be standing in their single line, almost touching one another, totally immobile. I wondered casually, knowing little of such things, where and how they mated and nested, how they fed and whether they roosted at night where they stood by day. How had evolution produced them from the primeval cell and made them so beautiful and for what purpose? No other animal could appreciate their beauty. Why should not some, at least, be misshapen and ugly? I reflected on the difficulty and clumsiness of the first stages of their flight. All birds fly on the principle of tucking their legs out of the airstream as quickly as possible and I began to understand why designers were making such efforts to produce mechanisms to retract an aircraft undercarriage.

At first it had seemed that Italian progress in their attack was so slow that delay by the League of Nations in the organisation of the next and final set of sanctions which would bring Italy to her knees was acceptable. However, some two months had elapsed since Mussolini had taken the fatal step, his almost unarmed opponents were faltering and it was clear that action, real action, was now urgent if Abyssinia was to be saved as the League had promised. All eyes were on Geneva and all ears tuned to signals from London and Paris whence the lead would come.

What we heard was so shattering that at first I could not believe it. I knew little of international politics and information in Aden was sketchy with English newspapers three weeks late, but the upshot was that the British Foreign Secretary, Sir Samuel Hoare, he of the passionate speech to the League of Nations, had passed through Paris on a short holiday. He had, quite naturally, taken the opportunity to meet with his French counterpart, M. Pierre Laval, then a powerful politician of the Right. Who was to know that this same Laval would be the most notorious of all France's long list of collaborators with her Nazi conquerors or that he would finally be shot as a traitor to his country and its cause?

These two, reposing no faith in the League of Nations to which they, and especially Sir Samuel had professed such passionate allegiance, together concocted a scheme which in their view would ensure peace, protect the Franco-Italian entente and be "acceptable" to the League, the world, Italy and Abyssinia. The latter would, of course, have no alternative but to agree to a "settlement" which would give Italy virtually everything she was demanding and leave Abyssinia a poverty-stricken rump which could not possibly survive in independence.

It was about as cynical and underhand a compact as has ever disgraced two great nations. It had the full approval of the French Government, who were probably concerned in its drafting, and, within a few days, it was approved in secret by the Cabinet of Mr Baldwin's newly elected Conservative Government, to be laid before the League in the names of its two most powerful members.

Before this could happen, however, the text of the agreement was leaked in Paris and became known to the world. The full impact of the press, public and political outcry when the Hoare/Laval plan became known in England was not apparent to us in the desert, although I believe the effect was little short of stupendous, so much so that the Prime Minister's position, within weeks of his overwhelming victory at the polls, was momentarily precarious. His Government had virtually announced, without consulting Parliament, that it didn't care a damn for Abyssinia or for obligations under the League of Nations Covenant or for the assurances given the electorate only three weeks before. "Honest" Mr Baldwin weathered the storm in his inimitable, pipe-smoking manner, dropping, but not discrediting his erring Foreign Secretary. Mr Anthony Eden, universally respected in Britain as the very epitome of the League was promoted to replace Sir Samuel and restore the country's confidence in collective security. Although he must have been a party to the Cabinet decision to support the Hoare/Laval Pact, he emerged unscathed, and in fact much strengthened, from the unsavoury episode. Sir Samuel became First Lord of the Admiralty within a very few months.

I was horrified that my country could be so devious. I was prepared to believe that there had been plenty of prodding from

France although M. Laval was not then the sinister and traitorous figure he later became. I could understand the French terror of Germany and their wish to keep their Italian alliance intact. As seen from Paris, Britain might be a prop and mainstay for France in a long war as her Navy and Commonwealth slowly became major factors, but it was France who would sustain the first shock. To push Italy into the German camp might mean an 1870-type suicide again.

So it was Britain alone who could take the lead to prove that collective security, by protecting Abyssinia against Italy, would be capable of protecting France against Germany. This vision, simplistic as it may have been, had become so clear to me that the news of the Hoare/Laval pact was a blow to the foundations of what serious reasoning there was in my light-hearted life. It would be an exaggeration to say that I was shattered. Too much of my being was occupied in the pleasure and happiness I derived from my own relatively fortunate circumstances. True, I had little money, but it was enough to sustain my marriage and indulge the tastes Joan and I both had for fun and good living, for literature, cinema, theatre, ballet and the visual arts, for sport, games and good company.

The Aden venture was an interruption, a hiccup, in my life. I took it seriously in the belief that a successful conclusion would ensure that life would continue on its reasonably progressive and, for me, pleasant way. The news from England and Geneva torpedoed that complacency for ever. My country's leaders had deceived the world (and myself) into believing that we were engaged on a crusade, only to find that we were the victims of a backstairs intrigue with an ally even less trustworthy than ourselves. The Americans had weakened the League of Nations when they abandoned their own creation. The French had been undermining it for years. But it was my country which now administered the fatal blow which killed the League and its ideals stone dead.

We went on drinking too much duty-free whisky and riding the Punjabi ponies past the supine flamingos. The Italians appointed a new Commander who galvanised their listless campaign into real activity. The Abyssinians persevered with the tactics which had defeated the Italians at Adowa in the last century. They met tanks and aeroplanes with rifle fire, charged machine guns with spears. They fell in thousands but even the mustard gas on their helpless, half-naked bodies didn't shock Geneva. I was at first impatient, then anxious, then angry and at last apathetic. I realised that I and the other millions who had signed the Peace Ballot had been living in cloud-cuckoo-land. The real world was the world of meaningless promises and election victories.

My last recollection of Aden was of the Emperor of Abyssinia, who had fled his defeated country and made his way to British protection. He stood, a pathetically small and slightly comic figure in a white cape and a huge British type sun helmet, on the bridge of the British cruiser *HMS Emerald* which was to take him on the first stage of his journey to Geneva, where his protest to the League would be "noted", and then to exile. The other ships in the harbour saluted and sounded their sirens and I think there was a genuine surge of goodwill and sympathy for the poor little Emperor. Certainly some of us who stood, glasses in hand, to wave him good-bye from the club which looked out over the harbour felt that to a degree his defeat was also ours.

By now my contract with the RAF was nearly finished. The international situation had already provoked a surge of expansion and an unprecedented demand for trained officers. The terms, however, were not particularly attractive, Joan was pregnant and in my disillusioned state I thought it better to try my luck in civilian life. I had had the best of flying and, with a family to keep, I had seriously to think of money and a home so I applied for and was given a passage home.

The brand new P&O liner *Strathnaver* was as large a ship as could then pass through the Suez Canal, and her speed was such that she had to waste a day in the Mediterranean in order not to upset the schedule of the older ships which still performed the bulk of the mail service to the East. After dropping many passengers off at Marseilles to allow them a precious extra week of leave in England, the *Strathnaver* cruised eastwards again and moored off Monte Carlo. Joan's parents lived in Menton so we disembarked and joined them, I for a week and Joan to stay a month. It was fortunate we did so since it proved the last time she saw her father whom she dearly loved.

After a week in the sunshine with the mimosa at its fragrant best, I reluctantly made my way to Marseilles to embark on the P&O *Chitral* for home. The contrast with the *Strathnaver* could hardly have been greater. There was no swimming pool, no grill room, no wide deck spaces. *Strathnaver* was a ship of the future for people who demanded pleasure, comfort, space, fun while they travelled. She was brilliant white, her funnel bright yellow. *Chitral* was a survivor from a harsher age, black with black funnels and a dull dark yellow superstructure. The cabins were small, the passages narrow, engine noise was everywhere and vibration continuous. The bar was cramped and dark, like a Victorian "snug" made for men to drink seriously together. There was an aura of the past which, although in Aden you were still conscious of it, you felt that in a year, two years, it would be gone. There was still the atmosphere reminiscent of the dhows, the queer European traders who lived native, the feel of a Somerset Maugham story, even a breath of Conrad's Lord Jim and sailing ships and dirty tramps sneaking in and out of queer unknown estuaries. All this you felt that *Chitral* had known and been a part of.

After the usual stampede to catch the train for England at Marseilles the first class was almost empty so I had no difficulty in getting a cabin to myself. No one had any interest in scraping acquaintance with me at that late stage in the voyage so I had time to come to terms with the radical change in my life.

It was the first time for many months that I had been able to think. Of course anyone can think at any time if he so wants, in the lavatory, in bed, driving a car, walking, waiting, any time when you don't need to concentrate your attention on a specific task. But since all the frolics and parties associated with my engagement and marriage, followed by the novelty of our little house, our rather spectacular holiday in Spain and the trauma of the end of that bit of life then the boat to Aden and the likelihood of war and the drinking and the drinking and the South of France where Pernod was still twopence a glass, all that had added up to the fact, not so much that I had no time to think, but that I had other things which I preferred to do. I didn't make time to think as the world made its way towards destruction and I and my like travelled with it, admiring the scenery and enjoying the fun which was plentiful.

There are times, sometimes as short as a day, sometimes as long as a year, when the progress of life seems to have halted and the normally remorseless grind of time hesitates to push you onward, content for the clock to stop and wait to be wound and press you on again. These curious intermissions are much less frequent now that ship travel is a thing of the past. For me, like the intervals between the movements of a symphony when the orchestra is ready to go on playing and the audience dares not speak or clap, they have always seemed tantalisingly long. I have never, however, found them profitable, never been able to use them as they should be used, for taking stock, for making plans and resolutions, for the washing clean of slates, and for preparing to be a better or at least a more coherent person. My time on board the *Chitral* was no exception. I did not ponder the farcical failure of which I had been a spectator nor did I care to contemplate what was to come except that I knew that I would be helpless to decide my own future or that of my dependents.

5

The Run-Up to War

"The Need is Pilots"

Back in England with only a few months of my contract with the RAF to go I expected to spend the time in some sinecure post where I might do a bit of flying for fun and have time to sniff around for a permanent civilian job which would provide a future for my family, due to have a third member at the year end. On arrival at the RAF Depot, however, I was surprised to find an immediate summons to report for interview with the Air Officer commanding the newly formed No.11 Fighter Group. Air Vice-Marshal Joubert de la Ferte was one of the most impressive senior officers I ever had dealings with in the RAF. He combined great charm with a comprehensive knowledge of Air Force matters and a more than usually shrewd judgement of the world outside. I was surprised and impressed that I was shown straight into his office at the exact time of my appointment, whereupon, after a social greeting, he embarked on a searching examination of my views and experiences as a participator in the events of the last six months.

After about a quarter of an hour of this during which I suppose he learnt what he needed to know about me, he switched to bringing me up-to-date on Air Force developments in England. He told me that the highest authority had at last been persuaded that some effective defence of Britain by fighter aircraft was now considered truly feasible and that, although bombers still had priority, his brief was to mould his Group into a going concern with reasonable expedition. He said that his

Commander-in-Chief, the redoubtable Air Marshal "Stuffy" Dowding, considered the international situation far more dangerous than the Government was as yet prepared to admit and was determined that his Command would expand and, more importantly, become fully efficient, as a matter of much greater urgency than had so far been officially communicated to him. The gaps would be huge until the wanderers returned from the Mediterranean and the Middle East, but he planned by then to have a framework in position in which an organisation two and perhaps three times the size of the old Fighting Area could take shape within a very few months.

I was flattered as a junior officer to be made privy to this sort of high level planning but I was even more surprised and delighted when Joubert told me that, in spite of my lack of seniority, he had decided to give me command of a squadron, No.23, stationed at Biggin Hill. He told me that No.23 had been stripped and cannibalised to make up deficiencies in the units going overseas in the *Cameronia*. I would find it now with only five or six aircraft, fewer pilots and only a cadre of ground crew. More pilots, probably all totally inexperienced, together with aircraft and ground crew would reach me during the summer. He could not say on what scale, but my job was to train and exercise whatever there was. I was to do this flat out so that the skeleton of that moment could quickly become a fully-fledged squadron in the great expansion he foresaw. He realised that I had only six months to serve but he hoped that if I made a success of what he offered I would stay in the service for a time at least with the real possibility of a permanency.

I was thrilled by Joubert's enthusiasm, and the importance he attached to what he wanted me to do and, of course, by the confidence he seemed to repose in me. Nevertheless when he asked me if I was happy with what he offered I had to be honest and tell him that I felt that my new family circumstances meant that I had to plan my future definitely and that meant finding a job outside the service. I said that I was truly enthused by the job and, if he would accept me doing it for only six months, I would put all I had into it for that time. He said that the Treasury was only allowing the RAF to plan on a short-term basis but that he accepted my position and I went to Biggin Hill determined to do all I could. Having decided to take my chance in civilian life and find a career outside flying, I did not feel inclined to change to another plan.

The station at Biggin Hill, normally home to two fighter squadrons and some smaller units, was almost deserted. When Joan arrived from the South of France I was able to rent a spacious, if somewhat gaunt, service quarter where we lived in some comfort while I strove to keep my word to Joubert. I flew quite a lot and worked at the administration and training of my slowly increasing complement until I could flatter myself that the squadron, although hopelessly under strength, was on the way to becoming an efficient unit.

It was a glorious summer, I was more or less my own master, and had plenty of flying and responsibility with good and willing people working for me. London was close, offering, so far as we could afford them, the pleasures of the town. The country around was still gloriously unspoilt, and we frequented some of the pubs later made famous by the Battle of Britain pilots who were to fly from our not altogether satisfactory field. Joubert's warnings of danger ahead stayed with me but nobody else seemed to be worried.

Almost the only blot on our horizon was the attitude of the Station Commander, a surly and disappointed individual who clearly felt that his exploits in the 1914 war had not brought him the success he considered his due. I fell out with him on the subject of a boat he was having built by servicemen in the hangar allotted to my squadron. Owing to the shortage of aircraft there was no real lack of space, in fact there was room enough to build a small destroyer without real disturbance to the squadron. It seemed to me, however, that this kind of activity in working hours in full view of those doing a proper Air Force job destroyed any hope of fostering a real sense of the importance of the RAF expansion. Perhaps mistakenly, I wrote an official letter asking that the boat be removed, pretending I did not know who was the owner.

The explosions which followed were phenomenal with accusations of insubordination and dire threats of the consequences. He could and did make life somewhat uncomfortable for me thereafter and, except for absolute necessity, he never spoke to me again but the boat was duly removed.

It is not always, or even often, that we know when we have reached the end of one of the chunks of experience which make up our journey through life. The last day at school, yes, you could foresee that, but the last innings at cricket, the last kiss, the last time to hear Figaro, of such as these we can never be quite sure that this or that one will really be the last.

It was within a few days of my transfer to the reserve when I ordered my Demon fighter to be got ready for me to fly. I was virtually sure on that September day that this would be my last flight in a service aircraft. On the reserve I would undertake to do a fortnight's training every year, flying small training aircraft to keep in some sort of practice. But the exquisite pleasure of the speed, the power, the manoeuvrability of a fighter aeroplane would not, I thought, ever come my way again. It had been a splendid time in my life and I had enjoyed nearly every minute of it, the fun of first youth, the drinking and the girls, the squash and cricket, riding and using a gun, theatre and ballet and the ups and downs of my engagement and marriage. These were the common lot of many young men of my ilk. But only a few of us had flying as an extra to the good things of life and what we had will never come again. The open cockpit, the helmet and goggles, the wind on your cheek at what was then great speed, the open exhausts so close to you, the sense of being separated from the earth your mother, the umbilical cord snapped as you savoured the freedom of the skies.

Well, this was the last of it. I had to go to Northolt to clear up some administrative chore and when I got back to Biggin Hill that would be the end of my flying as an active RAF officer. I climbed into the cockpit with a fairly heavy heart but I was convinced that my choice to try my luck in civilian life was the only rational one to cope best with my family responsibilities.

It was a fine autumn day with little wind and unlimited visibility. I chose to obey regulations and not fly the direct route over London but, keeping to the South, I followed the Downs and then struck North West until I reached the so familiar landmark of the Staines reservoir with the long pier which pointed to the aerodrome at Northolt. I remembered how often pilots, including myself, having been bewildered in bad weather by the maze of streets and railways in these parts, had been thankful to find at last the friendly stretch of water with its finger pointing unerringly to home. I turned and flew as the pier directed: there was the Harrow gasometer; there the shooting school; there the aerodrome with as yet no road along its southern boundary. With the wind in its customary south west, I came in low past the barrack blocks I had so often inspected and had only a few yards to taxi to the familiar tarmac.

When I had finished what I had to do and said good-bye to the friends who remained, I took off from the tarmac, gained speed low down, pulled up almost vertically, a stall turn, then a last dive on the mess where I had had so much fun, down, down, to roof top height to pull up, roll off the top and away, away, Northolt was no more in my life.

After my little show off, which I would not repeat at Biggin Hill for fear my *bête-noir* would be watching, I set a southerly course on the impulse of wanting to catch a glimpse of the sea, truly I suppose it was merely an excuse to prolong the flight. From ten thousand feet I saw Brighton, the South Downs, Portsmouth Harbour and the Isle of Wight, all so much part of my early youth, laid out like a map in the almost Grecian clarity of the day. Then northward towards the smoke of London and everything seemed to go quiet as if I were floating not flying as the light began almost imperceptibly to fade from the glare of the afternoon. There was Croydon with a giant (for those days) Imperial Airways liner slowly approaching to land. Dangerously close to Croydon was Kenley where Douglas Bader had taken off on his so ill-starred last flight. Having played squash with him and thinking that he would not play squash or fly ever again I felt a wave of pity at the penalty he was paying for a moment's rashness, little guessing how he would be able to turn that disaster into triumph. I was still flying too high to have any sense of motion over the ground and the sense of stillness, of being suspended alone in time and space was overwhelming.

I turned back towards the South, with an irresistible urge to do some aerobatics, just once more to feel the sensation of being one with the powerful machine which responded so smoothly and obediently to the easy commands of the stick and rudder. I dived and looped, did slow rolls, a flick roll, spins and steep turns with the wings vertical until I was almost giddy. Then back to the aerodrome, throttle back, sideslip to the left, sideslip to the right, hold off, stick slowly back, then right back in my tummy, wheels and tailskid touching ground simultaneously just as the book said. That, I thought, is the end of service flying for me. There would be some messing about in little training machines, perhaps some instructing and flights on commercial airlines but no more real flying.

Back at the tarmac for the last time, my fitter and rigger each holding a wingtip. Taxi slowly so that they need not run. Stop at the great door of the hangar, just a burst of engine to help with the last turn. Then petrol off, some sputtering, switches off, open throttle, more sputtering as if the engine itself willed me to stay, a last kick in reverse and the propeller was quiet. No other aircraft was flying, no engine running. I levered myself out of the cockpit, resolved to think no more of aeroplanes but of the new life. No more the fine machine at call, no more the three-dimensional freedom of the air. I had money to make and a family to rear.

At an important moment things went right for us. One day I was worrying that I might have to leave the Air Force with no job to go to, no house to live in and a child due in November. Then within a week I was offered a job in the City which seemed to have reasonable prospects and we were lent a delightful house rent-free for the whole of the winter. My City activities were not to start too seriously until the spring and we had a bit of money in the bank so we moved in to Aston Hall near Henley-on-Thames with a man and his wife to look after us. Charming as the house was, it was little more than an overgrown cottage and how it came by its pretentious name we never knew.

The baby, said to be due in November, obstinately refused to arrive although Joan was ensconced in an expensive London nursing home towards the end of the month, enduring all the tricks then known to the medics to "bring it on". I commuted daily from Henley to give what comfort I could while the bill swelled and we both fumed. Eventually we hit on the idea of getting her out of bed one evening and taking a box at the Palladium. There, with a surreptitious bottle of champagne, we were regaled by the "Crazy Gang", Nervo & Knox *et al.*, then at the height of their popularity. A splendid audience of devoted fans yelled with delight at every crack and quip and, between gulps of champagne, we laughed until the tears rolled down our cheeks. We left before the end, only just reaching Sloane Square in time for the beginning of the arrival of our daughter.

During the past summer rumours about the new King Edward VIII and his friend, the American divorcée Mrs Simpson, had reached even people as far from royal circles as ourselves and it was on the day of our daughter's birth that the Bishop of Bradford brought the rumours into the open, unloosing the full force of discussion in the press, which until then had nobly eschewed the story in spite of it being common knowledge outside Britain.

A day or so later Mr Winston Churchill led a huge meeting in the Albert Hall in pursuance of a campaign to persuade the Government to accelerate its rearmament programme. I was beginning to take an interest in such matters and would have gone to the meeting had it not been for my other preoccupations. As it turned out, however, Mr Churchill temporarily lost the interest of the public in his primary object by using the gathering at the Albert Hall to show that he strongly supported the cause of the King. There were those, amongst them some of our friends, who toyed with a romantic vision of a King's Party dedicated to keeping Edward on the throne and coming to some backstairs arrangement about his relations with Mrs Simpson. Mr Churchill may indeed have had something of the kind in the back of his mind when he made his impulsive but ill-judged gesture at the Albert Hall. If so, however, he quite wrongly gauged the mood of the majority in the country who, while sharing his affection for the King, were less inclined to tolerance of irregularity in high places. My personal knowledge of the King only extended to one casual meeting in the changing room at the Bath Club when, as Prince of Wales, he was playing in the Amateur Squash Championship. I was then less than impressed by his very offhand manner to other competitors and especially to the staff of the dressing room. While a supporter of the monarchy I felt that for it to survive as an effective political instrument, which I still believe it is, the behaviour, public and private, of its head people, must be not far from impeccable.

As the week wore on and Joan was still kept in bed in the nursing home, as was then the custom after childbirth to the considerable profit of the proprietors, I increasingly felt, in company with the bulk of the British people, that "The King Must Go". I was alone with the wireless at Aston Hall, when he made his dignified farewell broadcast. I felt sad for the good things he had done in the past but, looking back, I do not remember that I thought there was any possible alternative for him or his country.

Just about then came the startling, and to some superstitious people ominous, news of the burning of the Crystal Palace. The great glasshouse had stood on its eminence at Sydenham for nigh on a century, not very useful, but still something of a symbol of Britain's greatest period. At the time when our ancient monarchy was in a crisis more serious than any since the Civil War, the destruction of this great white elephant with its royal associations, could seem an ill omen for a country already racked with doubts and troubles.

We spent the rest of the winter in comfort far exceeding our means. I played a good deal of golf, reducing my handicap to single figures, we drank pretty copiously, went to parties and had a lot of fun. After a short spell in the South of France in February to play tennis and admire the mimosa, I acquired the lease of a five-bedroomed house in Chelsea at no capital cost and a yearly rent of about three hundred pounds, offset by letting off the basement for a pound a week.

From then until circumstances in 1939 dictated otherwise we lived in Oakley Gardens with a nanny and an Irish maid who cooked a bit, cleaned a bit and, given half a chance, talked a great deal. It was a happy little establishment and, for a time, we were able to ignore our inability to live within our income.

Those were good times for a young married couple in London. We had a car which for fifteen shillings a week I kept in a garage down the road, although it was generally accepted that the parking space outside every house was sacrosanct to the owner. You could visit your friends, who all lived not far away, without fear of serious traffic delay or inability to park. If you went to a theatre or cinema you went by car and expected to park close by and to find your car intact when you came out. Cocktail parties were frequent and restaurants not too expensive.

My city job was interesting but not demanding and we went to Ascot, the Derby, Wimbledon and Henley. I frequented Lord's and played golf or cricket at week-ends. In the winter I played squash in the Bath Club Cup and entered for the Amateur Championship. Perhaps best of all was my discovery of that king of games, real or royal tennis, at which I acquired a moderate proficiency. While modern lawn tennis is derived from the old game in that it is played with rackets and you hit a ball over a net, the contrast between the crudeness and monotony of the new and the subtlety and variety of the old is known only to the relatively few practitioners of real tennis.

It was in our first London spring that the Spanish civil war alerted even such pleasure-directed minds as mine towards the sinister atmosphere developing in Europe. At that time British people had very little knowledge of, and virtually no contact with, Spain. It remained an aristocratic, backward country, indifferent to, even proud of, its isolation from Europe. My maternal grandmother was Spanish and I had always had a superficial interest in the country. Granny was a remarkable old lady who wore an old Burberry mackintosh, never gave a hint that she was other than English of the English and every morning had a cold bath in which she would sing, or rather intone, with a loud but tuneless resonance, the while splashing water all over the bathroom with the vigour of a teenager. She was the daughter of a Spanish grandee, the last of his ducal line, but she never in my presence uttered a word of Spanish. The only faint indication of un-Englishness she ever gave was in the first war when the word 'queue' was passing into the English language and she would never give it anything but its proper French pronunciation.

The Spanish civil war had been in progress for some time when the bombing of Guernica brought it to the headlines of the newspapers and the forefront of even such unpolitical minds as mine. On our Spanish holiday in 1935, before the Abyssinian War, we had been to Barcelona to see bullfights or go to restaurants and nightclubs but we were totally unaware that, less than a year before, the streets of that fine city had run with blood in fighting between various political factions. We had been conscious of the hatred aroused by the *Guardia Civile* with their sinister, shiny, black hats and the firearms and daggers they carried at all times but, although we sensed an atmosphere of disquiet, we had had no inkling of the wave of hatred and cruelty which was soon to overwhelm the country in an orgy of self-destruction. Even less had we imagined that the cauldron would be stirred and replenished by the ideologies of the European dictators which to us were still only vague blots on the international scene.

Probably most English people, as far as they thought about it at all, were relieved that the 1936 Spanish election had thrown up a left-wing government rather than a successor to the repressive right-wing elements which had been in power. Little real attention was paid to events in Spain until it became apparent that the civil war was becoming the first of the surrogate wars, attracting active participation from the European dictatorships of right and left. Even then attitudes were of disapproval rather than of outrage, tending to excuse the behaviour of Russian or Italian/German intervention, according to the political views of the observer. In April of 1937 all that changed and there were few, even in easy-going England, who were not shocked and horrified at the appalling story of the bombing of Guernica.

This little town, precious in the history of the Basque country as the home of its ancient liberties, a place entirely without strategic significance or military installations, was almost totally destroyed by German aircraft attached to the forces of General Franco. The bombing was no ragged revolutionary operation but the calculated deed of a disciplined force of trained airmen using high grade equipment and weapons. Some 1,600 people, none of whom were taking any active part in the war, were killed and many others injured; the proportion of casualties to the total population was said to have been higher than that in the Battle of the Somme. The tale of this, the first obliteration raid in the history of war, has been told and retold, but never completely explained.

Guernica was the signal for me and many others to begin to think seriously of major war as a real possibility in our lifetime. Vigorous discussion was stimulated of the theory of warfare propounded by the Italian General Douhet who believed that a war could and should be won by an Air Force capable of destroying the social structure of an enemy by mass attack on his civilian population. This led to the view that a total change had come over war and that a country could be "bombed into submission" by heavy bombers aiming large loads at the greatest centres of population. By this means, against which it then seemed that there was no realistic defence, the defeat of the enemy's land forces had, according to the Douhet camp, become unnecessary since the civil population would insist on capitulation as soon as the bombardment became intolerable. The theory was more significant for Britain than for other nations because of the huge concentration of power and administrative machinery in London, near the coast and therefore vulnerable. It also made naval blockade, traditionally a primary weapon of British arms, too blunt and slow an instrument to be effective.

Now the Germans seemed to have given notice to the world that they understood and believed in this mode of warfare. Guernica, if it meant anything except senseless, sadistic destruction, meant that the Germans were proving to themselves, at the cost of innocent Spanish lives, that this new weapon could be effective and that they could wield it. They went on to use it, on a less effective scale, on Barcelona, Madrid and other large towns still held by the Spanish Government. The casualties in these towns were publicised and exaggerated by the world's press, which ignored the fact that the raids were not very effective in a military sense. It was the casualties and the obliteration of Guernica which resounded across the great democracies with a thrill of horror and, let us not disguise it, fear: real, naked fear of the German Luftwaffe.

The words of Mr Baldwin, now retired from the Premiership, were whispered everywhere. "The bomber will always get through," he had said, and people looked at their houses, their possessions, their children through rather different spectacles. What was one to do? It seemed there was nothing to do. Perhaps it would never happen.

The effect of the Guernica outrage on me was that it revived that active hatred of all things German which had so coloured my extreme youth. All the distrust of Germany and suspicions of her motives came flooding back. It seemed only too likely that what they had done in Spain was the preface to what they might do elsewhere. To threaten the peaceful world with terror bombing was a new method of achieving objectives and the idea was beginning to crystallise that German objectives might not be just to be rid of the irksome chains of Versailles. What if Berlin aspired to be the capital of Europe? Did the Nazis even dream of making Germany the greatest power in the world? Such thoughts boded ill for the peaceful and lethargic democracies.

In the early spring of 1938, my wife was staying with her sister and brother-in-law at their villa in the South of France, where I was to join them for ten days or so.

Travelling through France by train in those times, before airlines were common or autoroutes were built, one got a feel of the country from fellow passengers, from railway officials and sleeping car attendants, from the atmosphere on the stations where one hurriedly gulped brandy or coffee while the train stopped and from the talk of fellow diners in the restaurant car.

On this trip I remember an acute feeling of suspense, of waiting for something to happen. There was no particular excitement and the French with whom I spoke seemed more upset by the left-wing tendencies of their Government than by the activities of Herr Hitler. No one seemed particularly distressed by German and Italian activities in Spain and mention of Guernica was met with shrugs or expressions of disbelief. One was not, of course, testing any cross-section of French opinion. Those who staffed or travelled by the "Compagnie International des Wagons Lits et des Grands Express Européens" were quite likely to be waiting avidly for General Franco's victory and the emergence of a stable, right-wing Government South of the Pyrenees. A few Nazi aircraft in Spain worried them much less than a Communist Government there which they saw as certain to spread the contagion already rife in France. I took those I met to be representative of a fairly wide swathe of French opinion and they gave me no very favourable impression of the spirit of our greatest ally. A good deal was made of Herr Hitler's speech after the Rhineland occupation in which he swore that he had no designs on Austrian independence and no intention of effecting an *Anschluss*.

So what matter? On the lovely uncrowded coast the sun shone on the rocks of Cap Ferrat and the sea was blue as blue as we picnicked in a garden high up outside the old town of Eze. We played tennis in the afternoons and drank Pernod and brandy far into the night, sometimes in the boites and sometimes on our own balcony, closed against the cool night air. The gramophone and the pianists in the boites played endlessly the haunting tunes which had suddenly flowered in France to match the charm and talents of Charles Trenet, Yvonne Printemps, Jean Sablon, Maurice who needed no surname and the ageing Josephine Baker. One tune in particular, *Il y a de la joie*, sung by Jean Sablon, still haunts me from those times with the poignant lines:

> Dans les trains de nuit, il y a des fantômes,
> Mais il y a de la joie partout, il y a de la joie.

My brother-in-law's fine Edwardian villa with its terraces of orange trees behind and a huge border of carnations in front, was redolent of mimosa which flowered so profusely that we had no compunction in picking, picking recklessly, although it only lasted a couple of days in the house. The big orange tree by the terrace was the pride of my brother-in-law's gardener who had grafted onto it not only a branch of lemon but also one each of tangerine and grapefruit. I was immensely happy, with just that tinge of sadness which adds to happiness the edge that the joys we were savouring were by no means sure to last. Even our lazy hedonism could not entirely ignore the disquieting stories, each day getting shriller, of the doings in Vienna and Berlin, in Berchtesgarten and on the Austro-German border.

I left them there, genuinely I think, sorry to see me go since we had been good companions and had had so much fun in spite of the pall of doubt and decay that brooded over the France we had loved, now so visibly decadent, lacking even her own esteem.

The day I left was the day the German tanks drove into Austria to the acclaim of crowds who cheered the Swastikas which the tanks carried, and I had the impression that the French I saw on my way didn't care. At the larger stations there lounged idle poilus in ill-fitting khaki, dirty Gauloises hanging from their slack lips, slovenly caps askew as if they defied their own nation as well as the enemy. Their ancient rifles were clumsily held or carelessly discarded and I remember that, for the first, time I had some qualms about that fine French Army which was the pride and bastion of Europe. But, I told myself, these were only recruits or reservists, hauled from their homes as a gesture which neither they nor anyone else believed in. Somewhere behind them was still the greatest fighting force in Europe ready to defend not only the safety but the honour of France. Backed by the British Navy, a formidable Czech Army and a token British force, behind which stood the formidable potential of Britain and her Commonwealth and Empire, there was still a power in Europe which could and would substitute for the lost ideal of collective security, dead with the discrediting of the League of Nations.

Hurrying back to my part in the building of British air power, I wondered what the French Air Force was like. Was it rushing to arms like the RAF? Had it fallen behind as much as we had and was it catching up as fast? Did it have, or had it ordered, the new monoplane fighters which were changing the face of air warfare? The Germans already had them and the RAF had the first few squadrons operational, believing that they would be as good or better than the Hun. I caught my breath, realising that I was using the old word for the old enemy. Surely, surely our world was not going back to that. I, for one, did not then really contemplate the possibility in spite of my misgivings.

Back in England in some gloom I started to spend more days and week-ends at the flying school at Gravesend. For one thing it paid well and I wasn't making much in the nervous atmosphere in the City. The instruction of RAF Volunteer Reserve pupil pilots was necessarily a slow affair. For each step forward a pupil took at a week-end he would inevitably take half a step back in the fortnight or so which often elapsed before he flew again. He had to take pot luck with the weather and the aircraft and instructors available. It was often impossible to allocate an individual to a specific instructor and no one could say the system was as good as we would have wished. But we, and a number of such schools all over the country, provided the basic material for a real surge in the number of pilots which the RAF so urgently needed. But to make them ready to take the next step and become operational RAF pilots was, at the best rate we could achieve, going to take years rather than months.

For the pupils that was no matter. They took their flying as I had taken mine eight years before, as a marvellous free sport provided by the Government. Each flight, each step of progress, was an affair of the greatest fun. They were totally oblivious of being statistics in the books of hard-headed planners in Whitehall, faced with the impossible task of spectacular expansion for which the wherewithal was denied.

I was, perhaps, less carefree than the pupils because I was conscious that alarm bells were ringing, however distantly. I looked more often at the foreign news in the papers, listened rather more to the BBC, even sometimes read the Parliamentary debates. In the days when I was first in England after the *Anschluss* I heard, not without alarm, Winston Churchill's sombre forebodings as he expressed them to the House of Commons. It is fashionable now to decry those who ignored or disbelieved the warnings which that great man was trumpeting to the world by 1938, but I make no claim not to have been amongst them. It has to be remembered that the Churchill of 1938 was not the heroic and semi-infallible figure he became in the prime of his glory. We, who were only superficial students of politics, had never been exposed at first hand to his oratory nor to his personality. For most of Britain he was, inevitably, still the over-impulsive author of the Dardanelles disaster, the less than successful Chancellor who restored the Gold Standard, the implacable enemy of progress in India, the too emotional supporter of the impossible cause of Edward VIII and Mrs Simpson. That "cause" only existed in the imagination of a few impractical romantics out of touch with core British hypocrisy. You might despise that hypocrisy but as a practical observer you could not ignore it. I was perturbed by what Churchill said about Central Europe but they were the words of a failed politician out of office, words to be weighed against the views of those who were charged with the actual conduct of affairs.

The fact of having been in France at the time of the *Anschluss* made affairs on the Continent loom larger than usual in my thinking. To be physically near to a fault-line along which trouble may develop serves, in Dr Johnson's phrase, to concentrate the mind wonderfully. But it didn't last.

With the Continent cut off by those twenty-odd miles of sea, I was not alone in allowing the qualms raised by Hitler's actions and Mr Churchill's words to recede into the background. It was not difficult to allow the fears raised in France to be massaged away by emollient words and to conclude that Hitler's policies and promises might lead to peace. After all, if the Germans and Austrians were one people, and they both seemed to think they were, wasn't the unification of the two countries no more than a natural consequence of the end in 1918 of the hotch-potch of the Habsburg Empire? If self-determination had been right for the Czechs and the Poles and the Balkan muddle that was Jugoslavia, why was it wrong for the German-Austrians?

I don't now remember whether my carefree attitude in the spring and summer of 1938 was deliberate. I think it more likely that it stemmed from the circumstance that, although my long-term prospects were a bit doubtful, for the moment life was as good as could be.

Philosophers decry the role of pleasure in the pursuit of happiness. The concept of pleasure has been so blackened by puritanical moralists that the word has tended to conjure up visions of drug-laden brothels and drink-sodden inebriates heading for financial and physical ruin. To live for pleasure can be seen to invite such disastrous fates as overtook the young Rake in Hogarth's famous pictures. I am not ashamed never to have subscribed to such perverse ideas. I remember that leisurely summer as having been a time of real happiness and I have no regrets whatever that most of it was spent in the single-minded pursuit of pleasure. It is true that the Rake and his friends were little tempted by the joys of cricket, but I must surely have been very little behind them in the systematic consumption of alcoholic liquor.

I had at the time just about enough money to sustain our way of life, provided I kept up my flying. I could reach Gravesend from London in less than an hour and, on free evenings, I would often go there and do a couple of hours instructing which I thoroughly enjoyed and which, since it was well-paid, provided a welcome addition to my income. I was happy to be contributing to the urgency of rearmament, but in the main I flew for fun and for the cash.

In spite of Mr Churchill's warnings and the misgivings I had felt when in France, I was at one with most of my contemporaries in not appreciating the real significance of the *Anschluss*. I knew it was a violation of the Versailles Treaty but, like most Englishmen, I had no very high opinion of that document and some sympathy with the German attitude towards it. As for Austria, what of the cheering crowds who greeted

Hitler on his triumphal progress to Vienna? Careful watching of
the film of this event produced no evidence that the enthusiasm
was anything but genuine and widespread. So, in company with
my wife, who was a good companion, we pursued a pleasant and
frivolous life. When I was not flying we spent week-ends in the
country, often with my brother at Sunningdale where we played
golf or cricket. In London I played squash and made good
progress with my real tennis. As the fine summer wore on and
there was little doing in the City, we stayed often with my
brother-in-law in Wiltshire where we played good cricket with
forays into Dorset and Somerset. The tranquillity and beauty of
those countrysides are with me still. We played our matches
on well-kept grounds, often in the shadow of an ancient church
or quiet manor house or on a green where the pub and the
post office watched over our activities. Events in Europe were
forgotten and we spent far more time over the *The Times*
crossword puzzle, which then had a strong predilection for
cricketing clues, than over the news pages of that journal.
Cricket was king and, at the drawing of stumps as the light
diminished and we strolled slowly off the field, sweaters over
our shoulders, beer and bonhomie in front of us, it was true
to say that we didn't have a care in the world. If, as was only too
often the case, we had hangovers in the morning, that was soon
cured by brandy and ginger ale before we set out for another
day's cricket, able to doze in the back of a large car which my
brother-in-law's sympathetic chauffeur drove with due regard for
our delicate heads.

Even mentally wrapped in my cricketing cocoon, I suppose I
had known that Hitler was up to no good in his dealings with
Czechoslovakia, which, like the rump of Austria which he had
swallowed, was a child of Versailles and therefore, in the
German view, had little legitimacy as a nation. Unlike Austria,
Czechoslovakia was a fiercely democratic state, having close ties
with France and deep suspicions of Germany, not lessened by the
burden of a sizeable German-speaking minority in a vital position
bordering its great and greedy neighbour.

Back in London I soon became unpleasantly aware that the world around me had little relation to the dream existence in the quiet West Country but was a place where the erratic and raucous activities of the Austrian ex-corporal played the lead part. I remember that, for the first time, members of the British Government were busily proclaiming that no-one in Europe wanted a war and that, therefore, there would be no war. I was sophisticated enough to be suspicious of that reasoning. Why, then, talk of war? Why should we need these reassurances?

Three years earlier I had had no difficulty in contemplating a war with Italy but that war, if it had come, would have been a crusade on behalf of the League of Nations backed by the world. I was then still imbued with the belief that the Kaiser's war had been the war, if not to end war, at least to end giant conflicts. I knew that that struggle had been triggered by the assassination of an Austrian grandee, who, although heir to a great throne, was not in himself an important enough figure to justify the disasters which followed his death. And now, however loud the assurances that it was not going to happen, the war that was being contemplated was of the old traditional sort, a contest between rival alliances which, like its predecessor, would kill millions who neither knew nor had been the slightest bit affected by, the issues which caused it. This was so diametrically opposed to all that I had believed for so long that I was quite unable to come to terms with the idea that such a war might actually start within a very few weeks.

I remember that, at Joan's insistence, we pored together over the map of Europe and found Czechoslovakia, a "pistol pointing at the heart of Germany". Even to such a tyro as myself, the strategic importance of the country was obvious, as was its strategic weakness now that Austria was a part of Germany.

While we were cricketing and junketing in the amiable Wiltshire countryside, I had been vaguely conscious that the British Government was taking an unaccustomedly active part in events in Central Europe and that a well-known shipping magnate had been sent to Czechoslovakia, a country without a coastline, to concoct some sort of report. I had little idea of his mission except that it was to do with the hysterical threats of Herr Hitler and the weak and pusillanimous Government of France, which was having second thoughts about the French commitment to defend Czechoslovakia through thick and thin.

Some of my recollections of that confused and confusing autumn are clear enough. I remember being bewildered by the famous, or infamous, leading article in the The Times which the knowledgeable said signalled what amounted to British support for German demands on Czechoslovakia. Like most of my countrymen I had reasonable confidence in the Government led by Neville Chamberlain, the man of peace, and I saw no reason why some honourable compromise in Central Europe should not be contrived.

Ever since I became a grown man I had, largely unconsciously, absorbed much of the tolerant creed of the prevalent classical liberalism. This dictated, among other things, that such generalisations as lumping together the inhabitants of a specific area or the speakers of a certain language as necessarily having certain qualities or defects in common was a fallacy. Nationality and even patriotism were at a discount; a certain internationalism, typified in the ideals of the League of Nations, was the cult of the time. With this spirit guiding me, I had been at pains to suppress or destroy the anti-German sentiments with which I had grown-up in and after the war of 1914-18. But now it was becoming clear to me that the Germans, whose behaviour had dominated so much of my childhood, were again the big bad wolf of Europe.

By the autumn of 1938 the Nazi Party and its Leader dominated the news around the world. The Annual Rally at Nuremberg was awaited with trepidation in the Chancelleries of Europe and the parlours of pacifists but it was a godsend for the media. It was the lead story in every newspaper and radio channel and provided the newsreels, whose fortunes had been flagging, with a shot in the arm.

That year in Germany unbelievable heights of theatricality, propaganda, and nationalistic hubris were reached in the frenetic hero-worship of the Führer. The underlying theme that Hitler had restored Germany's faith in herself and her mission and was destined to lead his Party and his country to ever greater heights of renown and power came to a head at Nuremberg at the beginning of September.

Displays at the annual Nazi Rally there by the greatly expanded German armed forces proved beyond question that under the Nazi regime the standards of discipline, drill and dress, which had characterised Prussian armies since the days of the Great Frederick and his militaristic-mad father, had been revived. Important and impressive as was the new Wehrmacht, even more significant was the succession of regimented bodies, many in great numbers, representative of every aspect of German life, each proudly proclaiming its adherence to the Nazi Party. Men and women, boys and girls, from every conceivable organisation and age group, all perfectly disciplined, either dressed in Nazi uniforms or displaying swastika regalia, marched and counter-marched to the strains of such heavily martial patriotic music as only the massed bands of Germany can produce.

The effect of sheer power, of vigorously devoted youth and solid maturity alike giving themselves body and soul to a cause and to the man who had called them to his service, was unmistakable, even at second hand on the radio. This extraordinary spectacle, seen on every newsreel, was the epitome of deliberately engendered mass emotion. The lusty singing, the slogans and banners, the weaving of intricate patterns of drill, were calculated to have a hypnotic effect on spectator and participant alike. As dusk fell, quantities of torches outlined the movements of the masses as with one voice they sang in their thousands the German national songs, culminating in the Nazi anthem, the not very tuneful *Horst Wessel*.

The climax came when, after an almost unbearable minute or more of silence, Hitler, alone and dressed in his plain Nazi uniform, stepped into the floodlight which now illuminated only the dais to which, with slow dignity, he advanced. There he stood, right arm raised in the Nazi salute waiting for the frenzied shouts of "Sieg Heil, Sieg Heil", to die away into silence, a silence again deliberately prolonged to accentuate the suspense before he started to speak.

At that time I knew no word of German, a language which I later discovered is admirable for song, cumbersome for conversation and a uniquely powerful medium for the rhetoric of threats and hatred. I have occasionally heard other Germans exercise this quality, if quality it is, in their language; but I am sure no one has ever equalled, or even rivalled, Hitler in the sheer hatred he was able to convey or the brutality of the threats he uttered.

This was the first time that I had heard his voice and I remember being conscious even at second hand of the extraordinary hold he had on his listeners. I have since been told that, although it was he who sanctioned the cold-blooded planning of the rally for the purpose of raising the crudest mass emotion, he himself was almost as much affected as those he was manipulating. Certainly, as his speech progressed, I could feel the reality of the hatred he conveyed in every word of his snarling rhetoric and it was not only revulsion that I felt but a wave of almost physical fear at his ranting. Interspersed as it was by the deep, concerted, baying of "Sieg Heil, Sieg Heil" from his increasingly frenzied audience, I felt that his threats against the Czechs were also directed, if not at me personally, certainly at my country if it stood in his way. Even if I could persuade myself that the foul, almost animal menaces Hitler distilled out of crowd hysteria were artificial and possibly hollow, I could see that they were concerted and controlled by a technique new to the world. Delivered with the hideous power of his oratory, they conveyed, even over the ether and without my having understood a word that was said, an impression of potent, active evil that was beyond anything in my experience. I was unpleasantly conscious that in this phenomenon which had arisen in Germany my easy going, indifferent country was up against something for which it was unready, and almost certainly unfitted, to deal.

In our London house. Joan and I, in our different spheres, were both acutely aware, in the aftermath of Hitler's Nuremberg speech, of a sense almost of impending doom hanging over the great city, breathless in August after the summer heat. Everyone, I think, felt a surge of sympathy for the Czechs combined with the awful frustration that their French ally, committed by treaty to their defence, was impotently in the throes of one of its frequent political crises. This seemed to be thrusting Britain, then reputed the leader of the world, into a position which she neither desired to occupy nor knew how to handle. We did not seem able to exert an iota of power to help our new friends.

I was deeply worried for my country and also for myself and my family. The futility of my journey to Aden and the fact that Italy, not the most credibly warlike of nations, had defied the League of Nations and the world, weighed heavily. So where stood the League of Nations now in the face of this greater threat? The answer was that it wasn't standing at all. It was cowering in a corner. All depended on Britain. And somewhere in the background of London's collective mind lurked the bogey of air power and the word "Guernica".

Joan and I discussed whether she and Nanny and our daughter should leave town and go to her family in Wiltshire, but we decided that that savoured too much of panic and we would have "business as usual", anyway for the time being.

All sorts of rumours and counter-rumours circulated around London, some emanating from, others contradicted by, the press or the BBC. The atmosphere was fraught with a dreadful feeling of powerlessness, of not knowing what was being done, least of all what ought to be done. Not that that stopped every Tom, Dick and Harry from demonstrating on tables, on carpets and most especially in pubs and clubs, what THEY would do. Match-boxes, ash-trays and cigarette packets gyrated on bar counters, representing military or aerial formations of whose existence there was little certain knowledge and of whose likely behaviour, none. Conscious as I was of my own ignorance, I was bewildered by all the rumours and views I heard. These ranged from what my brother, who was a member of White's Club, picked up from the indiscretions of Cabinet Ministers and the fears and follies of financiers, to the denizens of the public bar at the Leathern Bottel in Cobham where the Gravesend instructors would congregate after flying.

Joan was very determined to be with me as long as possible and I agreed that she and the family should stay in London for the timebeing. I was pretty sure that London would not be bombed in the early stages of a war. The Luftwaffe would be fully occupied on the Czech front and in repelling the attack in the west which France, with at least some military and air help from Britain, would mount in support of her ally.

Things seemed to be going from bad to worse until Mr Chamberlain took the initiative in suggesting that he should talk personally with the German Chancellor. When the Austrian ex-Corporal replied that the Prime Minister of Britain would have to fly to the farthest south east corner of Germany to see him, the snub was ignored in the general relief at the respite.

Mr Chamberlain was then nearly seventy years old, Hitler twenty years younger. The Prime Minister's enterprise engendered varying degrees of support, admiration and bewilderment, all emotions I shared.

Civil flying was not then the commonplace activity it has since become nor was a sudden trip abroad by a Head of Government a normal way of doing international business. But I realised that the gentle merry-go-round of diplomatic protocol had been overtaken by events and I think almost the whole country respected the old gentleman with the umbrella who was overturning convention and using the tools of the twentieth century in his search for peace.

The news of his visit to Berchtesgarten was profoundly depressing since it clearly meant that Britain, because of France's political inaction, had taken the lead and, without being under any legal obligation herself, had been able to persuade or compel the Czechs to give in to Hitler's demands and the French to abandon their ally. Appalling as was the morality of these proposals, the prize was that there would be no war.

I remember a mood of uneasy relief and that I shared Mr Chamberlain's belief that he had little alternative to recommending that the predominantly German districts of the

Sudentenland should be transferred to the rulers of their own race
as the majority of inhabitants seemed to wish. There was enough
of the element of natural justice in this policy to appeal to the
fair-minded. Hitler's ranting about the oppression and sufferings
of the Sudeten Germans under Czechoslovakian tyranny did not
ring particularly true but there was some excuse for a feeling of
no smoke without fire. However much the Czechs disliked it, this
seemed the obvious solution, provided, of course, that Germany
accepted it as final.

My feelings at the time which I think were shared by, and
possibly derived from, the feelings of a majority of English
people, were that, even though the transfer left Czechoslovakia
without a defensible frontier, if there was to be no war it
wouldn't matter that much. Since Germany guaranteed the
frontier surely that was, if not perfect, the best that could be
expected. It was not then obvious, as with hindsight it now is,
that Hitler had no intention of keeping his word to the Czechs or
anyone else.

I knew little of Germany and the Germans except that I had
grown-up in that atmosphere of induced hatred from which, over
the years, I thought to have successfully escaped. I still tried to
deny the force of my instincts and to judge matters by reason as
far as I was able, but the sound of Hitler's ranting and the
mindless yells of approval of his audience at Nuremberg could
not but revive my adolescent feelings of Germany as the enemy.

No one could deny the enormous achievement of Hitler and
the Nazi Party in having overcome huge unemployment, built
some of the finest roads Europe had ever seen and generally
restored confidence and purpose to a people battered into the
ground by the rigid adherence of hostile neighbours to the harsh
terms of the Versailles Treaty of twenty years before.

But what Mr Chamberlain brought back from Berchtesgarten
was only a draft agreement said to be acceptable to Hitler if the
Czechs, French and Russians, (who had been ignored
throughout), agreed to it. It still remained for Britain to effect
this. Distasteful as it might be, it seemed a road to peace, the
buzzword of the time.

6

Training in Wartime

A Visit to a Bomber Station

I assumed that the Prime Minister's second flight into Germany to meet Herr Hitler was simply to tie up minor matters following French and Czech acceptances, however reluctant in the latter case, of practically the whole of the basis of agreement which Mr Chamberlain had brought back from his talks at Berchtesgarten. There was no particular reason for elation at the way things were going but no need to panic. I remember my brother saying to me that the reaction of some of his friends at White's had been that "when war comes we shall weep for thirty Czech divisions". But surely, I thought, war isn't coming?

Yes, I did think that; but all the same in my heart the question mark persisted.

With Mr Chamberlain at Bad Godesburg for what seemed to be the final stages of Hitler's "negotiated" triumph, (although the evidence of any negotiation was nil since Hitler was to achieve everything he wanted), suddenly the atmosphere, which had been fairly relaxed, returned to maximum tension. It was apparent that all was not as well as had been thought. In fact all was very bad indeed. Hitler, it appeared, had reneged on the assurances he had given at Berchtesgarten. There he had obtained all he asked for; now at Bad Godesburg he wanted more.

The "peace at any price feeling" which had been prevalent in England noticeably retreated. The idea that the Prime Minister had acted in good faith and had been dishonestly outmanoeuvred was rife. The Czechs had mobilised and there were signs of warlike preparations in England, although these were far short of mobilisation, except that the fleet had been brought to readiness. Tension grew by the hour.

On an evening of that very harassing week, Joan and I went, as we quite often did, to have some drinks at a pub off Sloane Square much frequented by people of our sort. The Prime Minister was to broadcast to the nation and we felt we would prefer to hear what he had to say in the company of others. The fact that he was to broadcast was in itself indication of a major crisis.

Almost all of us there, men and women, were of fighting age. Probably many of the men had reserve or territorial commitments. The girls and married women alike could not tell what war would mean for them; it would bring excitement, perhaps distinction, for some but separation and tragedy for many. As the hour approached, conversation slowed and the pleasant atmosphere of young middle class life was stretched and tense in an uncanny silence, broken at length by the chimes of Big Ben dominating the bar and then a voice, (was it Alvar Liddell's?) announcing simply, "The Prime Minister".

His speech was flat and uninspiring, but how else should he have spoken? Joyfully? Rabble-rousing, jingoistic? Calling the people to fight for King and Country? Which the Oxford undergraduates, not without a good deal of support, had pledged themselves not to do. We weren't going to fight for King and Country in the way all classes had enthusiastically risen to do in 1914. But we knew we had to fight just the same. Mr Chamberlain's words have remained the most famous he ever uttered:

"How horrible, fantastic, incredible, it is," he said, "that we should be digging trenches and trying on gas masks here because of a quarrel in a faraway country between people of whom we know nothing . . . " Included was a half hearted-warning to the dictators but his final words were, "war is a fearful thing, and we must be very clear, before we embark on it, that it is really the great issues that are at stake".

It was about as depressing and uninspiring a speech as it has ever been my misfortune to hear on a great occasion. It might have been deliberately designed to encourage the Germans. And were those Germans really a faraway people of whom we knew nothing? The Prime Minister and his advisers at least must have known something about them. The pub emptied quickly and I drove Joan home in silence, except that I remember saying that whoever had cruelly suggested that Mr Chamberlain would make a good Lord Mayor of Birmingham in a bad year, wasn't far out.

After much anxious consultation we still decided that the family should stay on in London for the timebeing and, like everyone else, we went about our business in a sort of dream until that dramatic moment in the House of Commons when, as the Prime Minister was telling the House of his effort to get Signor Mussolini to intervene, he was handed a note. There was a pause while he read it and the House scarcely dared breathe. Then, with as near as his nature could get to a tone of exaltation, he told his enthralled listeners that he now had an invitation to meet Herr Hitler again, this time in Munich. The House was echoing the feelings of the whole country when they cheered and cheered, encouraging their ageing leader to make one more throw for peace. The rapture in the House reflected in full the feelings of the whole country. Everyone knows the results which have, with hindsight, made Munich a dirty word in English history.

On the day Mr Chamberlain came back from his travels, I had been swimming at the Bath Club where the story was rife that there had been an agreement and there would be no war. Everyone was relieved, and on my way home in the car, feeling curiously drained, I was suddenly peremptorily waved to a standstill by a policeman at the intersection of Sloane Street and Pont Street. Traffic going the other way was also stopped for no reason that I could see, there being no car visible in Pont Street. A small crowd had gathered from nowhere, on the pavements and spilling over onto the road in obvious excitement. I heard shouting and cheering coming from the west, gradually getting louder and nearer and those around me started to wave and cheer as a car came into view, driving slowly past me. The Prime

Minister, his normally haggard face transformed as he smiled and acknowledged the plaudits, was waving a piece of paper which he held in his hand.

Later we heard that he had appeared on the balcony at Downing Street and was greeted, as he had been at Heston aerodrome and along the route to London, by an ecstatically cheering crowd. In Downing Street he told them that the paper he showed them contained Herr Hitler's signature to an assurance that the German and British peoples would never again go to war with each other. He said that this was the second time in fifty years that "Peace with Honour" had been brought home from Germany. He believed it was "Peace for our Time".

I dived into my neglected history books to discover what similarities there might be between the Congress of Berlin when Disraeli and Salisbury had claimed "Peace with Honour", and Mr Chamberlain's sortie to Munich.

It was true that in each case there was a quarrel in Europe between a large, powerful nation and a weak one and in each case the outcome was likely to have such a substantial effect on the future of Europe that the most powerful third-party nations felt they had to be directly and closely involved.

It seemed to me that any resemblance between the two cases ended there. The outcome of the Congress of Berlin was clearly in favour of the Western Powers and particularly of Britain, whose interests in the "faraway area" and her policy of propping up Turkey were an important feature. But Russia also received enough concessions to make her reasonably satisfied with the results. It was a negotiated settlement. In the case of Munich, except that war was for the timebeing avoided, there was no genuine negotiation and no gain for anyone except Hitler. In the one case British interests and the interest of Europe in curbing Russia, a potentially over-mighty state, were served. At Munich the state which two years earlier had been prostrate had obtained exactly what it wanted and was now well on the way to becoming far more over-mighty in Europe than ever Russia had been in the nineteenth century.

I have since wondered whether in suggesting the comparison Mr Chamberlain, who undoubtedly believed that he had some personal influence with Hitler, was mindful of Bismarck's comment in his diary about Disraeli that, "Der Alte Jude, das ist der Mann", (the old Jew is a real man). Did Chamberlain think that Hitler, like Bismarck the most powerful man on the continent of Europe, was making a similar assessment of the old gentleman with the umbrella?

For the moment the British people breathed again and put faith in their brave Prime Minister and the promises he seemed to have obtained at the expense of the Czech nation from the mysterious, hysterical genius who ruled Germany.

We breathed again, but for many it was pretty uneasy breathing. Parliament had rapturously approved Mr Chamberlain's actions and the only resignation from the Government, that of Mr Duff Cooper, made little immediate stir. The House managed to ignore his telling resignation speech, in which he fulminated against Hitler's repeated demonstrations of bad faith and total disregard of solemn affirmations and promises. Votes against the Government were negligible. Mr Churchill and a few others criticised and abstained. But Peace with Honour?

This seemed like peace and we could be thankful for that but . . . Peace with Honour? Disraeli and Salisbury could claim in 1878 that they had gone back on no undertakings to the Turks. It was true that Britain had given no formal undertakings to the Czechs so on the face of it British honour had been saved. But what of the French? What of the League of Nations? Had we not underwritten the formal French treaty obligation to the Czechs? And what of Russia? Sinister and communist she might be, but she was there. She hadn't been "there" at Munich.

It was difficult not to be troubled, not at the fact of peace which I could and did accept with something like enthusiasm, but at the manner by which we had come to that peace. I have subsequently met many who claimed to be vociferous opponents of the Munich settlement but they were very thin on the ground at the time and although my heart was heavy with uncertainty I do not claim to have advocated any different policy.

I know I read the papers and Parliamentary debates with more attention than had been my wont and that I was profoundly unsettled by Duff Cooper's speech and disgusted by the jackals of Poland and Hungary whom Hitler encouraged to the further dismemberment of poor miserable Czechoslovakia. My anti-German instincts revived but I could not be anything but unhappy at the performance of our French allies. And I was not alone in being impressed, even overawed, by German strength and determination, German technical ability, German thoroughness, German military and aeronautical skills. Nor was I the only one to feel some guilt about Versailles and the three or four million Germans in the Sudetenland. It was much later that I realised that these had never been part of Germany and that their real grievance was that in the Austrian Empire they had been favoured over the Czechs, favours naturally withdrawn under rule from Prague.

With all these great events pressing on me I still had a life to lead and a family to support. I could not forecast the future so all I could do was cast about for the best way to direct my activities to allow for the possibility of either war or peace.

It had become clear to me that it was most likely that the Prime Minister's hope of Peace in our Time was not a prophecy but a pipedream. The future I began to see for myself was the short-term prospect of active service in the Air Force and for this I set about preparing. I had been pressed to take the job of Chief Flying Instructor at Gravesend if the school expanded and I agreed to this on the basis that I would work four-and-a-half days a week there, including week-ends, and nights as needed. I would fit in two-and-a-half days in the city in order not to lose touch and to keep my seat warm. This gave us a bit more money with rather less leisure but within the limits imposed by my Gravesend obligations, we had as happy a time in a curious way as I have known either before or since. I had a lot of satisfaction in my work of trying to improve efficiency in training of the young reservist pilots at Gravesend and instilling into them something of the importance of what they had volunteered to do. It wasn't easy for them since they were only available to fly at week-ends and summer evenings and their progress could not be other than erratic. But there was a splendidly keen atmosphere, the Chief Instructor was a close friend with whom I worked with great ease and pleasure and I think Gravesend was a unit which produced more than its share in the considerable British effort to gain air power, the only positive result of the Munich "settlement".

Joan liked to spend time at the beginning of the year with her sister and brother-in-law in Menton, where her mother and her brother also lived and I managed to join them for a few days in March, this being all I could spare from my flying. My activities in the City were very slack and I could take as many days off as I liked from there.

The coast that year seemed unbelievably beautiful with the mimosa more prolific than I had ever seen it. One easily understood how our Edwardian forebears used the Côte d'Azur as relief from the cold and fog of England after the best of their winter sport was over. To wake in the train at Marseilles with surprise that you were (quite naturally) going backwards out of the terminus was as exciting as ever. Equally lovely was the first smell of salt; the lovely clear air; the warm barren country as the train made for the coast; the first glimpse of the blue, blue sea at Fréjus, followed by the hills and tunnels with tantalisingly short views of sea and rocks; the well-known, but still romantic, names appearing on the stations; a prolonged stop at Cannes, where the fashionable travellers with their maids and trunks were met by smart chauffeurs; then much more sea; Juan les Pins, a beach with a few houses and pensions, one hotel and lots of mosquitoes; Antibes, still a picturesque village; and on to Nice, brash and vulgar with the little harbour, the boat for Corsica alongside. We always laughed at its name, the Commandant Quer.

It was a happy time in Menton, all too short. The oranges and tangerines were ripe to pick off the trees in the garden and the sea and sky were so blue and tranquil it was hard to believe that the world was not also as beautiful and tranquil as that lovely coast.

Before I had left England there were rumblings and rumours that "that man" was up to his tricks again and as I made my way back the train was continually being held up. There was talk of troop-trains having precedence and again on the stations were the slack mouthed, cigarette smoking poilus: lounging, dirty, untidy and bored. Hitler, we heard, had made his way to Prague and done what he had expressly promised the British Prime Minister he would never do. By now a puppet government had been installed there which had "invited" the conqueror in, so the Anglo-French guarantee of the Munich frontier was not worth the paper it was written on.

After the final rape of Czechoslovakia even the British Prime Minister began to lose faith in the policy of appeasement which until then had been approved by the large majority of Members of Parliament and by the British people as a whole. From that time the increasingly menacing shadow of Hitler hung over all activities in Europe and in England. At Gravesend the determination of the RAF to expand was reflected in our redoubling efforts to increase our output. The same applied to thousands of organisations all over the country; but as the Government was not prepared to organise full mobilisation of the national resources or decree the removal of financial inhibitions on production and manpower, the expansion could not keep pace with that of Germany.

Hitler, in spite of his having so often sworn that he had no further demands in Europe continued to assert that Danzig, League of Nations, controlled after the Versailles Treaty, was a German town. The Prime Minister, and a great many British people with him, abruptly changed course. For the occupation of the Rhineland and the rape of Austria there had been no war although the Versailles Treaty had been flagrantly violated in both cases. For Czechoslovakia the French, with British support, had wriggled out of their obligations, and Russian attitudes had been dependent on the French.

Now, however, we were told that we would fight for Poland. When Mr Chamberlain spoke in the House of Commons to that effect, he added that His Majesty's Government had informed the Polish Government of the decision and that France had formally associated herself with the pledge. Even the least knowledgeable among us could hardly forbear from saying: where, oh where, are those thirty Czech divisions? And who now controls the output of the famous Skoda Works in Pilsen, Czechoslovakia? We went on with our routine, flying ever more intensely, trying not to drop standards, yet pushing, pushing the pupils forward. The Territorial Army was to be doubled but who would want to join when the equipment, the drill halls and, so some people thought, many of the officers, dated from the Boer War? The introduction of conscription brought no immediate strength but it was at least a gesture to the peoples of the Continent that Britain was in earnest, although the decision of His Majesty's loyal Opposition to vote against it on a Motion of Confidence didn't exactly help. Anyway, there was still cricket.

I was lucky enough that summer to do a refresher course at the RAF Central Flying School which qualified me as an RAF instructor. CFS was one of those thoroughly élitist British institutions, like Eton, the Brigade of Guards, White's and the Foreign Office, which were so established in their superiority that they had no fear of criticism. The standard of flying was very high and the spirit and friendliness, as in all such elitist institutions, was beyond reproach. The time I spent there was as happy as any in my service life and what I learnt from my instructor, a sergeant pilot years younger and with far less flying time than myself, was invaluable. I graduated with the usual "B" or "average" with which I was quite satisfied at the time although all instructors had designs on an "A2" or even the rare and coveted "A1".

Instructing doesn't have the glamour, excitement or variety of the operational branches of the RAF, but for some pilots, of whom I was lucky to be one, it is nevertheless of absorbing interest. Although, as the reader will see if he or she bears with me, I eventually tired of training, I never regretted having spent time and effort in my various instructional jobs.

The summer of 1939 is often compared with that of 1914, but I do not think the shadow of what could only be a long and disastrous war hung nearly so heavily over Europe in 1914 as it did in 1939. From the spring onwards there was much talk of coming to terms with Soviet Russia to check the expansion of Germany since, whatever you thought of communism as a creed, without Russian help there was no alternative to accepting Nazi Germany as the arbiter of Europe. But dislike of communism was paramount in the British Government and ordinary people had little faith in the outcome of the negotiations. The simple, unanswerable question was whether, if Russia were enlisted to balance German power, all of Eastern Europe would be lost to communism.

I was one evening discussing this with a friend who had a background of European travel and experience of Eastern Europe and its problems. The slow and secret talks with the Russians had as yet produced no result and Archie, who had lately written an excellent book about his travels in Poland, Czechoslovakia and the Balkans, tapped his nose and said: "My dear Peter, there is only one certainty in European politics, and that is the ultimate untrustworthiness of the Russians."

Was he right, or was it the implacable hatred of the English ruling class for communism which propelled Stalin into the infamous Molotov-Ribbentrop Pact which, in spite of the poor progress of the low level British delegation in Moscow, stunned and horrified almost everyone in England and showed that war was even closer than I had thought.

Before that ghastly dénouement and in spite of the general unease, there remained a gut feeling that a European War was just so stupid that it couldn't happen, so for such as me it was not difficult to continue to eat, drink and be merry. There was cricket and fun and we talked, drank and loved into the nights without too much thought for the morrow.

My cricket season ended with a tour of the Channel Islands where the sense of ease and stability was stronger than in

England. Their proximity to the Continent was a boon, bringing a strong whiff of France to combine with their passionate Englishness. It simply never occurred to anyone that the coast to the east would ever be other than friendly. The great French Army was just across the water and no one thought of defending the Islands. Our cricket, if not of the top class, was enormous fun.

On the boat going home I spent an hour leaning on the rail with a very pretty girl talking of everything under the sun except of Hitler and war. She knew about books and the beauty of places and the fun of travel and I was sorry when she rejoined a party for dinner. Nevertheless I was totally surprised when later, without a knock, she slipped quietly into my cabin. I was in my bunk reading and, before I could say anything, she had taken my book away and pressed her lips against mine. After a time with a cry of delight she threw off her dressing gown and was nakedly pushing for room in the tiny space of my bunk.

When at length we lay tired but blissfully happy I couldn't not ask her why she had come. She was so obviously not the sort of girl who rushes willy-nilly into men's beds, nor for that matter was I the type who invites or expects such encounters.

She went quiet at that. Our love-making had been of smiles and laughter and fun but now she was serious. Propped uncomfortably on her elbow, she looked down at me with something like sadness in her eyes. She told me that somehow she had become sure that this would be the last holiday she would spend outside England and she wanted all the memories to be happy. She had been happy while we talked by the rail and looked at the sea and suddenly she had thought that "this" would make it complete. I hope and believe that she went away content.

On 1st September any confusion about Hitler's intentions *vis-à-vis* Poland vanished with the German attack in great strength across the Polish border and violent air attacks on Polish Air Force bases. The British Prime Minister still managed to maintain uncertainty about British determination to overcome French equivocation and implement our guarantee to the poor wretched Poles.

Joan being six months pregnant with our second child, I had thought it prudent a few days before that the family should go to her sister in Wiltshire before I was called up and lost control of my life. We shut up the London house and I stayed in the cottage on the edge of the marshes near Gravesend which I was renting by the month.

Flying had stopped at Gravesend, our service-type Hawker Harts had been returned to the RAF and we had been warned that we might have to evacuate with our Tiger Moths at very short notice. In war a training school operating within the front line of the air defence of London would be unacceptably confusing to the defenders on the ground, at sea and in the air. In the safe was a sealed envelope which I was to open on the declaration of war. It would contain instructions as to what we were to do and I was to lead the flying squad to whatever destination had been allotted us.

It is amusing to remember the vague rumours current at the time about our defences. In aviation circles there was much talk of some kind of "ray" whose operation was only vaguely guessed at but was assumed to be something to do with the modern developments in electronics. Many believed it was a "death" ray which, when pointed at an enemy aircraft stopped its engine, and there were serious tales that somewhere on the South Coast a guinea-pig pilot had had his engine stopped by the "ray" and had to force-land at RAF Tangmere from a height of twenty thousand feet. Alas, no such invention was available, but maybe the rumours weren't so far out after all because the mysterious buildings which prompted them were the radar installations without which the country could not have survived in the Battle of Britain.

The drift towards war was notable for the total lack of enthusiasm or jingoism on the part of anyone. The crowds in the streets of Berlin and Paris were said to be as silent and depressed as were those in London. But in England if they did not cheer, neither did they jeer. The British people as a whole felt rather than thought that something wrong and evil was afoot in mainland Europe and had, somehow, to be stopped.

On that Saturday evening, with general mobilisation in progress all over the British Isles and war apparently inevitable, there still seemed to be indecision in Westminster and the Quai d'Orsay, but we pilots, with plenty of time for drinking and discussion, reposed great, if uninformed, confidence in our Polish allies, whose perfidious behaviour towards the Czechs after Munich was forgotten. We believed that they would defend their country with tenacity and skill and hold out while we and the French exerted pressure on the Nazis from the west.

Churchill was back in the Government and there was talk that the Prime Minister still hoped to avoid war, that the French were thoroughly unhelpful but that the Labour and Liberal Parties, who had so assiduously opposed rearmament, were now prodding Mr Chamberlain towards more positive action.

We drank long and deeply to the health of the Polish people and their gallant army which was, we were confident, holding the Nazis in check. Although some thought the Germans had a case over Danzig whose population was overwhelmingly German, we gave our support entirely to the Poles and did not doubt for a moment that Britain and France would act and save that unfortunate nation. We drank many health's to the Polish General, sometimes called Schmidley-Ridz and sometimes Ridz-Schmidley. Then, on a news bulletin, came the news that the Polish Air Force had been virtually destroyed on the ground and some of the drink died out of us. But we still believed that the threat of the great French Army would yet make Hitler draw back.

On 3rd September 1939 I awoke with a hangover to the news that a British ultimatum had at last been sent to Germany. This was to expire at eleven o'clock and if no satisfactory reply had been received by then and no German action had been taken to reverse the aggression against Poland, Britain would be at war with Germany. The news from Poland was not good and, although I was not then fully able to filter the equivocations and inexactitudes by which in war disasters are temporarily concealed, it wasn't difficult to tell that things were far from rosy on the Polish front. And where were the French?

If war was declared our instructions were to evacuate
Gravesend aerodrome immediately and I was to open a sealed
envelope giving the destination to which our remaining aircraft
were to be flown. The Prime Minister's broadcast was timed for
eleven-fifteen, a quarter of an hour after the ultimatum had
expired so I decided we would listen to the broadcast ready to
fly. The ground crews were to start the aircraft as soon as we
emerged from the hut where we had a wireless set. I was to lead
the flock and the others would follow.

At the appointed hour over the air came, once again, the tired
uninspired voice of a man already defeated. Mr Chamberlain
remained determined to undertake the task he loathed and for
which he must have known that he was totally unfitted, but
never, I think, has minister offered less of leadership in
committing his country to so obscure and dangerous a future.
I was not alone in that I went to war in a vacuum, with no idea of
what I should do or become, or of what sort of war it would be.
It was all unreal and distant. Poland was in truth "a faraway
country of which we knew nothing".

I made hasty calculations as to the courses I would fly,
strapped myself in, ran up the engine and taxied out for take-off.
When everyone seemed in position I raised my right arm, saw
them all acknowledge, dropped my hand to the stick and we took
off in a wide gaggle. We were finished with Gravesend and I, in
common with millions of others, had lost control of my life.

I first set course southwards towards Reigate to keep clear of
London before turning west for Hullavington in Wiltshire which
was our first destination. We were to refuel there and then fly
north to Castle Bromwich, near Birmingham, where, apparently,
lay our wartime task. Virtually all flying in England was
prohibited and our roundabout route was specified so that we
would not confuse the defences on the east side of the country.

It was a beautiful day with unlimited visibility and I had
reached about two thousand feet when, looking around to see that
all my flock were following, I was riveted, and I admit appalled,
by an extraordinary sight. Over the southern suburbs, and behind
them over all London, the balloon barrage was rising. The

ungainly shapes, dozens of them, all fully inflated, were slowly rising to their operational height. Seen from the air it was a truly awesome spectacle, not least because of its implications. The only conclusion that I could draw was that, even before the British declaration of war, a German air fleet had taken off, almost certainly to raid London. If they had been reported by the Observer Corps, that faithful bevy of old gentlemen scanning the skies with their field glasses which, as far as I then knew, was our only early warning system, they must be pretty close. It was very unlikely that the balloons would be trying a full-scale training exercise so I could only think that my assessment that there would be no early attacks on London had been quite wrong and that there was a real air raid afoot.

When the raiders had dropped their bombs it was quite likely that they would dive out of the target area, possibly in a south-easterly direction in which case they could well coincide with us. The glee of well-armed bombers meeting such slow and helpless victims didn't bear thinking about.

I considered various plans. I was not so much concerned by the chances of meeting enemy aircraft as by the likelihood of people in England getting trigger-happy at an alarm and firing off at any aircraft they might see. In the end I decided to continue on our way, climbing higher to be out of range of casual small arms, and hope for the best. It was a considerable relief when we were to the west of London and there were no signs of bombing in the city.

At Hullavington all was quiet, there was no flying and I was told that the Air Raid warning which had sent the balloons skyward had been a false alarm. A small private aircraft returning to England had put the fear of God into innumerable breasts. It was the first farce of the "phoney war". I was soon to experience the second and third.

When I asked for petrol the answer was a flat "No". RAF orders were that no petrol was to be issued except to RAF aircraft flown by RAF personnel. That ruled us out and we could not get to Castle Bromwich without a refill. I repaired to the Mess where I found old friends who offered to try to get the ban lifted but as there was a civil aerodrome nearby I thought it would be quicker not to stir this particular pot and just hop over a few hedges to where we could be refuelled on a commercial basis.

The third farce was that when I arrived at Castle Bromwich to which I had been specifically directed, I found another balloon barrage flying. My appearance near the field was greeted by red Verey lights and Aldis Lamps flashing red signals, denoting that under no circumstances could I, or anyone else, land.

It was an awkward predicament since I knew of no other aerodrome in the immediate vicinity nor could I communicate in any way with the ground or with the dozen or so aircraft following me. On balance I decided that, since all were fairly experienced pilots, they would avoid the cables and, to a veritable barrage of red Verey lights, I landed and no one came to any harm. All in all the day made a queer beginning to the greatest war of all time. We had a good laugh, although the locals operating the balloons stood on their dignity and affected not to see the joke. I suspect that they may have been slightly disappointed that their balloons had not claimed a victim from the intruders.

Nearly a week passed before we managed to obtain a decision as to our next destination. This turned out to be a small civil aerodrome only a few miles away, on the site of what is now the capacious and excellent civil airport of Birmingham. Here we were absorbed into another school and, as often happens in such shot-gun marriages, the spirit and camaraderie of our Gravesend operation evaporated in an atmosphere of petty controls, red tape and a much smaller commitment to getting on with the job.

These were the first days of the "black-out" in which the fear of air raids, I suppose stoked from Whitehall, reached horrendous heights among local authorities, the police and, indeed, the public at large. The tiny slits of light which, at the beginning of the war, were all a car's headlights were allowed to emit must have been responsible for a plethora of pedestrian deaths and damage to cars and property.

A good example of this near-panic was when the workers at a factory in Birmingham refused to work the night shift on the grounds that the black-out of some skylights was not effective. In vain the management poured more black paint on the suspect windows, the workers insisted that they and their vital factory were being exposed to mortal danger.

It was decided that personal inspection was the only way out of the impasse and that permission should be obtained from Air Ministry for a single aircraft to inspect the factory which would be unmanned but with working lights switched on. Nobody particularly relished the job since no lights on the aerodrome or anywhere else were to be allowed, but I suppose I was the obvious "volunteer". For take-off and landing I was allowed two small "gooseneck" flares, invisible above one thousand feet or further away than a mile or so. I was to climb to ten thousand feet above Birmingham and then flash my navigation lights on and off, whereat a pilot stationed on the factory roof would direct an Aldis lamp at me so that I could locate the factory. When I had acknowledged he would switch off and I would see whether there was any sign of light from the area.

It was a pitch black night and without navigational aids or wireless the whole exercise was distinctly unnerving. However, I was able to assure the workers that their blackout was fully effective and had the satisfaction that shift work was renewed.

I soon grew impatient with idleness in the small niche I was asked to fill at Elmdon. It was made very clear that suggestions from new brooms likely to interfere with a leisurely way of life or inject any spirit of urgency into the flying programme would be unwelcome. I, therefore, pulled some strings and got myself formally called up into the mainstream of Air Force life. Within a month I was posted to Drem, not far from Edinburgh but, more importantly, on that fine North Berwick coast where are situated some of the finest golf courses in Scotland and, therefore, in all Britain. I say more importantly because, having arranged my transfer in order to be able to do more useful flying, at Drem flying had been stopped altogether.

This was not through any lack of keenness but because in the first days of the war a German reconnaissance aircraft had appeared off the Firth of Forth which was a prime defence area. It was Gravesend all over again and I, therefore, resigned myself to playing golf every day at Muirfield, a lovely course little used since most of the membership was fully occupied on war work.

This too idyllic interlude lasted a month, after which I was posted to South Cerney in Gloucestershire. I made my first flight there on my thirty-first birthday and from then on I did at last become an active part of the Herculean efforts the Air Force was making to catch up from the lethargy of peacetime.

During the "phoney war" all England lived in a state of curious suspension, knowing, after the debacle in Poland, that we faced a frighteningly powerful and ruthless enemy but finding it hard to believe passionately in a war in which there was no "actual" fighting. I think no-one at that stage visualised the shape of the war to come, but the exploits of the Lutwaffe in Poland, where the Polish Air Force had been virtually destroyed in a single day, made it clear enough that all might be won or lost in the air. We in Training Command had our brief loud and clear. It was to use every available aircraft and every available flying hour to produce every new pilot we possibly could. No-one had any illusions as to the urgency of our task.

However good and plentiful the new aircraft coming on stream might be, without pilots they were no more than lumps of very expensive metal. There was a growing danger of a large pile of those lumps of metal, with all their elaborate equipment, lying idle because the pilots who could make them into weapons of war simply did not exist. To increase the numbers of the lumps of metal was not easy but it could be done by the introduction of shifts, longer working hours and improvement in methods. Much of this was being done and next year was vastly accelerated by the appointment of Lord Beaverbrook as Minister of Aircraft Production.

To increase the number of pilots was much more difficult. The erratic weather in the British Isles is often unsuitable and sometimes impossible for flying training. To take too many risks leads to more accidents and losses of aircraft. Worse than losing aircraft is the loss of the effort which has been put into training pupils and, worst of all, the loss of almost irreplaceable instructors. The balance between excessive caution and taking too many risks had to be struck with great care and nobody got it right all the time. There are limits to the amount of good teaching in the air an instructor can do in a day, a week or a month without getting stale and dropping the standard. A pupil pilot, however keen, can only absorb so much at a time which is why instructional flights have always been limited in duration.

General Wavell has said with much wisdom that ill-feeling between Staff Officers and those in the operational field is as old as warfare and the Air Force was no exception to that shrewd General's assessment. I have known many examples and, since I managed to survive the war without occupying a Staff Officer's chair, I ought to be prejudiced. In that time of the phoney war, however, I thought that the staff from the Air Ministry downwards worked well with those who did the flying. We grumbled at the targets they set and they grumbled at our failures to meet them but in the outcome the supply of pilots, always a critical factor, was enough, but only just enough, to meet the awful needs which arose in the years to come.

After a time I found an adequate house near South Cerney which I could rent for my family, then living expensively in an hotel. I arranged for our furniture to be brought down from London and, since the arrival of our second child was inconveniently signalled on moving day, I had the day off and, in thoroughly inexpert fashion, supervised the unloading. Domestic help had by then dried up for newcomers to the district so I cheerfully but inexpertly made my bed and slept alone in the house. I woke in the morning with a raging temperature and feeling like death. Luckily I had a telephone installed for service reasons and could get a doctor who diagnosed double pneumonia due to sleeping in damp sheets. How was I, a male ignoramus, to know that sheets needed "airing"? I had heard the word but hadn't the slightest idea what it meant. Thanks to what was then a new remedy called "M&B", I survived, but it wasn't pleasant.

At South Cerney there was no slot for me as a senior instructor but I was glad for the time to do a junior job in which I could get used to the twin-engined monoplane Oxford trainer which was a very different aircraft from anything I had flown before, and to the conditions of flying in wartime.

There was one important hurdle which I had to overcome. This was that the monoplane, which was clearly ousting the biplane, did not respond to the controls as sensitively and elegantly as had the biplanes. It had relatively little "feel", so you had to discard the old belief that flying by feel was the only safe and proper way to fly. You had to forget the kind of snobbery which said that using instruments, even as a check, was unworthy. In biplanes a skilled pilot could and did know his air-speed and the correctness of his flying by "the seat of his pants" as the saying went. With a monoplane it was absolutely necessary to refer continually to instruments, without, of course, relaxing the look out for other aircraft.

This was specially important in night flying. The horizon on fine nights can be exceptionally well-defined and visual flying is no trouble. But on many really dark nights there is no horizon whatever. In peacetime with plenty of lights on the ground this was tiresome but not really troublesome, but in the very strictly enforced conditions of blackout, the world outside the cockpit was a wall of utter blackness giving no visual indication whatever of earth, sky or direction. For those, like myself, who had done a lot of flying in aircraft with rudimentary instruments and had normally flown visually, it was quite an effort to train yourself to do the one thing you had been teaching pupils not to do for years, to fly by instruments with your head in the cockpit.

This has now become so normal that it is hard for anyone now to conjure up the difficulty, even the horror, of having to discard all your familiar instincts and sensations in the air. Through many hours of using those feelings their messages had become inordinately strong, however rigidly you disciplined yourself to discard them. But discard is the wrong word because you couldn't discard them. They were there, telling you often quite the wrong thing. They would even deceive you by making the engine noise sound as if you were diving or climbing when you were doing nothing of the sort or even the opposite.

Taking off on a dark night was the ultimate test. For training purposes we used the standard flarepath of two flares at fifty yards apart and three at hundred-yard intervals. They were not the old "money" flares which gave quite a lot of light, but "goosenecks" which gave very little light indeed. They provided the absolute minimum guidance needed for take-off and landing but, being designed not to attract hostile aircraft, they were not nearly as helpful as to what we were used to in peacetime.

On take-off, the Oxford at full power would be just leaving the ground as you reached the last flare but had not then attained a safe climbing speed. It was at this moment that the pilot had to forget all idea of seeing where he was or what he was doing and concentrate on his instruments, raising the undercarriage, keeping dead straight and gradually increasing his speed while still remaining in a climbing attitude. The Oxford had little spare power and if you tried to climb too quickly by easing the nose up, you would reach a semi-stalled condition from which you could only recover by pushing the stick forward. You then lost height, perhaps too much height and the invisible ground would be hard. It was not unreasonable for pupils with little experience of flying by instruments to have nightmares about their introduction to night flying and even some instructors (including myself) had worries.

There were many crashes in Flying Training that winter, nearly all avoidable. They were due to carelessness, over-confidence, bad weather and sometimes, I am afraid, lack of proper supervision. Some were trivial, some serious, some fatal. One of our instructors and several pupils were killed on night flying. Any accident put back the training programme while, as the winter ended and the war became active with the German invasion of Norway, the requirement for trained pilots increased daily.

The news from Norway which had been sustainedly optimistic for a time, suddenly reversed and it was clear that we were faced with defeat. Norway was going the way of Austria,

Czechoslovakia and Poland. Hitler's so-called "Peace Offensive" had prolonged the unreality of the war after the fighting in Poland was over. Now it was much closer and one's friends were in it. The makeshift attempt to operate obsolescent fighters from a frozen lake savoured of the French comment on the Charge of the Light Brigade, "c'est magnifique mais ce n'est pas la Guerre". But this was war indeed and, as naval activities were reported, the names of the ships we had often seen and sometimes visited at Portsmouth rolled off the announcer's tongue, *Warspite, Renown, Repulse, Resolution, Furious.* The Admiral, Geoffrey Layton, was a friend of my mother's and we had known the family well when I was a teenager. There was nothing for us but to redouble our efforts to produce the pilots.

One picture comes back to me from those days. It is of my mother sitting by the fire in the drawing room of our village house after a not very happy news bulletin. She sat, as she always did, head slightly on one side and bowed as she stared into the fire and I was suddenly struck with a vivid realisation of her predicament. Her husband, my father, had been killed in the very first months of that other war and she had not married again, dedicating her life to his children. Now, a quarter of a century on but before she had become an old woman, had come another war with the same enemy. Her two sons were of fighting age, one in the Army, the other in the Air Force. Now that it had ceased to be a Phoney War and looked sure to be a shooting war, how could she expect that those sons would survive? She felt my eyes on her and looked up and smiled. She was a brave lady.

It was soon clear that the Norwegian campaign was a disaster and Parliament, Press and BBC were much occupied with speculation about the Prime Minister's capacity to lead the nation in war. Along with many others I did not comprehend our danger. I had lived long with Charles II's famous Article of War that "It is upon the Navy under the Providence of God that the safety, honour and welfare of this realm do chiefly attend". Just lately the cry "The Navy's here!" had echoed through the country when *HMS Cossack* had rescued British prisoners from a German ship in Altmark Fiord. But without proper air support the Navy had not been able to achieve success in Norway. So more pilots . . . more pilots.

It was our custom, in order to save valuable time, that after giving a pupil dual instruction, the instructor would get out of the aeroplane at the edge of the tarmac, despatch the pupil for his solo exercise and walk laboriously back to the hangar, his heavy parachute still on his back. One May morning I was proceeding thus when my Flight Sergeant, quiet and undramatic as he always was, greeted me with, "They've gone into Holland".

I remember a great surge of fury. Until that moment, in spite of many horrors, there had always been an air of distant unreality about this extraordinary war. I had not really hated the Germans, only Hitler. There had always been a little cool voice in the background, uneasy about French lack of generosity in victory in 1918 and the British and American failure to check the not unjustified vengeance they sought. I had believed in international order and justice and the League of Nations. An individual nation which erred should be brought to justice, yes, but police and judge don't, or shouldn't, hate criminals while they bring them to punishment.

Even at the awful attack on Poland and the horror stories of the bombing and occupation, I had stepped back from the brink of real hatred of the German nation. I felt that the war had to be fought with dedication to a principle but not with hatred of a nation. That way the settlement at the end could be just and fair and productive of long-term peace.

Somehow the Flight Sergeant's "they" and the venom with which he imbued the word finally changed all that. I hated Hitler and I hated the Germans who loved him and made him their near-God. I did not forget the manifold sins of my own country but I knew that these were peccadilloes compared to this dreadful and cruel German disregard of all standards of decency and civilised behaviour. At the simple sentence, "They've gone into Holland" my heart turned over. I had never been to Holland nor ever known a Dutchman but that small neutral country with its close links with Britain and the English crown had a special niche as an island of peace in a turbulent world. And the Flight Sergeant's "they" had been infinitely expressive. It could only have one meaning; it meant the villains, the arch-enemies of mankind, the Nazi Germans. I was surprised but not shocked at the wave of hatred that swept over me.

I soon learnt that the Flight Sergeant's message had not told half the news. The Germans were also across the borders of Belgium and Luxembourg in huge strength. The objective was obviously not the subjection of those small and helpless countries which were flies beneath the Nazi boot. It was in essence a re-run of the famous Schlieffen Plan of 1914, a gigantic "right hook" attack on France. My mind went back to Brightwell and the hushed company in the hall and the pretty Belgian refugee girl who had seemed to my childish eyes a being from another planet.

I then thought, quite confidently, that the Germans would be stopped as they had been at the Battle of the Marne, although I did think also of Bismarck's war when the Germans weren't stopped. But this time surely there was the great French Army, the finest in Europe, and its invincible Maginot Line .

I had no great opinion of the morale of the French nation but, like most ordinary people in England, I had great faith in the invincibility of the French Army, supposed to be the best in Europe. They had built the impassable Maginot Line, constructed with heaven knew how many thousands of tons of concrete and equipped with the latest heavy guns which could deal with any number of tanks. What I, and those many who thought like me, did not know was that the Maginot Line did not defend the Franco-Belgian frontier, also that the French, and to a lesser extent the British, High Commands were still fighting the war of 1918. Most of the German Generals had a much more modern outlook, largely culled from the writings of the British writers Liddell Hart and Fuller. The Allied armies in France were circumvented and defeated because of the genius of two German generals who had imbibed this doctrine, General von Manstein who formulated the plan of attack and General Guderian who spearheaded the Panzer advance.

I soon realised that the news from France was bad but I had no idea quite how bad until in the last days of May. I was flying tranquilly at a few thousand feet above Oxfordshire and, far away to the east, I saw a huge black cloud, of whose significance at the time I had no idea. It had risen over Dunkirk. The small British contingent in France was decimated and its equipment lost, although many of its men struggled home. Within weeks we had no French ally. We were alone.

There is no more galling predicament for an able-bodied member of the armed forces than to be helplessly but safely ensconced in a rear area when his country is heavily engaged in a desperate losing battle in which every man and machine is needed. Such was my situation throughout the Battles of France and of Britain. I lived in the comfortable farmhouse we rented in Gloucestershire with my wife, our nanny, a three-year-old child and a baby. We had a "daily" and a man to work in the garden twice a week. When, in response to the Government appeal to "dig for victory" I made him dig up the beautifully manicured lawn in order to plant potatoes, he could have killed me since he had tended, mown and weeded that lawn for years. Alas, we never ate the potatoes nor knew who did.

It was harassing for me, as a pre-war fighter pilot, to be spending those anxious days trundling my Oxford or ancient Hart trainer round an aerodrome miles from the battle. My contemporaries were fighting, even the young inexperienced men whom I was training would soon be flying the fine new Spitfires and Hurricanes, while I was still blundering around Gloucestershire, testing, encouraging, polishing or rejecting their successors. But it was clear that no one any longer had the right to consult his own preferences.

Someone, I think it was Storm Jameson, wrote a novel about that time called *Cloudless May*. I do not now remember the book but the title has stayed in my mind, so calm and beautiful was the English countryside in contrast to the terrible events across the water. The weather held pretty well all through June, July and August when it was difficult to grasp the realities of the great battle in the English skies. All we could do was fly, fly, fly, and keep the pupils flying and working to make themselves ready for what was before them.

The wastage of resources through accidents was a constant worry in training circles in the RAF. The schools were bombarded with directives to take more care, ensure flying discipline and maintain standards. But equally we were under severe pressure to produce a greater output of flying hours and trained pilots.

Often when I was lying awake, too tired to find sleep quickly, I would fret my brains to find ways of improving the standard without slowing the process. RAF flying training was then, I think, accepted as being very good, probably the best in the world. It had been built up since the days in the first war when I had watched from Stubbington playing fields the crude machines from Gosport curvetting in the sky. The "Gosport Tube", through which instructors communicated with their pupils, dated from those days. Now the Central Flying School, responsible for training instructors and laying down procedures and standards, commanded great prestige and respect throughout the world.

When I left CFS I had not been conscious of any deficiencies in the course, only of my own failure to achieve the complete mastery it offered. Now, thinking again, I realised that, as flying had developed, a gap had opened which, while it had mattered little in peacetime, was now very important indeed. It concerned the teaching of flying by instruments.

The syllabus of flying instruction had been built up over the years. There was a standard "patter", elaborate and detailed, which described the exact methods of using the controls to effect the manoeuvres of which the aircraft was capable. Instructors had to master this in order to pass on the skills in handling aircraft to their pupils. But for instrument flying there was no syllabus. There were various methods for different aircraft to reproduce the effect of flying "blind" and every pupil had to do a certain minimum of time "under the hood" while his instructor acted as safety pilot. But there was no laid-down set of exercises to be carried out, with the result that much of the time spent "under the hood" was either wasted or even, sometimes, imaginary. Testing of pupils in the skill was desultory or non-existent.

I came to see this attitude to instrument flying as a serious fault in the system because of the wartime factor of more flying in really bad weather and night flying in blackout and poor visibility, both of which called for an enormous improvement in the ability to fly by instruments alone. I decided to inaugurate a system in my own flight to try to improve matters.

Accordingly, I made out a list of exercises to be done under the hood which included doing accurate turns, the important skills of climbing and descending with varying degrees of flap and the undercarriage down as well as up and finally of taking off "blind". I soon had no doubt of a great improvement in standards. All my instructors took to the idea with great enthusiasm as something they had unknowingly been waiting for and all reported on it favourably. When I was satisfied I told a friend on the staff what I was doing. He was enthusiastic and I was called for an interview with the Group Commander who had expressed interest.

I did not altogether relish this since he was Air Vice-Marshal Park who for a time had been my Station Commander before the war. I well knew that he had cordially disliked me as a wild and unruly young man, little susceptible to discipline and unlikely to be a credit to the service. He had only very recently been posted to the Group from No. 11 Fighter Group, which he had commanded with immense distinction throughout the Battle of Britain. To be sent to command a Training Group was a transition which could only be seen as demotion. Since he had played an outstanding part in the most harassing days of the Battle of Britain and his Group had borne the brunt of the fighting, it was widely rumoured that he had been unfairly ousted by a less successful rival. He had every reason to be a bit disgruntled and I felt it was very unlikely that I should find him any better disposed to me than he had been before the war.

He was a bigger man than I had credited. Greeting me in the most friendly way, he listened to my scheme with close and rather flattering attention. When I had finished he was immensely enthusiastic. He had enormous drive and a high reputation as a pilot and he used all the weapons of his considerable authority to push the scheme. The result within a very few weeks was that the first ever Instrument Flying Syllabus was promulgated by the Central Flying School for use in all training units throughout the RAF.

Towards the end of 1941 I was appointed Chief Instructor at the Advanced Flying Training School at Lyneham in Wiltshire and promoted to Wing Commander. My previous excursions up and down the promotion ladder had each been hindered by unforeseen complications. This was no exception.

Until the war aerodromes had always been grass fields, fairly level, reasonably immune from obstructions but often unusable after heavy rain or snow. So, from early in the war, with aircraft getting heavier, operational aerodromes were laid out with two concrete runways, a long one for use in the prevailing wind and a shorter one crossing at an angle. Existing aerodromes were increasingly being converted to this pattern and it was odd that since at the new stations the flying area was almost entirely covered with concrete the decree went forth that aerodromes were now to be known as airfields. No sooner had I started work in the new School than we were told that Lyneham was to be equipped with runways and we were to move out, quick. After a few days of not knowing our future we were offered a substitute aerodrome in Lincolnshire and I was deputed to inspect it and confirm its suitability for our purpose.

When I got there I was really appalled. There was one long runway completed and a second nearly so. It had been intended for use by Bomber Command but apparently had been refused by them as unsuitable for their use. The accommodation and facilities were awful, mostly unfinished. There were taxi tracks and dispersal sites designed for a bomber squadron but totally unsuited to a training unit. There were none of the assembly rooms, lecture rooms and so on absolutely necessary to complete ground training. As for flying training, there were no huts or accommodation for flight offices where pupils could be supervised when not actually flying.

Flying training, which entails large numbers of take-offs and landings, had always been carried out on a grass field with plenty of room on either side of the centre line dictated by the wind, so that several take-offs and landings could, with reasonable care, be done simultaneously.

The idea of training on a runway airfield had never crossed anyone's mind because with a single runway in use only one aircraft can take off or land at one time. A runway has to be clear of one movement before another can safely take place. This means that all movements have to be controlled from the ground and instead of five or six landings and take-offs being possible at one time, all the time, each movement would have to be controlled from the ground and could take anything up to five minutes to complete. Training aircraft were not fitted with radio so control would have to be by the old crude method of signalling by Aldis Lamp. On a runway airfield the wind will seldom be exactly aligned with a runway, so many landings and take-offs have to be done slightly crosswind, which would be most unsuitable for inexperienced pupils.

My report could only be to the effect that it would be difficult to find any location in the United Kingdom which possessed fewer of the attributes normally considered essential for a training airfield. When the runways were completed there was still a good deal of work to be done on the perimeter track and dispersal sites. The main runway had a very nasty slope which was presumably why Bomber Command had turned it down.

The reply came that there was nowhere else available and if we could not accept Ossington the School would have to be disbanded. Confronted with this, I said, on reflection, that although the output would be lower than that of a normal training school, I thought it might be just possible to establish methods and procedures by which we could get by. Having made this rash statement, with which no one either on the staff, in the active instructing world, or even my own commanding officer agreed, I was told to make it come true. It was noticeable that literally no one on the staff was prepared to associate himself positively with the gamble.

The School was lucky to have the services of four or five very experienced instructors of whom two, in particular, I knew to be of exceptional quality and, despite misgivings, which I shared, they threw themselves whole-heartedly into the enterprise. Although the technical flying problems were truly formidable, the whole exercise was a good example of a fascinating rule well-known in all three services, that the more isolated and uncomfortable a unit may be, the more likely it will be that, if left to itself it will overcome almost any difficulties.

Everyone of us was daunted and shocked by the idea of trying to operate when there had been no proper preparation, and the facilities for living and for ground instruction were totally inadequate. As for flying, the idea of teaching and practising take-offs and landings, often crosswind, on these runways was regarded as absurd. But our Commanding Officer, although he had been as sceptical as anyone, backed us to the hilt and the sense of a joint effort of which everyone was an integral part was overwhelming.

Just before we started work the German battle cruisers *Scharnhorst* and *Gneisenau* ran the gauntlet from their hiding place at Brest back to their base in Germany, coming within range of Dover guns, of many torpedo-carrying destroyers and small craft and of shore-based aircraft. They and their escorts completed the hazardous journey without apparent damage in spite of determined and repeated attacks by all arms. Although the weather had been terrible, giving the German ships wonderful concealment, the country was dismayed that we no longer seemed to control even the narrow seas so close to our own coasts. The Government came under heavy criticism and national morale fell catastrophically. I think that this fresh setback at a time when, although we had a new ally, everything still seemed to be going wrong, stimulated us at Ossington in the task we had undertaken.

It was necessary to ask everyone to work unaccustomed hours as well as accepting the very difficult conditions but, with the skills and effort and suggestions of our most experienced instructors and the goodwill and effort of all, including the pupils, the exercise slowly and unexpectedly started to come to life. When the first pupil was sent solo we had a party to celebrate. We were, to everyone's surprise, on our way.

Since it was now clear that most of our pupils would be destined for Bomber Command which needed a steady flow of replacement pilots, advanced training schools were constantly exhorted to step up the hours of night flying. As the night flying consisted of circuits and landings and no lights were allowed, it was usual to have only three aircraft on at once for fear of collisions since all were flying at circuit height, i.e. fifteen hundred feet. It was even more difficult for us because of the taxying problems with our single runway. However, we got over this by inventing a system whereby we could have twice the normal number of aircraft in the air, sending three aircraft at a time to do what we called an "aerodrome survey". This meant that each one climbed to a pre-arranged height of 2,500 feet or more and stayed at his height until given permission to descend. There was some risk attached to it, especially if there was an air-raid warning and we had to douse the aerodrome lights, but since I and all the senior instructors did our full share of the flying, everyone accepted that it was worthwhile. For several months we far exceeded the amount of night flying carried out by schools with much better facilities. Eventually the penny dropped and our system was put into general use.

There was one snag, however. We were very much in bomber country and the heavy bombers at nearby airfields were now taking off and landing at fairly close intervals owing to new tactics of concentration. This meant that quite a few heavies would be lumbering through the air, clumsy and unmanoevrable, climbing very slowly because of their huge loads, and would not find it acceptable to avoid the airspace round Ossington. A couple of Oxfords at fifteen hundred feet some miles away from their airfields had not constituted any danger, but when we started to fly at four or five thousand feet it became a different matter because they might need to climb through those heights. Since nobody was allowed to show any lights, our aircraft presented some danger to both bombers and themselves.

The Wing Commander in command of the nearest bomber squadron came over to see me and we arranged that his flying control staff should notify us when they wanted our flying restricted to below two thousand feet for general safety. He was extremely enthusiastic about our new methods, saying that it was a universal complaint on the squadrons that new pilots had not nearly enough night experience, making the first part of their operational careers distinctly dicey. A few extra hours on Oxfords would obviously not solve the problem, but it would help.

We got on well together and he asked me to come over to lunch the following week, with the proviso that if they were "working" he would postpone. No message came and I went over by car, not wishing to waste aircraft time. Arriving at the mess I was conscious of a general air of happy elation and a good deal of convivial noise. No one greeted me and I proceeded into the ante-room where there was a considerable assembly and much talk and laughter. I looked round for my host who was invisible in the throng but a young officer took pity on me and politely asked whether I was looking for someone.

I explained that the Wing Commander had asked me to lunch. I hoped he was here?

"Oh, he's here all right, sir, don't you worry. But its a party. Bit of a do last night and a stand down tonight. I'll get the Wing Commander . . . "

He extricated my host, a small man, from the middle of the largest and noisiest group which he left with obvious reluctance to greet me with somewhat exaggerated bonhomie.

"Yes of course I remember," said he, which was manifestly untrue. "Splendid to see you. Come and meet the chaps. Wizard prang last night. Here waiter . . . a pint for the Wing Commander. Come and meet the chaps. Bill, Johnny, Lazy . . . this is Wing Commander . . . oh dear I must be drunk, I've forgotten your name . . . Come and look at the photos . . . They're the best ever. Teach those bloody Frogs to play along with the Boche . . .

The night photographs were remarkable indeed. They showed clearly the Renault works on an island in the Seine just outside Paris. He pointed out target indicators descending and all the prints showed explosions, smoke and fires. From the photographs a layman would have said that the factory was a complete write-off and that it would hardly be worth the enemy's while to try to recover significant production from the chaos which, to the untrained eye, seemed to cover the whole island. It seemed incredible that any human being who had been in the factory could have survived.

I asked about this and was told that they believed that, in common with most French and German factories, there was no night shift. There were built-up areas all round and naturally some of the bombs would have fallen outside the target. But, after all, there was a war on. And the French hadn't behaved all that brilliantly . . .

"NEWS". A shout so stentorian as to quiet even the rapidly increasing din of laughter and talk, was followed by a chorus of "Sssssshh, ssssshh. Tankards in hand, everyone gathered round the radiogram while a signals officer adjusted the tuning and volume.

"I bet we're on first," said someone.

"Unless they've murdered ole Hitler!"

The cool, measured tones of the BBC announcer gave this, the most outstanding success of Bomber Command in two-and-a-half years of war, pride of place.

When the bulletin turned to other news it was soon drowned by talk, laughter, shouts for the steward and calls for more and more beer which seemed to be in ample supply. (Ours was strictly rationed.) I decided I must sneak out, not that I was averse to such parties but, until you get a bit drunk, they aren't such fun when you are the outsider. I made an excuse about having to see a visitor from the staff which was greeted with shouts of "Fuck the staff". "Teach them to fly" and so on. Missing my lunch, I made my way back to my familiar work in the grip of much deep thought. The difference in outlook and way of life between men with roughly the same background and wearing the same uniform was very striking. What I had seen was, I realised, something of a "one off", born of the exceptional success of the night's operation, but I was very conscious that the camaraderie, the sense of being an exclusive band of brothers, in this, the first wartime bomber squadron I had known, was something quite apart from the rest of the service. I also knew that only a few nights before they had been to Berlin and the casualties had been heavy. They had every right to celebrate the success on an easy target, but behind the laughter it was impossible not to know that the inevitable question was lurking as they looked around the cheerful, familiar faces; who, who, was going to survive. Not all, that they well knew.

Much of my thought revolved around my own situation.

From the start of the war I had accepted that there was no chance of my being released from training duties to return to my first love, fighters. With the advent of the Hurricanes and Spitfires there had come totally new flying techniques and I knew that my peacetime frolics on those beautiful biplanes were now totally irrelevant. By the time the Battle of Britain was joined the urgent need was for young pilots in the lower ranks, not for older men who would have to learn from the bottom. I appreciated that the training job, unspectacular and often frustrating, had to be done and done well. Those who, like myself, could obviously make a real contribution, were not likely to be spared.

In early 1942, however, much had changed. The supply of pilots, thanks in part to the huge overseas training programmes, was up with events. It was now only necessary to keep up the numbers and improve standards. I felt, although it may seem self-satisfied to say so, that I had made an adequate contribution. I had been in charge of several units whose efficiency had been acknowledged. I had triggered off an important development in the teaching of instrument flying and I had done a good deal of flying myself, much more than was normally expected or required of a Chief Instructor. I still had this very important task on my hands to prove that an Advanced Flying Training School could be operated from a runway airfield. I was pretty sure that we were on the right track and that it was, against all expectations, going to come off. If I was quite sure of that I felt I could legitimately put in for a change of job. I was thirty-three years of age and I did not relish the idea of going through the war without seeing any action. I started to lay my plans.

I had some knowledge of the intricate and often devious methods by which vested interests in the various Commands kept or acquired those officers whom they considered would be of value and disposed of those with whom they were less impressed. Postings in the rank of Wing Commander and above were carefully vetted and arranged. Private "Empires" became the rule rather than the exception. Great men leading big formations made it clear that they knew best who would serve them best. Although this led to favouritism, it produced teams of officers who stuck together with a fierce personal loyalty which served to relieve the awful strains of war on their masters. Those outside the system criticised but those within knew that it worked.

To get where you wanted to be, therefore, it was necessary to discover what avenues you could best use and what strings you could best pull. If an application for posting was turned down, it was no good putting in another for at least a year, probably more.

My Station Commander, an old acquaintance, had become a friend and, although I knew he would want me to stay, I also knew that he would not stand in my way. In June he agreed with me that the experiment which we had so doubtfully undertaken was a roaring success and, with his blessing set the wheels in motion for my move.

I managed to get an interview with the AOC No. 5 (Bomber) Group which controlled the squadron I had visited after the Renault raid. He was friendly enough but questioned me closely and shrewdly on my service record and my flying and administrative experience, making it clear that he preferred to make new Squadron Commanders from officers in his Group who had considerable operational experience. To send someone with no experience of bombing to command a squadron was on the whole unfair both the experienced pilots in the squadron and to the officer himself. I could not help seeing his point and my heart sank.

However, in the end he said that, if I put in an application soon I might expect to finish my courses at the Operational Training Units in time to come to the Group before the great bomber offensive which should start in the spring of 1943. He gave me no definite assurance but said that, if my course results were satisfactory, and if there were a vacancy, he would probably be able to accept me. It was really the best I could expect.

After the interview I left in a rather muddled state of mind. I had a foot in the door and that was good, very good. But I was uneasy at some of the things the AOC had told me. He said that the Manchester, the heavy bomber planned to re-equip his Group, which still had some pre-war Hampdens, was a complete failure and was being withdrawn. So his force was likely to be temporarily grounded when the country, in spite of now being sustained by Russian and American allies, badly needed the stimulus that spectacular results in the bomber attack on Germany could give. The war was going badly. He said that the Commando raid on Dieppe had been nothing short of a disaster and the campaign in Africa was little different. The Germans might reach Cairo with all that that implied. The fall of Singapore had been nothing less than a fiasco and the loss through incompetence of the fine old *HMS Repulse* and the spanking new *HMS Prince of Wales* with virtually all their crews was a disastrous blow in the Pacific. A huge offensive by Bomber Command was, he said, the only immediate way in which, now that the glory of having "stood alone" was wearing thin, we could attack the enemy. Only thus could we give some help to our hard-pressed ally the Soviet Union, which had lost great numbers of men and quantities of equipment without as yet stemming the German advance towards the Caucasian oilfields.

There was a new Commander-in-Chief at Bomber Command, whose determination and energy were known throughout the RAF, as was his reputation for rudeness, bullying and single-minded intention to have his own way.

It was clear to me, as I drove away from this, the first of many visits to No. 5 Group Headquarters, that what I knew

of Bomber Command was very superficial. The AOC had spoken
of the thousand bomber raids of which he said only that on
Cologne had had any success and I was a little uneasy at his
analysing success in terms of "acres" of the town "devastated".
This savoured more of the indiscriminate bombing of London or
the deliberate terror bombing of Guernica than of the near
annihilation of an important part of the Nazi war machine that
I had glimpsed in the photographs of the Renault works.

I went back to my office, shut the door, looked at my "In"
tray, as usual filled with a mound of paper, and had no impulse
to empty it. Instead I concocted a letter applying to be posted to
Bomber Command, giving as my reasons that I had been
instructing for the whole course of the war and a couple of years
before. I pointed out that I had done nine hundred hours on
Oxfords and in that time had flown with over eight hundred
different pilots, largely testing or assessing pupils and
instructors. It worked and within a month I was given a date a
couple of months ahead to report to an Operational Training Unit
in the unaccustomed role of pupil under training for transfer to
heavy bombers.

The last couple of months of my long stint on training were
uneventful although the pressure for more trained pilots was on
as never before since aircraft production, especially of heavy
bombers, was at its peak and keeping pace with the heavy losses
in attacks on Germany.

Before I left Ossington I was a passive witness to an incident
which has stuck in my mind, leaving a picture which haunts me
to this day.

I was in my office one afternoon when a duty officer
telephoned me to report that there had been a crash not far from
the aerodrome. He gave a description of the approximate position
and how to get there. We had, as usual, a lot of aircraft flying
and the odds were that it might be one of ours. From my window
I could see the horrid tell-tale plume of black smoke which
indicated a fire so, ordering an ambulance and fire engine to
follow me, I set out to investigate. Nearing the spot I could see
some smoke coming from within a wood though it was not the

heavy plume I had seen from my office. There was a track which could take wheeled traffic and I soon found the place.

It was in a small clearing. The fire had died down and the wood was utterly quiet as I turned the corner into the open space. I have seen many crashes in my flying life but that day I was confronted with what was, by a long way, the most macabre sight I have ever seen.

In the middle of the clearing, which was about seventy yards square, was a Moth trainer aircraft. It stood exactly as if it had made a perfect landing there but although it had the shape of a Moth it was only the ghastly ghost of an aircraft. The Moth was of metal construction with the wings and fuselage covered in fabric. On this ghost every scrap of fabric had burnt but the metal construction, twisted in places, had survived to show the perfect outline, the skeleton, of the aircraft. In the cockpit, fully visible, sat a figure, dressed in flying clothes, helmet and goggles and charred boots, sitting exactly as if he were still in control of the aircraft, one arm stretched forward with a gloved hand on the control column as if he were capable of flying it. The hideously lifelike position was as awful as a magnified detail from a painting by Hieronymus Bosch.

The pilot's fireproofed flying overall had kept the shape of his body intact. His helmet was fitted tightly onto his head so that, although it was charred it had not burnt. The goggles, askew, were still in position. I did not dare look at what was under them.

I supposed that what had happened was that the pilot had had the idea of landing in the clearing, which was manifestly impossible. The aircraft had probably stalled, hit a tree and, turning a double somersault, had come to rest in the landing position as it burst into flames. At least the pilot must have been killed or unconscious before the fire since otherwise he would have struggled to get out. I put a guard on the wreck, telling them to touch nothing and wait for the accident investigation people whom I would alert.

I left Training Command with no regrets. I felt I had made a contribution to the important work of improving flying standards and accelerating output. I had written and instituted the first ever instrument flying syllabus, admittedly a pretty crude affair which was much improved when the Central Flying School took up the idea. I had succeeded, where it would have been easy to fail, with the school on the runway, and while doing that, had initiated a new standard of night flying training. I had worked hard, had had plenty of fun but it was time for a change.

The prospect of moving into a new and totally different Air Force did trouble me a bit. What I was leaving I knew so well. I was on top of the job, understood the people, the instructors under me and the Staff Officers who watched me. But Training Command was totally unlike the strange world of the bombers, which I had no more than glimpsed. Would I be accepted, I wondered, and could I ever become a part of anything so foreign to me? Would the young aircrew find me old, cold, aloof, trying to seem superior because of my rank? I would know no-one. I was on my own. I had never flown a large, heavy aeroplane. I thought I could cope with that but I was no technician. And what of the operations? Would I have courage? How much was necessary? Some of the descriptions in the more lurid papers and the citations of the deeds of heroic proportions were, I felt, beyond me. I could not guess how I would feel or how I would behave.

There was one other wrench in my leaving.

Clare (that was not her name) and I had met at a charity party promoting some good cause which was trying to improve the crude and uncomfortable living conditions at some of the local RAF stations. I was there representing the RAF. She was sitting alone, very well-dressed, quiet and beautiful, thoughtfully distant from the assembled company. She sat gracefully and naturally and looked immensely elegant. She caught me looking at her, smiled spontaneously and quickly looked away.

I was conscious of her scrutiny while I made my little speech thanking the company for their interest in the RAF and for what they were doing to make the lives of our men more tolerable. Later we were introduced and exchanged banalities appropriate to the occasion. She had lived here with her widower father until she was grown-up, then married and lived in London. Now she was evacuated with one of her daughters, living with her father again to be away from the bombing. And so on. Came a silence and we looked at one another. Spontaneously we both laughed as a current flowed between us. "What rubbish one talks," she said, "and yet . . . "

"Could we meet and perhaps not talk rubbish?" I asked.

"I could if you could," she said, "but I know its difficult for people like you with a war on and all . . . "

"Not impossible," I said.

"Well," she said, "let's try. I could be here at half-past six tomorrow," and was gone.

"Here" was the hotel in the market place of the local town, five miles from my aerodrome. At that time RAF aircrew got a small allowance of recreational petrol for their private cars so it wasn't too difficult for me.

In the month after that first meeting we started to see one another regularly, at first once, then two or three times, a week. When recreational petrol for cars was withdrawn from the RAF except for those on operations, I bought a power-assisted bicycle for which you got a tiny ration. Clare would ride on the back, laughing and swaying precariously but swearing she enjoyed the air. We had to be careful because her father would not have countenanced our doings for a moment so I would collect her and drop her back at the end of the drive. She disliked lying but had to tell him she was doing some new "war work". We would only go to pubs where she would not be known, and she would share my occasional day off when, if the weather was nice, we would have a picnic in some solitary place.

In spite of the immense attraction we felt for one another our relationship was pervaded and curiously enhanced by the unspoken knowledge that there was no future for us. A permanent love was impossible so we accepted the next best thing, not speaking of love but feeling it deeply, knowing that in war life may be short and must be difficult. We hardly ever managed to share a bed but our love making was fervent as our talk was engrossing. She was a lovely girl.

When the time came for me to leave, neither of us could pretend that it was not the end for us. War had thrown us together but when war parted us it could only be permanent. There was no way we could correspond or meet and keep our lives intact. Our last evening before I went south for short leave with my family before joining my Operational Training Unit was desperately sad but at the same time redolent of all the enormous happiness we had had. When we came to say goodbye at the drive gate we kissed and kissed and she cried a little. Then suddenly through her tears she cried, "A reprieve! A reprieve!"

"How?" I said, a little suspiciously. We had talked long and earnestly about a clean break.

"Meet me here tomorrow," she said, "and I'll come as far as Grantham with you and come back by train. What a marvellous idea. I'll bring a picnic . . . "

So we snatched some more hours and it was a lovely autumn day and we lay on a rug in a cornfield and it wasn't an anti-climax at all.

7

The Whirlwind of Bombing

A Letter not Sent

Knowing some senior officers in the right places marvellously helped my transition from Training to Operations. Within three months I found myself in command of a Lancaster squadron in No. 5 Group, now commanded by Air Vice-Marshal Ralph Cochrane with whom I had had many dealings in Training Command and who was much more willing to employ me than his predecessor had been. I was conscious that, however well qualified I might be for the general duties of command, in the all important matters of operational skill and experience I was a complete novice.

To my flight commanders and other hardened bomber pilots in the squadron with fifteen or more operations behind them, my long flying record and the high rating I had obtained on my training courses were of no interest. They were even a disadvantage since this was a young man's war and these young veterans would naturally be wary of a newcomer, older than them, who might think he "knew it all". They would have preferred a new CO from among their own fraternity, speaking their language, knowing what they knew.

My squadron operated from a satellite aerodrome, two runways with a perimeter track and dispersal points, a mass of concrete thrown down at short notice onto the Lincolnshire mud. A collection of temporary huts served the necessities of sleeping, eating and an absolute minimum of the office and technical accommodation needed for a bomber squadron. The crudeness and discomfort of the facilities had clearly conduced a rather special spirit of comradeship and enthusiasm not found in centres of greater cleanliness and comfort. I had seen enough of such locations to know how tender was this plant of high morale. It flourished against odds but could wilt at the first sweep of a new broom. I knew I had to play it very softly while I was learning.

As was customary, I was to do my "second dicky" trip for operational experience with one of the squadrons at the neighbouring base to which we were an appendage. Here there were full peacetime facilities, excellent accommodation for officers and men, squash courts, playing fields, fine hangars and technical buildings. Here were stationed two Lancaster units, one a newly formed special duty squadron which did not participate in day-to-day operations.

The captain of the crew detailed to initiate me suggested that I accompany them on the flight test of the aircraft which took place before it was bombed up and made finally ready for the operation. He was a saturnine young man well into his second tour of operations and gave me the impression of being under some stress. It was clear to me that neither he nor the rest of the crew relished having a surplus passenger on the trip, especially one of my, to them, relatively exalted rank.

On the test the pilot rather apologetically told me that he and his crew were in the habit of calling each other by Christian names and not, as was laid down, by their functions, navigator, wireless operator, captain and so on. I would, however, answer to "second pilot" if it became necessary to address me although it was made quite clear that conversation from me would not be welcome. When we were in the air I asked him to do a couple of steep turns so that I could have an idea how, in emergency, I should maintain my precarious standing position behind his seat and I sensed a first note of approval in his voice as he complied.

After testing their aircraft, aircrew were free until briefing which would be in the late afternoon. We could not leave the station nor communicate with anyone outside and for me it was an awkward few hours to fill. However, at lunch the Station

Armament Officer, an old acquaintance of mine, suggested that I might come with him and see the operation of "bombing-up".

Driving round the perimeter track we encountered numbers of tractors drawing long trains of trolleys, each of which, he explained, formed the bomb load of one of the aircraft at the dozen or so dispersal sites in use for that night. When we reached the machine in which I was to fly, the bomb train had just arrived and the trolleys were being shunted to positions from which the bombs could be transferred to the cavernous bomb bay in the belly of the Lancaster, doors open to receive the load.

The Armament Officer pointed out the four-thousand pound bomb which each aircraft would carry. I had, of course, often heard of the famous "cookie" with which Germany was being scourged but I was unprepared to find it looking exactly like a glorified dustbin. The Armament Officer looked at it with positive affection. "This'll explode just before ground level," he explained, patting the great cylindrical object affectionately. "That's for maximum blast. Makes them keep their heads down while the incendiaries light up." Unused to the proximity of large quantities of high explosive, I was slightly alarmed at his cavalier treatment of such a lethal object although I knew it couldn't possibly explode except by courtesy of its detonator. Next he pointed out big black containers, each of which held ninety small incendiary bombs of four pounds each. These would be emptied in succession by the bomb-aimer's control. The incendiaries were small rectangular boxes of black metal, their cases as thin as possible to allow for the maximum filling of magnesium based incendiary material.

When every position in the yawning bomb bay was filled the NCO in charge called to an airman in the aircraft to close the bomb doors and after a few words with the cheerful armourers, all obviously devoted to their task, we were back in our car.

I decanted him by another aircraft and returned thoughtfully to the Mess. With some time to go yet before briefing, I turned over the pages of one or two of the feeble periodicals of the time, but my mind was churning over what I had just seen.

I knew comparatively little about bombs and aerodynamic shapes, or about the different terminal velocities and characteristics of falling objects. It was a rather abstruse science of which I retained little knowledge but I did remember that bombing accuracy depended largely on the shape of the bomb. It was surprising to discover that the bombs we were going to use that night, and which Bomber Command normally used in large quantities, had almost no aerodynamic shape at all. If you aimed them at Battersea Power Station you might hit Westminster Abbey or St. Martin-in-the-Fields or the slums behind Notting Hill Gate . . . That, I reflected, pretty well corresponded with the Blitz on London. The Nazis had sown the wind.This was the start of the whirlwind they were to reap.

In the briefing room I sat with my crew, their chatter contributing to a cheerful hubbub which mitigated but did not conceal the tension in the atmosphere. We faced a dais, behind which a big map of Western Europe showed main defended areas covered with red ink. A hush greeted the entry of the Station Navigation Officer who, with red tape and pins, started to mark on the map the route ordered for the night. From our aerodrome the thread led to Mablethorpe on the Lincolnshire coast, thence to cross the enemy coast at Egmond in Holland. Next came a position north of the great red blob which showed the heavily defended area of the Ruhr. This elicited some facetious groans from the audience, growing to a crescendo when the next short thread and a red marker proclaimed the target as Essen, home of Krupps, the greatest armament factory in the world.

We all stood up as the briefing officers filed onto the dais, headed by the Station Commander, whose DSO and DFC ribbons proclaimed that he had two tours of bomber operations behind him. I suppose he was five years younger than me. He motioned us to sit and the business of briefing to proceed.

First came the Squadron Commander announcing the target as Krupps of Essen, already, he said, considerably damaged and he hoped tonight would complete the job so that we wouldn't have to go there again. This was greeted with discreet groans as an old joke no longer very funny. He proceeded with precise details of the plan, giving times and heights, the route into and out of the target area, the colours of the target indicators to be used by the Pathfinder Force, all the complex operational details which had to be dovetailed into an exact programme for each individual crew. The target was to be marked by the comparatively new "Oboe" method by which, we were told, Mosquitoes of the Pathfinder Force could drop their markers with immense accuracy. It was this method which was revolutionising the effect of bombing on short distance targets in Germany, mainly those in the area of the Rhine/Ruhr valleys.

When we came to general information the emphasis was all on Krupps. Krupps the villains, Krupps a primary begetter of Nazism and supporter of Hitler, Krupps who made shells and guns and aircraft cannon which took toll of our bombers, Krupps the merchants of death. The aiming point was the centre of the great works, some three hundred acres in extent.

The Intelligence Officer, a formidable lady who minced no words, was particularly passionate in her exhortations. "Yes they've been damaged," she cried, "but make no mistake, they're still turning out the guns and shells aimed at YOU." The "YOU" was so fervent that I was momentarily reminded of the posters of Kitchener pointing his finger at the nation in the first war against these same Germans.

"So you've got to get them this time," she proclaimed, her voice vibrant with hate. "The flak's going to be worse than ever. Its been reinforced, so its no good my promising you an easy time. Krupps supplies its own guns." She gave details of the searchlights and other defences, pointing with a wand at the many areas coloured red on the map and concluded with a final outburst, "They're going to give you HELL," she spat, "see that you give it them back!" and she sat down, visibly affected by her own vehemence.

Half of me found this excessive hype by a non-combatant a bit distasteful but the other half, while somewhat alarmed by the prospect of the evening's work, was impressed by the knowledge that my first taste of operations was to be against the notorious factory which was such a significant part of the Nazi effort.

Watching the assembled aircrew, including those with whom I was to fly, I realised that they were almost totally untouched by most of what they had heard. If, indeed, they had heard, since for parts of the briefing many eyes had been shut and others had been concentrated on papers in front of them, oblivious of the eloquence to which they were being exposed.

Later I realised that this was not indifference but an inevitable result of the new methods of bombing. Targets were now marked by the Pathfinder Force with long burning Target Indicators, brilliantly coloured fireworks, red, green and yellow. The main force had simply to aim at whichever indicators they were directed to bomb and these instructions, to bomb a marker, introduced a curiously impersonal factor into the act of dropping huge quantities of bombs. I came to realise that crews were simply bored by a lot of information about the target. What concerned them were the details of route and navigation, which colour of Target Indicator they were to bomb and what they could do to make sure they arrived on time and got home safely. I concluded that evening that, while the fierce lady was probably convinced that she was striking a significant blow in the great struggle, for the bulk of her audience she was whistling in the wind. I made a note not to follow her example.

Take off was at dusk and an unnatural calm brooded over the Lincolnshire countryside as we were driven to our aircraft. Some of the crew waved to friends waiting at other dispersal points as we passed. I had a strange feeling of the loss of freewill. For nearly all the war I had been more or less my own master, giving rather than receiving orders. Now I was the creature of circumstances over which I had no control whatever.

The crew indulged in a good deal of facetious conversation as we climbed slowly up to our operational height of twenty-thousand feet before setting course eastwards, but crossing the North Sea all fell silent, bracing themselves for their task. When the bomb-aimer announced "enemy coast coming up," it took me a little time to focus on the faint white line he had seen some time before.

"Give me a fix when we cross, Johnny," said the navigator, and "Flak ahead, skipper," answered the bomb-aimer and as he spoke I saw the anti-aircraft shells bursting in front of us. They were distant, flickering stars, momentary flashes, leaving a harmless puff of black smoke where they had been.

"Coast dead below . . . NOW," called the bomb-aimer and, after a minute or so the navigator called, "OK Paul, on track and on time. Course for position A two-nine-three for twenty-two minutes." Position A, north of the Ruhr, was where we were to turn onto the course to take us into the target.

For me it was a very long twenty-two minutes in the absolute blackout, more effective even than in England. For the first time the Captain addressed me. "Second Pilot?" "Here." "Keep a lookout to port for fighters or our own aircraft." I acknowledged, peering into the blackness.

After a quarter of an hour the bomb-aimer announced "Paul, I've got yellow markers ahead and a bit to starboard." The pilot dipped the starboard wing nearly upsetting my balance and I could see the yellow markers dropping. It was uncanny that what had been just talk in the briefing room was now, over enemy Germany, reality. As we reached the position A and the navigator gave the course into the target only the uncanny silent flares gave any indication that there was anyone or anything on or over the earth except ourselves, suspended in a black vacuum. We turned in accordance with the navigator's direction and as we did so suddenly the area towards which we were now flying sprang into life.

Instead of the pitch dark there was suddenly a mass of searchlights, slowly, methodically, scanning the sky over a huge area. At the same time streams of tracer, some white, some coloured, followed the searchlight beams at quite low heights and lastly, at levels from well above our height to four or five thousand feet below came a dazzling display of twinkling stars, the Ruhr barrage of heavy ack-ack. There seemed to be hundreds of bursts almost simultaneously. You were quite unconscious of the invisible but lethal load of shrapnel each burst vomited into the sky; all you saw in the light of the searchlights were hundreds of round puffballs of black smoke, harmless enough but still ominously threatening. What was daunting was the sheer size of the defended area. Essen itself was somewhere in the middle of the huge tent of light, but the searchlights and the flak were coming from an area far greater than that of a single town.

"I'm going to weave," called the pilot. "Watch out for fighters everyone and for our own aircraft." His turns got steeper and more prolonged as we headed towards the astonishing display of light and smoke concealed in which, I had to believe, lay Essen and Krupps.

Now the action had begun in earnest and amid the constant winking of gunfire and the streams of tracer I saw the first red markers descending slowly, slowly. Almost at once they were followed by some greens, how close to the reds I found difficult to assess. Our instructions were to bomb the reds dropped by the Oboe Mosquitoes or otherwise the green "backers up", less certain to be accurate, dropped by Lancasters aiming at the reds in order to keep the marking going. Now there were more flashes on the ground and long strips of silver light betokened the first sticks of magnesium-based incendiaries.

It seemed an age before at last the navigator called, "George here, three minutes to ETA. (Estimated Time of Arrival)". Very soon came the bomb-aimer saying "OK Paul, I've got a red and some greens straight ahead." The bumps from the flak became more persistent and searchlights flashed across our wings, momentarily lighting up the cockpit. "Hell," said the pilot, "they're getting too bloody close." He turned quickly to starboard, then back again. "On course, all yours, Johnny," he called to the bomb-aimer. "Hurry up, for Christ's sake."

"OK, bomb doors open," from the bomb-aimer. Jerks and rumbles as the bomb doors opened with maddening deliberation. "Left a little, left, left, steady, steady, OK, bombs going." I felt the aircraft lighten as each component of the load was released. I could see green target indicators to our left but the bomb-aimer's view directly below was obscured for me by the aircraft's nose.

With bomb doors shut again we turned steeply for home and it seemed that we would never get out of the defended area. We were rocked continuously by the blast from exploding shells. I looked back at where green target indicators were still falling, rather randomly now; some must have been many miles apart, and there were still streams of silver from incendiaries and flashes of guns firing and bombs exploding. Great areas were now covered with black smoke and the livid dark red of fires. I strained to see if I could see any ground detail but could make out nothing definite, only fire and smoke and the flashes of guns and the occasional larger flash of a four-thousand pound bomb exploding among the searchlights. It seemed incredible that so many aircraft could fly through that barrage of fire and light and survive. We were still in the searchlight area but the pilot was weaving, turning, diving and climbing and using plenty of throttle so that the probing beams never rested on us for any length of time. There were still continual bursts of exploding shells above and around us and one of the gunners suddenly yelled "fighter astern and to port" and both turrets fired long bursts of tracer while the pilot wrenched the aircraft into a steep diving turn to port in which I nearly lost my hold on his seat.

A few more minutes and the searchlights were behind us and we were out of the defended area, the weaving was less frenzied, the fighter, which I had not seen and which must have been well astern in a blind spot for me, had apparently lost us. The shell bursts became more sporadic and ahead there was nothing but a blessed blackness.

"Well done, John," came from one of the crew as we left the lights behind us. "You got us out of that a treat."

Over the sea and nearly home the crew gave vent to their relief with wisecracking about tomorrow's likely stand-down (a day with no operation ordered), and the prospect of meeting their "popsies" at the Saracen's Head in Lincoln. As soon as we were below oxygen height a strong smell of cigarette smoke pervaded the normal metallic atmosphere of the aircraft. The Flight Engineer, standing near me, lit one for the pilot and offered to do the same for me. I didn't smoke cigarettes at that time anyway, but the idea of anyone breaking the absolute taboo of smoking in or even near aircraft which had been inculcated into me from the first time I set foot on a tarmac came as something of a shock. But it wasn't my business.

At debriefing the crew, chattering and pleased with their continuing lives, ranged in a semi-circle before one of the Intelligence Officers. On the outskirts, I listened to their answers to his questions and found myself surprised at how much, in my inexperience, I seemed to have missed of the events in which I had, albeit passively, taken part. They had infinitely more positive impressions than I could pretend to, were much clearer in their memories of what target indicators they had seen and of the concentration of incendiaries around them.

The Station Commander was strolling from one group to another and, looking over the Intelligence Officer's shoulder, he scanned the reports of our crew. "Did you have a good trip?" he asked them.

"Yes, sir, wizard." "Poor ole Krupps," came from the more articulate members. "Spot on, I think, sir," more soberly from the Captain. The Group Captain turned to me, "How about you?" he asked. I saw that he hadn't the faintest interest in what I, a beginner, might think, so I answered equivocally, "I expect everyone finds it a bit bewildering on their first trip, sir." He nodded vacantly, looking over my shoulder at a crew behind us who were engaged in an excitable rendering of their adventures.

At my own airfield the Operations Block was just closing down in broad daylight. The Intelligence Officer was anxious to know about my trip, confident that the results had been good. One of our aircraft was unaccounted for. In bed at last I was overtired by what had been a fairly gruelling day. The nightmare picture of the target area, like a huge marquee of light in a dark garden, haunted me. What I had seen revolved endlessly in my brain and I tried to calm myself by an analysis of four separate pictures. The first was of the scene conjured up at briefing by the measured descriptions given then of the target, Krupps Works. I had imbibed an impression that it would appear as an entity quite separate from the town of Essen. In fact I had not the slightest impression of either. Then I thought of the prophecy of red target indicators, dropped by the magic of Oboe, which would be on or very near the aiming point in the middle of Krupps with green target indicators clustering round the reds. I had not visualised the wonderfully deep vivid colours of the target indicators but nor had I anticipated the erratic way they appeared, nor the slow, inevitable way they moved when around them the flashes, the smoke, the fires, all seemed static. Then I had imagined the arrival of the main force, us, piling our bombs on the reds or greens, annihilating what was left of the evil of Krupps. My actual impression was only of many patches of bright silver, many far apart and none seemingly connected with the target indicators but gradually turning to red under the black smoke. Then the defences. The warlike WAAF Officer, had not concealed their strength but had given me not the slightest impression of the huge area they covered nor of the long time needed to fly through them. At briefing the whole thing had sounded fairly simple.

Of course it wasn't simple at all. In war a commander may decree how, when and where his forces shall engage in battle but once the engagement is made he has no influence on what the enemy does and little on what actually happens. The only certainty is that there will ensue a degree of chaos while the two sides struggle. Only afterwards, usually quite long afterwards, if at all, can it be proven what occurred, how the orders were obeyed, how frustrated, how interpreted or ignored. The battles waged by Bomber Command over its German targets were short, less than an hour in my time and often only thirty to forty-five minutes, but they obeyed these rules. I, as spectator participant in this my first battle, had to admit that my picture of our objective had been totally overlaid by the confusion of the constant flashes, air and ground, by searchlights, flak, the threat of fighters, sudden changes of course and attitude, the extraordinary brightness of the long lines of incendiaries burning with that same intense silver light as the fireworks out of superior Christmas crackers.

I had to admit that I could not begin to analyse the distances
apart and relationships between the positions of the many target
indicators I had seen. The gauging of distances on the ground
from twenty thousand feet is difficult at the best of times and
these could hardly have been described. I tried to visualise the
size of an aerodrome as seen from twenty thousand feet. It would
appear as little more than a pinpoint. Nevertheless that was
bigger than Krupps.

To project such an imprecise concept onto my imprecise
vision didn't mean much but perhaps it would send me to sleep.
It was staggering to think that there must have been more than
five hundred of those luminous tails of incendiaries. No question
of counting, but it was true that the silver trails had been
everywhere, covering a huge area for a time as brightly as the
searchlights and then merging into the red and black of fires and
smoke.

As I lay sleepless I reflected on those marvellous photographs
I had seen of the Renault works on the Paris island. Probably
nothing comparable had happened to Krupps but, even so, I felt
fairly sure we had done real damage, delivered a real blow to the
enemy's potential. It was a step at least in the great campaign to
which Bomber Command was committed and of which I could
now feel myself a member. It was stimulating indeed to be a part
of an enterprise which could, and I believed would, paralyse the
enemy's ability to maintain the huge production he needed if he
were to defeat our Russian allies. Even more vital, if not so
immediate, our efforts could so drain his strength that when, not
this year but perhaps next, we and our American allies landed on
the Continent, they would liberate the captive peoples of Western
Europe from their enfeebled conquerors without the awful
bloodletting which an attack on the full strength of the Reich
would have entailed.

It was a dream, perhaps, but not an ignoble one.

Then suddenly I wondered, "Why all those incendiaries?
What would they do in a great armament works?"

It was relatively rare for the Photographic Reconnaissance
Units to get good photographs of Ruhr targets because the whole

area was nearly always obscured by smoke and industrial haze. After the two raids on Krupps that March, however, there were some excellent results and it was clear that the great works had been severely damaged.

After Krupps, Kiel.

The Battle of the Atlantic was then at its height and the news we had was not good. There were ominous rumours, in fact ill-founded, that the war was being lost to the U-boats. So an attack on Kiel, aimed at the docks, the ships and U-boats and their repair and assembly yards, would be a significant contribution to success in the Atlantic on which all depended. Buoyed by the apparent success at Essen we set out for Kiel in high hopes.

It was acutely disappointing on approaching the target to find the whole area entirely covered by cloud. We had been warned at briefing that this might be the case and if so the instructions were to switch to an alternative method of attack, code named Wanganui.

This development of target-marking by the Pathfinder Force was designed to allow bombing of some reasonable accuracy when the main force were not able to see target indicators on the ground. In this technique specially equipped aircraft dropped "sky markers", which floated above the cloud some thousands of feet below the height of the bombers who would "aim" at these markers while flying on a predetermined course. The markers were supposed to be so placed that our bombs, if correctly aimed, would at least fall in or near the target area. The expected accuracy was better than nothing but only the most sanguine enthusiasts had real faith in the probability that a Wanganui attack would produce anything but a wide scatter of bombs.

We obeyed instructions but it was impossible to hope that, except by some stroke of luck, the heavy attack would produce results enough to affect the vital Battle of the Atlantic. However, some such setbacks were only to be expected and this first one in no way undermined my faith in the mission of Bomber Command.

I had been in command of the squadron for just over a fortnight when a message came from Group Headquarters that a VIP (Very Important Person) was to be with us for the night's operation. As I was not flying myself I was to show him all details of operational procedures, preparations and briefing. He would remain with us until the aircraft returned and would be present when the crews were debriefed.

Visits of this sort, although inevitable, were less than welcome since many large or small contretemps requiring urgent action could, and nearly always did, arise in the course of the day and these were apt to interfere with the courtesies a distinguished visitor might expect.

In this case the VIP was Sir Kingsley Wood, Chancellor of the Exchequer. Unlike many such visitors he was not without knowledge of the Air Force since he had been Secretary of State for Air for a time before the war. He was a chubby little man, bustling and personable, with rimless spectacles, a small but jolly paunch and a benevolent expression. He was pink and well-fed and comparison with Mr Pickwick was irresistible.

His visit was uneventful except for one incident which stayed in my mind but not, I think, in his. We were in the Intelligence Block when the Senior Intelligence Officer asked Sir Kingsley whether he would like to see photographs showing results of recent raids. When these were produced the little Chancellor inspected them closely using the three dimensional magnifying glass through which the flat aerial photos were converted to something very like reality. When he got used to using the glass he started to chuckle with satisfaction, muttering "Capital, capital. This is really getting somewhere. I do congratulate you." I looked over his shoulder at the print he was examining and caught my breath in amazement.

In the stress of adjusting to my new job, getting to know my squadron and making myself fully competent on the Lancaster I had not yet explored every corner of the station under my command. Although I necessarily had spent a good deal of time in the Intelligence Block and had seen the photographs of considerable damage at Krupps, the operation against Kiel had been frustrated by cloud and there were still no results known. I had not thought to look up past results so these photos, which the Intelligence Officer said had been taken of Düsseldorf a few weeks back, were a new experience for me as well as for my guest.

I had never seen anything like them. Seen through the stereoscopic glass the detail was staggeringly clear, showing just rows and rows of apparently empty boxes which had been houses. They had no roofs or content. This had been a crowded residential area, long streets of terraced houses in an orderly right-angled arrangement, covering virtually the whole of the six-inch square photograph. There were one or two open spaces but the chief impression was just those rows and rows of empty shells, a huge dead area where once thousands of human beings had lived. There were no craters, simply those burnt-out houses. It was devastation on a huge scale and it was impossible to see from those photographs how human beings could ever live there again. There were no factories or large buildings except what was possibly a roofless church, the streets seemed to hold no traffic and as I gazed fascinated at this my first real bombing photo, I remember saying involuntarily, "God! The Germans will never forgive us for this".

The remark wasn't meant for anyone, it was a kneejerk reaction of astonishment, but the little Chancellor picked it up like a flash.

"What do you mean, forgive us?" he snapped. "Let me tell you it's we who'll have to forgive the Germans and what's more, I hope we don't do it too quickly. Germans forgive us indeed!" He was very belligerent and I could only apologise for my unfortunate little outburst which was not a rational or considered comment but the result of shock at seeing that photograph. My visitor was noticeably cool for a time but as the night wore on he appeared to forget my outburst and eventually he departed in the dawn with quite fervent expressions of gratitude for the success of his visit.

With Krupps believed to be seriously damaged it was almost inevitable that, while the nights were still long enough to allow deep penetration of enemy territory, we should be given as a target the great armament works of Skoda near Pilsen in

Czechoslovakia, then thought to be the greatest contributor after Krupps to the supply of German war material. We made two attacks, both of which cost dear in losses of men and aircraft. I had reason to understand the difficulties of attacking such distant targets with the navigation aids available at the time since, on the second attack, our navigation was faulty and for some time we were lost. Eventually we arrived over the target area ten minutes after the raid was timed to finish. This meant going through the defences alone and we were lucky to get out with little damage. Unfortunately the marking was faulty and the attack failed. A week or so later over Stettin on the Baltic my aircraft was "coned" for the first time. I had seen others undergo this alarming experience and did not relish it for myself. It happened all too frequently in defended areas that when one searchlight managed to fix firmly on its target there was apparently some device which enabled others to follow and all would "lock on" to the bomber. The near blindness induced by eight or ten of these very high-powered beams coming from every side produced a frightening sensation of being caged by light. No matter how you struggled, the dazzling beams would hold you and you lost all sense of movement. It was as if you were motionless in the sky, shells exploding all around you, waiting for the one which would destroy you, knowing that every fighter in the area had marked you for his prey. It was the moment of truth for us all, five hundred miles from home.

I felt the soundless but united plea from the crew by that telepathy which establishes itself in a bomber over enemy territory but there was no need for anyone to warn me of our danger nor to tell me they were all willing me to get them out of it.

"Hold on for corkscrew" I called into the intercom. This was the only known way out of our predicament, by a series of the most violent diving and climbing turns, emulating the shape of a corkscrew. We had practised this many times in order that the crew could learn to continue their functions in spite of the manoeuvres.

The Lancaster was, for a heavy aircraft, quite tractable but the physical effort for the pilot and the discomfort to the crew in a prolonged corkscrew is considerable. I began to fear that we were too securely held in the searchlights ever to get out. It seemed they were locked onto us like a vice, and pull and push the control column as I would, taking us into almost vertical turns and the steepest climbs and dives I dared risk, they clung to us as if they were glued to our shape. The rear gunner warned of an aircraft following us but I was already doing the most violent manoeuvres of which I and the aircraft were capable. Then suddenly one of the searchlights left us and then another and another . . . somehow their co-ordination had been upset although three or four still held us. Sweating and with my arms, forearms and wrists aching with fatigue, I kept the throttles at maximum and, miraculously, they lost us. Still close, the beams kept brushing over our wings, probing, probing until, suddenly, they all went out together. It was a queer sensation to be back in the merciful dark.

I could hear the relief in the rear gunner's voice as he said "Well done, skipper," which was praise indeed since he was far more experienced in his job than I in mine. Alas, he did not survive the war.

Soon after this the summer nights became so short that the only targets in Germany which could be attacked in darkness were those in the industrial area which stretches from Dortmund and Unna in the east to Duisberg in the west and Cologne in the south. So was unleashed what became known as the Battle of the Ruhr, in which attacks were made almost every night that weather permitted. The enemy naturally reinforced the area and the barrage became so formidable that on some nights every aircraft in the squadron would sustain some damage. Strong and wonderful aeroplane that the Lancaster was, most such damage could be quickly repaired and the aircraft made fit to renew the attack, often on the following night. Fighters were, however, the major cause of our losses and we had reason to bemoan that our ·303 Brownings were outranged and outgunned by the enemy cannon and large-calibre machine guns.

The Way we Were. – The author (*right*) and his brother the late Sir John Johnson, 6th Baronet of New York, at Brightwell, 1912.

The author (*standing 4th from left*), members of his air and ground crews and their Lancaster 'D' of 97 (Pathfinder) Squadron.

Rare photograph of a Lancaster dropping a 4,000lb bomb and incendiaries on Duisburg, No. 101 Squadron, 1944.

Rare photograph of a formation of Lancaster aircraft on its way to attack targets in Northern France.

Two views of the Town Centre of Essen taken by German photographers in 1943.

Joseph Bato's drawing of St Paul's Cathedral standing proudly above the destruction of the 'Blitz' on London.

Hitler and the Young Idea.

The Entrance to Belsen, June 1945.

Belsen, April 1945.

Date: 8th February, 1945.   R A I D   S C H E D U L E   Officer i/c Flying:

AIRCRAFT		CAPTAIN		FLT. ENGINEER	NAVIGATOR	AIR BOMBER	W/OPERATOR	MID GUNNER	REAR GUNNER
					PRIMARY BLIND MARKERS				
1. FB.706	D	G/C JOHNSON	(28)	F/O RATCLIFFE	F/L HATCH	(P/O MOIR) W/O SYMONDS	F/S GREENLEY	F/S GARROD	F/S WATTS
2. FB.410	J	F/L EATON	(44)	F/S SHEPHERD	S/L CAMPBELL	F/L DOBBIE	F/S SPRIGGS	P/O FUTER	F/S GAFFREY
					FLARE FORCE I				
3. F3.408	O	F/L SHORTER	(47)	F/S BETTS	F/S BAYNES	(F/L THOLSON) F/L BILLINGTON	W/O WITHERS	W/O BATHO	F/L ROBERTS
4.	H	F/L HINES	(26)	SGT SINCLAIR	F/O McQUILLAN	F/S MARRABLE	SGT MORONEY	F/L RAY	F/S PALMER
5.	F	F/O WATSON	(49)	SGT KILMAN	F/O JAMES	F/O NOBLE	F/O ROLFE	F/S MILFORD	F/S CLARSON
6. FB.276	S	F/O NOON	(25)	SGT PITT	W/O HIGGINS	F/S HALLETT	W/O THORPE	F/S DOUGLAS	F/S HARVEY
					FLARE FORCE II				
7. FD.965	K	F/O RYAN	(32)	SGT KIRBY	F/L SABINE	P/O MATTHE	F/S WHITEHEAD	F/S WALSH	F/O BURNHAM
8. 83/I		F/O WARBROCK	(16)	F/S ALLISON	F/O HENDRY	F/S CHOLERTON	F/S TURNER	W/O CHANNON	W/O LENNON
9.	M	F/O IOW	(13)	SGT CHAMBERLAIN	F/O MUDDLE	F/O ORRELL	F/O WILLEY	SGT BRITTAIN	F/S McNEILL
					FLARE FORCE III				
10. FB.881	L	LT. ADDISON	(13)	SGT NELSON	P/O DURAND	F/S BILLINGTON	SGT ROGERS	F/S ROPER	F/S HUNT
11. ND.569	T	F/O MAY	(15)	SGT GARROCH	F/S BARLING	F/S GEORGE	F/S MATHER	F/S WILLIAMS	F/S HALL
					EMERGENCY				
12. FB.422	P	F/O GREENING	(21)	SGT NUTT	W/O CAIRNS	W/O BLACKBURN	SGT NEWSOME	F/S DEAN	F/S BELL
13. ME.623	G	F/O ROBERTSON	(18)	SGT SAXBY	F/S SOAR	F/S SOULLARD	W/O MORGAN	F/S BACK	SGT HERON
14. ..975	C	F/O COTTMAN	(18)	SGT CROSS	F/S MURRAY	F/S COSTER	F/S ARMEY	F/S PETSCHEL	F/S BULL

T. Auer F/O

W/ Group Captain, Commanding,
No.97 (Straits Settlements) Sqdn.

A typical Raid Schedule of 97 (Pathfinder) Squadron.

There was great pressure for more and more operations and a Squadron Commander had plenty to do in keeping his squadron able to provide the maximum number of aircraft for every operation, seeing to the advanced training of new crews, directly supervising the preparations for the night's operation, watching the progress of his crews in relation to the stresses under which they worked. He had to keep an eye on the welfare of the ground personnel without whom the squadron could not operate. The loyalty of his crews and the spirit of the squadron depended in part on his doing his fair share of operations himself. Life that summer was lived at a very high level of intensity. When we were not "working" (the euphemism for operating), I spent what time I could spare with my young officers who generously came to accept me as nearly one of them. I don't believe I really spoilt any of their fun in spite of the difference in our ages.

This curious war we fought, between sessions at the White Hart or Saracen's Head in Lincoln, was something new in the history of warfare. We saw no enemy, knew little or nothing of our casualties. The slender effects of the missing were collected and despatched, the letters of condolence written, their beds occupied by replacements.

It was a strangely impersonal war. The defences which threatened us were visible enough, the twinkling of innumerable shells exploding in the barrage, the probing fingers of the searchlights, the constant threat of fighters against whom we had little defence. All these we knew, but we were not really fighting against them, we were simply trying to evade them. And our own part in the fighting was quickly over. In the glare of searchlights, with the continual winking of anti-aircraft shells, the occasional thud when one came close and left its vile smell, what we had to do was search for coloured lights dropped by our own people, aim our bombs at them and get away.

Concentration on target indicators was the be-all-and-end-all of our "fighting". The crux of our every operation lay in the few minutes when the bomb-aimer kept the clear beautiful colour of a target indicator in his sight, gave his directions and ultimately loosed our load at a firework made in England.

It was during the Battle of the Ruhr that there was a change in our operation orders. In the space for "Objective" it had been usual to have such target descriptions as "to destroy an enemy factory". Then these changed to such euphemisms as "to do maximum damage to an enemy industrial centre" or "to do maximum damage to an enemy port" but soon the usual order was the clear instruction "to destroy an enemy city". Even I, who saw the orders in their original form by teleprinter, did not at first notice the change in emphasis, being intent mainly on such vital detail as the colour and timing of the target indicators and the route there and back and the defended areas on the way.

The spirit in the Lancaster squadrons at this time, in spite of losses very near to the supposedly prohibitive mark of five per cent per operation, was very high. Our new aircraft, the new marking techniques, the new navigational equipment, the new radio countermeasures and the fact that we were the only people in our island who were actually attacking the hated Nazis, added up to an inspiration all of us felt. We believed that we had the capacity, if not to finish the war ourselves, at least so to weaken the Nazis that their ability to defeat us would be gone for ever. If we performed our duties adequately we would make a significant contribution to winning this hateful war without those terrible casualty lists which I dimly remembered from the other war.

The Battle of the Ruhr continued from April to the middle of July, by which time the Rhineland cities of Düsseldorf and Cologne as well as the Ruhr towns proper, Duisberg, Dortmund, Essen, Wuppertal, Remscheid, Bochum, had all been attacked, some of them two or even three times. The defences intensified with the progress of the attacks and some of our losses were grievous.

Cologne was the target which, after the one-thousand bomber raid, had been held up to the public as the example of a town disabled by bombing. In fact, the damage had been scattered and Cologne was subjected to three further attacks in 1943, each one heavier in terms of bombs dropped than the one thousand raid.

The first of the three took place in bright moonlight, conditions which had been so disastrous for us that for some months very few operations had been ordered against Germany in moon periods. This night the moon was so bright you could have read a book in the cockpit. The attack was asking for trouble from fighters, but in addition as we approached the target area I was horrified to realise that the Lancasters at our height were emitting those white vapour trails which had been such a feature of the Battle of Britain and which you now see laid by civil jets at heights much greater than ours over Cologne. The trails were bright and persistent and the four separate lines from the four engines were plain for anyone to see. All a fighter had to do was to follow them and, as he was at least one hundred miles per hour faster than us, he could not fail to find a bomber at the end. It was an unnerving experience. By luck I was unscathed but the losses were high and included a new flight commander in my squadron on his first trip. He was an experienced officer whom I had been hoping would relieve me of some of my load but he had not been with us a week. After this the policy of not attacking German targets in the full moon was reinstated.

On the second Cologne attack, in the dark this time, my aircraft was hit with a resounding crash when over the city. I can still sometimes hear in the night the sepulchral tones of my flight engineer saying over the intercom as I recovered control, "the starboard outer's on fire, the port inner's losing revs and I don't like the look of the port outer". I feathered the starboard outer (i.e. stopped the engine and put the propeller into the fore and aft position where it made least drag). We lost some height getting out of the target area and it was soon clear that, with only one engine giving full power, it was unlikely that we would be able to avoid losing more height. Our base seemed a long way away.

At about ten thousand feet, well below our operational height, in consultation with the flight engineer and after throwing out every bit of surplus weight, we jiggled the three engines so that we were very nearly maintaining height. But this wasn't necessarily going to get us home and of course we were in the unfortunate position of being alone, slow and unable to manoeuvre without losing precious height. After about a quarter of an hour the rear gunner gave warning of a fighter apparently tracking us so, not very happily, I did a quick diving turn. It cost valuable height but luckily he lost us and we approached the Belgian coast with about enough height to have a sporting chance of reaching England if, and it was an if, the good engine which had already done an hour at full throttle, did not falter, and the two doubtfuls held up. I gave the crew permission to jump over Belgium if they wished but none accepted.

We struggled across the sea and mercifully the weather was fair because a second engine gave out just before we reached our base. However, we were lightly loaded and had enough height to go straight for the runway and, putting the wheels and flaps down very late, we just made it although the third engine packed up before we had actually stopped. The Lancaster was a fine aircraft.

After that I was tired enough for my body to take charge and wind a soft blanket of obliteration around the uneasy mind which fought nervously against the rest it needed. But next day I woke with that uneasy feeling which sends the brain too quickly searching for the ill-circumstances of the day past and the day to come.

The squadron had lost two aircraft and I thought "Oh Lord, that means fourteen letters of sympathy" and then, "Don't be so bloody callous, thinking about the bother to you of putting pen to paper a few times. These were flesh and blood, think of their friends and relations, their wives, mothers, sisters and girlfriends. How dare you demur at writing a few letters, each of which, if you couch it well, will mean some real comfort to someone".

When I had a mood of depression and I doubted whether what we achieved was worth the sacrifices, I found difficulty in writing these letters. However sure you are that your cause is just, the feelings of a wife or mother at the loss of her husband or son are too tender for the words of a stranger to soothe. Was it worse or better for them that in most cases it was impossible to know whether the missing were dead or prisoners of war. The uncertainty often lasted for months and sometimes was never fully dispelled but in the letters I wrote I usually emphasised that there was ground for hope. But when the operation had been a failure, the young lives lost just a gain for the enemy, how difficult it was to write sincerely.

One couldn't say "Your son/husband was lost owing to the incompetence of the Staff in routing the force through a dangerous area in which a number of our aircraft were seen to be shot down" or "Your husband/son was an excellent tail-gunner and had the respect and admiration of his crew. His captain was a competent and steady pilot but I always had doubts about their navigator and, from reports I have received, it seems likely that the aircraft was badly off track when shot down . . . "

The bedside telephone rang. We were "on" again to-night. I put the past out of my mind for the moment and thought of the present. Those two new crews would have to go. I would have liked them to do a couple more training trips first but, with aircraft available, they'd have to be on. The powers-that-be wanted maximum effort all the time. Maybe they were right. But we might do better, hit more where it hurts, if we trained a bit more? The rapier, not the bludgeon. Or are the losses mostly luck? Not really. There's plenty of luck but the better ones have more luck.

And Bryant. Should I stop him from going tonight? He's done twenty-nine trips. One more to go. Twenty-nine is surely fair enough when they're all tough. How awful if he went missing on his thirtieth and he's got the jitters good and proper. But if I start stopping people at twenty-nine it means the tour is twenty-nine and not thirty and then you'll be stopping them at twenty-eight. Oh hell! He'll make one more. I wonder what's the damage to my aircraft.

After the Ruhr, Hamburg. The great port on the Elbe was a good deal further from our bases than the Ruhr but towards the end of July an extra hour or so of darkness made it accessible without flying over enemy territory in daylight.

The Battle of Hamburg was at that time the heaviest and most concentrated attack Bomber Command had made on a German town. After four attacks, and with some contribution from the US Air Force, we were told that, in spite of the last attack having been almost completely abortive because of weather, we had won the Battle. Over half, perhaps up to three-quarters of the most densely built up parts of the city had been virtually destroyed and the docks and shipyards severely damaged. Most damage had been done by huge fires which had swept through the town on a scale never before even contemplated. It was being said that almost the whole population had fled to the open country outside the city. It was clear that the contribution of this great seaport with its significant manufactures, contributing perhaps a quarter of total U-boat production, was at a standstill. There was a sense of elation throughout the Command. We had known of vast damage in the towns of Ruhr and Rhineland but in no case had the reconnaissance and Intelligence reports claimed a complete stoppage of all industrial activity.

Perusing the reports and photographs after the attacks, I spent a good deal of time contemplating their possible effects. There was little doubt that reports of the total stoppage of activity were accurate and no one could deny that this was a significant success for Bomber Command. The areas of burnt-out houses, were even more sensational than those in Düsseldorf and the Ruhr towns.

The gloating of the Press, the comparisons with the Luftwaffe attacks on Coventry, Warsaw, Rotterdam, Belgrade, London were perhaps not unjustified. The frequent references to Coventry took me back to the night in November 1941 when I had stood for many shivering hours on a dark and silent landing ground in Gloucestershire. I had taken a party out for night flying training when an Air-Raid warning, caused me to douse the flare path. Unfortunately, the warning came too late to prevent a German bomber from unloading its bombs on us. A less than pleasant operation since we had good reason to suspect at least two unexploded bombs from the load which had straddled the field. Thereafter we could do nothing for the rest of the night but listen to the seemingly endless stream of German bombers flying northward in what we learnt in the morning was the famous attack on Coventry. The damage to the town was too immense for the news to be suppressed and the media were forced to admit near disaster. All production was stopped, many people were killed and injured, huge fires had raged out of control. People fought to leave the area. "Lord Haw-Haw", the voice of German propaganda aimed at Britain, announced that all British cities would suffer the fate of being "Coventrated". Mostly his broadcasts were treated as a sick joke but this was one of the few which was all too clearly based on truth.

I had little time in the summer of 1943 for reflection but it did occur to me that after Coventry, which was probably comparable in damage to what we had done in the Ruhr and in Hamburg, production had started again on a small scale within a week and was now believed to be at full stretch. When the family of a serviceman or woman was "bombed out", their house wrecked, someone killed or badly injured, the serviceman or woman was allowed five days special leave to go home, fix things up, organise the neighbours, or visit the hospital. Five days leave, then back to duty. I remember very few complaints or applications for extensions. That was the spirit of England under bombing. Was there any reason to suppose it would not be the spirit of Nazi Germany? We had put Hamburg out of action for a week or a month but surely the Ruhr towns, like Coventry, would now be recovering and their outputs grimly increasing?

Two main facts dominated the lives of the aircrew who fought this extraordinary war from the mostly improvised and uncomfortable airfields which dotted the plains of eastern England. These facts were the risks they ran and the casualty rate which gave them an even-money chance of survival. The tour for those who "finished" was generally about five or six months and, during this time, there developed a typical defensive attitude. Pushing the main facts into the background, they treated their life on the operational station as unreal. It was as if they had been given a loan of a life apart from their own reality and during these months their own lives were in cold storage elsewhere. They had little interest except in the immediate task or what to do with their considerable periods of comparative liberty. In the short term they would use these to drink, to wench or to sleep.

They slept enormously. But what made life bearable was a leave entitlement far and away greater than almost any other servicemen enjoyed. Although they might have a small ration of "recreational" petrol, it did not as a rule take them home. For that they needed the railway and the free ticket to anywhere in England, Wales or Scotland which was part of the leave entitlement.

Since the war the British Railway system has been the butt of a huge volume of criticism, often crystallising among commuters into absolute hatred. It is quite hard to visualise that, during the dark days of Hitler's war, when the railways reached a nadir of dirt, discomfort and unreliability far beyond what now obtains, they were held in respect, even affection. There was a certain romance in the undermanned stations, dingy and uncared for by day, unlit, unwarmed and silent by night. People waited, waited. Often staff had no more idea than the public whether a train would come or where it was going if it did come.

There was no petrol and virtually no buses, so the railway was for nearly everyone, most especially for poorly-paid service men and women, the only lifeline which connected them with their other real existence. All who were away from their normal homes and loved ones relied on cheap or free travel by rail and most were deeply appreciative of the railway's efforts, sometimes under attack from the air, always starved of equipment and manpower, to provide some sort of service to the many who genuinely needed it.

A disproportionate number of journeys seemed to be done at night because people were desperate to reach the atmosphere of home and were willing to travel all night to gain a few extra hours. Trains would persevere until, hours late, they reached their destinations. On the darkened stations weary would-be travellers waited, waited. Couples, huddled in doorways or sheltered by empty slot machines, held hands or embraced. Some stared miserably into the darkness praying that the invisible train wouldn't come to separate them. When it did come, the sighing of escaping steam proclaimed that men and machines were weary, but not yet seeking rest. Some blinds would be lifted, others, hoping to discourage new entrants, stayed firmly down. A few passengers would leave the train to stretch their legs but there was no coffee, no alcohol, not even a stale bun to be had. War, in all its dreariness, came more completely to the railways than to almost anywhere else.

You can exaggerate the wonder of the comradeship, the stoicism, the sense of purpose of the British people in those wartime days but it existed and was to be seen at its best in the difficult milieu of the railways. There was even some breakdown of traditional British reserve and phlegm. People were known, especially on dark nights when air-raid warnings were prolific and the trains ran anyhow, to talk with strangers.

It was on one of those nights that, having to do a local journey by train, I talked with a stranger.

Our love affair was short and passionate. Although I was over thirty, married and not without experience of "affairs", I had never known a relationship of such vitality and intensity as developed between me and this stranger. When we first saw one another in the corridor of the silent train, London-bound but immobilised between Grantham and Peterborough by a "red" warning, the strength of the current which flowed between us obliterated everything except ourselves. For me, she was beautiful, yes, but it wasn't entirely, or even mostly, that. We talked spontaneously, even intimately, but it wasn't that either. It was something which at once seemed inevitable, part attraction, part natural friendship, but above all instant, instinctive trust. This was a casual pick-up in a train, but we both knew, and each of us knew that the other knew, that it was not a casual pick-up.

I had to get out at Peterborough, the next stop, and the dilatory train roused itself only too quickly. She told me she had been visiting her sister in Grantham and was going back to London, where she lived. As the train grunted and shunted, anticipating Peterborough, I was desperate at losing her but, with the train stopping, I simply had to move towards a door when, suddenly, catching my arm, she said breathlessly that she could be in Grantham again in a week's time. But not with her sister. Could I make it? The train stopped. I had to go, but I had time to say "Yes. Six o'clock on the up platform from London, I'll be there. I promise". We kissed, and I think we were both determined not to lose what we had so oddly found.

We were honest with each other. I told her I was married with two young children. She that she had been married, disastrously, then worked in a dress shop, which she hated, and then in a book shop, which she liked but couldn't live on the pay. She had been an Air-Raid Warden in the blitz and then she had met a man. He was a wide-awake who had something to do with the Government but not directly and something to do with the arms industry, she didn't exactly know about that. He had taken her on as a sort of assistant secretary-cum-driver. It was a reserved occupation but she still did her job as Air-Raid Warden. That was part of the bargain because she was friends with the others at her post. She had dreaded going into the services and communal life. Her man was kind and not demanding and gave her a flat and some money to spend.

"All right," she said savagely. "I'm a whore, but there it is. Its not nice but its better than the other. Its not so much that I want things, I honestly don't. But I loathe poverty and dirt. I'm sorry," she said, "but its better you should know. Do you mind? I can leave him if you want me to."

How could I mind? In war one's vision was pretty blinkered. You saw what you had to see and partly, I suppose, what you wanted to see. Nothing was for sure and nothing was for ever.

In any case, perhaps we weren't really in love. We whispered many words, lying together in the dark. She was a demanding and passionate lover but among the many words we whispered as we lay in the stuffy, blacked out hotel rooms which were our refuge, we never said the three crucial ones, never said "I love you".

There was, in truth, much love between us as we both knew. But I suppose we were truthful people and to have said those words would have committed us in a way that neither felt able to be committed. There was no hint of sadness that this was so and no mention of it, but it was so.

I never knew her address. She said it was better I didn't and I only used her Christian name, Shelagh. "No Irish blood," she said, "just a whim of my parents but I stick with it."

Our few meetings, stolen days and nights in a difficult time, were a huge comfort to me. The intimacy in which we lived, never for more than two days together, utterly severed from the rest of the world, gave me a happiness and peace of mind I had never known. The simple fact that she was there miraculously quelled the tensions of my life as bomber pilot and bomber Squadron Commander. We never talked of our other lives but I hope and believe she felt that what we had together also helped with the difficulties I knew lay in her life in London.

Our poor little story would have no place in this account were it not for its ending which was thus.

I had known from the beginning that this was a war of science and technology, of organisation and planning, of concentration and work rather than of great deeds. If England was to win through against the fearsome odds we faced, every resource had to be used at the highest efficiency and this applied to men and women as much as to petrol or coal mines or armament factories.

In that context I had seen and accepted that my best contribution was in the use of my experience and the skills I had acquired in training. For three years I had worked really hard and I think quite successfully at what I knew I did well. I had brought some useful innovations and new thought into the training process and had been able to squeeze something very near to maximum results out of the units I had led. But I was always conscious that such a contribution held little personal risk and no contact with the enemy. There had always been a sneaking feeling that I, like many others, stayed in Training Command because it was safe.

So when I achieved my aim of being for a time in the front line of attack on Germany I felt an immense relief that I could make a direct, as opposed to an indirect, contribution to the ultimate defeat of Nazi Germany.

For the first months of my time as a bomber the fascination of mastering the many aspects of my new occupation and trying to ensure the efficiency of my squadron kept me more than fully occupied. It was, by any standards, a rewarding task.

Towards the end of the Ruhr Battle, however, I began to wonder whether I was fighting the type of war I had visualised that lunchtime after the raid on the Renault works in Paris. I saw the Nazi Germans as the incarnation of the power of evil, the new essence of a nation which, twice in my lifetime had, through greed, overwhelming ambition, lust for power and contempt for non-German humanity, abruptly stopped any progress in Europe towards those ideals of human progress and happiness with which I had grown-up. But now that I had been given what I asked for, with the examples of London, Coventry and other British towns behind us, I began to question whether this wholesale destruction of German towns was efficient. Perhaps the horrors the Nazis had unleashed on the world removed the old traditions of warfare. This was total war indeed. They had sown the wind, they were reaping the whirlwind. But still I wondered . . .

Looking back at my few months on bombers, we had failed at Skoda, Krupps was obviously not destroyed and most of what I had to show for my urge to join the battle was the rows and rows of burnt out houses in a dozen German towns. Of course there had been damage to war industries and the like, but the primary result seemed to be in those rows and rows of empty boxes.

I was disturbed, almost frightened by my own thoughts. Although we heard much of the miracles of production being achieved across the Atlantic and were conscious of the strength our great ally was pouring into Britain, I knew enough of our enemy to realise that the war was far from being won. The possibility of the Nazis producing some technological war-winning weapon always loomed. The Russians were holding their own, forcing the German lines slowly back, but they were not yet winning the war. Only Bomber Command, with increasing participation by the US Air Force, was striking at the heart of Germany. Perhaps by the wholesale destruction of German towns we were forestalling some frightful development of weaponry. The Russians complained endlessly that they were bearing the whole burden but the diversion of German effort to the defence of towns must be having a considerable effect. And yet I wondered.

We were only doing on a larger scale what they had done to others. Would you, I asked myself, rather win the war by dubious methods or allow it to be lost? I had no difficulty in answering that we HAD to win. But . . .

In the main I told myself that there was little to be uneasy about. We were delivering large quantities of bombs on the Reich. That was the task allotted to us in the general plan of allied strategy to defeat Hitler. Surely that was enough. I was partially reassured.

But then in Lincoln one day I bought a book, an illustrated book which was apparently not of interest any more since it was remaindered. It cost me five shillings and I have it still but at the time its contents thoroughly upset me. I did not show the book to anyone or describe or discuss its content. But I most urgently felt the need to share the burden of what it implied for me; and only Shelagh, my lover and my intimate who had no part in the mainstream of my life, generous and loving girl that she was, could be the one to understand. She would know that I did not ask reassurance or advice from her, nor even discussion; she would simply accept the burden of the knowledge of my predicament and in doing that infinitely lighten my load.

I was loath to tell her by word of mouth or show her the book in one of our all too short but ecstatically happy times together. I could imagine my confession hanging between us like a dark cloud which we might not be able to disperse in the fleeting hours we had together. By some clumsiness of discussion we could cloud the idyll of our relationship and that I could not bear. I did not know her address, that was part of our pact, so I could not post her a letter and a letter was really the only way I could tell her my inmost thoughts without provoking a reply I did not need. All I wanted was that she should know. So I resolved that I would write my letter and next time she came I would give it to her as we parted, asking her to read it in her own good time. By just reading it she would be doing for me what no one else could.

In the event we never said that good-bye. With the letter written I heard that Shelagh was dead, killed by a falling beam in a burning house from which she was trying to drag an unconscious child. The letter I had from her friend concluded:

"I think she knew she was going to die. She told me that you were the only person she wanted me to tell. She never talked of you but I always knew you were there. I think maybe she loved you. I hope that perhaps you loved her a bit. She was worth it but, poor Shelagh, she had no luck."

So here is the letter I never sent:

Darling,

This letter will say things I ought not to say, tell you what I too often feel when you're not there. After I have been with you for even a short time I don't worry about such things. That's the wonder of what you give me. But when you're not around these ghoulies crowd in on me and for good or ill I must tell you of them.

I bought a book this afternoon and stupidly I have let it thoroughly upset me. You, my darling, who are so practical and intelligent and balanced, wouldn't let that happen. I can't imagine that you, so bright and shining, would ever let yourself, or me, feel that the world was grey and hopeless because of an idea.

You see, the book I bought was a book of drawings, rather good drawings, of London in the blitz. They were done by a foreigner, Joseph Bato, a Pole who, although he certainly has affection for the country which has taken him in and for the town which is the mainspring of the fight against his country's enemies, yet can hardly have the feeling of a true Londoner for his village. Nevertheless the drawings and the short captions and descriptions which accompany them are vivid and compelling.

For instance . . .

The third drawing is of a row of houses, typical London houses of three or four stories; the first floors have little balconies and you can imagine the pleasant L-shaped drawing rooms behind them. The next floors are smaller with good unostentatious windows, open at the bottom as they would be so that the nice couples who slept there should not feel bunged up in the morning. The higher floors are smaller still, a bit cramped perhaps but pleasant enough. You feel that nurses, children, parlourmaids and such had led a happy and ordered existence there.

But in the midst of this pleasant terrace one house has "caught it" as the saying is. The whole front has been blown away, exposing horribly to the street the shattered remains of the quiet, decent life that went on in that sort of house. The ceiling that once separated the drawing room from the dignified dining room below with its good mahogany table and silver candlesticks is now bent awry. You cannot see the dining room but balanced on the remains of the ceiling are two loose doors from upstairs, one with a coat, a horribly upstairs sort of coat, hanging from it.

Above, beams and floorboards, carpets, clothes and sticks of furniture, torn lampshades and broken cupboards lie about in an aimless, intimate litter, some hanging drunkenly between one floor and another. A bath lies on its side. In the top or nursery floor everything is broken unrecognisably.

It is drawn without any over-emphasis. This is just an "incident", that horrible word so expressive of the attitude of authority to private tragedy and destruction of personal things.

On the opposite page is the artist's comment, for the picture has no name. It is only an "incident". He says, "Revolting, deadly revolting, this mad crushing of civilian things, civilian life. The murder of women and children, of harmless people. I started to put on paper what I had seen. As a protest, as . . . as if making a long list, an endless and strange list of things which have been destroyed; a list which must be presented to somebody, some day . . . some day of Justice."

I suppose this picture and these words arouse a fine normal spirit of resentment in English people. Murder, you see, darling, is a strong word and a murderer is not, on the whole, a very nice person.

Do they keep lists in Germany I wonder? And do they also look forward to a day . . . a day of Justice? There are, after all, women and children in Hamburg and Cologne, there are baths and stair carpets and lampshades in their houses, civilian things, civilian life. There are children and nurseries on their upper floors. Of course the Royal Air Force aims for military objectives, but, darling, you've seen the photos, haven't you? "Revolting, deadly revolting, this mad crushing of civilian life".

And I swear to you, my sweet, that nothing that ever happened in London in any way approached what I saw in Dortmund on a summer night last month. "A long list, a long and strange list of things," said our artist.

Oh, darling, I need you tonight. It is weak and stupid of me but for once I need comfort and quiet. If you were here I wouldn't be telling you all this, of course. I wouldn't even mention it to you. I should just know by your fair hair in the crook of my shoulder, by the touch of your lips in the hollow of my neck, that I couldn't be what this book says, a murderer, a killer of women and children, a member of Bomber Command.

The captions go on, each one opposite a drawing of destruction.

"They hurled down their bombs, large and small no matter where they fell. They knocked down the House of God." (The drawing is of Chelsea Old Church.)

"They smashed the house of the poor." (A tenement building with the whole side torn away and the remains of rooms with iron bedsteads and cheap furniture exposed useless in the street.)

". . . and the house of the rich." (The In and Out Club in Piccadilly.)

". . . hospitals." (A ruined part of St Thomas's.)

". . . and pubs." (One near St Paul's with a skyline of empty shells of houses and the proud Cathedral intact behind.)

"Is the Temple a military objective?" (The fine dignified old buildings with empty windows, jagged skyline and a heap of debris in front.)

"The Hall where Shakespeare once played. If crippled will it help to defeat Britain?" (Middle Temple Hall, partly destroyed.)

"Is it a soldierly virtue to kill people on a dance floor? Is it a military effort to murder young women and girls while they are amusing themselves in a restaurant?" (The remains of the Café de Paris. Chairs and tables higgledy-piggledy, the pillars broken and lights and fittings hanging anyhow. A champagne bucket drunkenly bent in a corner and, more or less intact, the balcony where I have often had supper.)

"The Tower is overlooking dreamily the senseless destruction. It has witnessed many a cruelty, killing and murder; hardly ever anything so ghastly, anything so mad." (The Tower of London stands as background to a scene of destruction.)

"This night they came down to the tube without mother. She had been murdered by a bomb." (Two young people asleep under a rug.)

There are hard words in this book for the Germans who bombed the English cities, aren't there? Read them back, darling, read them back for me. Savour them and think about them and tell me if they are true of the English who are destroying Germany and the Germans as they tried to destroy us. Darling, tell me if they are true of me? They are not pretty words. Read them back.

"Murdered . . . so ghastly, so mad. Senseless destruction . . . cruelty, killing and murder, murder, young women and girls in a restaurant . . . arson . . . revolting, deadly revolting . . . "

But I tell you, my darling, that no German pilot ever looked down on London and saw the obscene red mass of flames that was Dortmund last

*month or Hamburg last week. And this is only the beginning, for
nothing can stop us now. Nothing but the end of the war can stop the
destruction of practically every city in Germany, destruction that will
make Bato's drawings look like the record of a peevish child bored with
its bricks; destruction that will make those words sound like a mother
scolding a spoilt child compared with what they will say of us.*

*Is it true, darling, what Joseph Bato said about them? Will you tell me
whether it's true? Because even if it is true it's no good our saying "Oh
well, they started it."*

*Is this boring you, my darling? Probably it is. Perhaps you're saying
with womanly reason and logic, "What's he got to worry about? He's
only doing what he's told. For God's sake get on with the job."*

*Now I've hurt you, I know. Because you hadn't even thought of saying
that. You're far too sweet and understanding not to worry a little if I'm
worried.*

*The introduction to the book is by Mr J.B. Priestley. By his writings he
is a man of great common sense, integrity and has much understanding
of what you might call "the ordinary person". He has fought in one war
and done much at a difficult time to help people to keep their courage
and spirit alive in this one.*

See what he says in his introduction:

*"The fact remains that this indiscriminate mass bombing is a terrible
and obscene business. It belongs to the nightmare side of things. It is
like some old, ugly dream come true. It cuts deeper, as I know from my
own experience, than fighting at the front. And for this reason, that it is
warfare at its foulest, all mixed up with women and children, with
familiar surroundings, with houses and shops, libraries and hospitals."*

Although I missed her terribly I am glad now that my poor
darling Shelagh did not read my letter. It would have caused her
distress far above the selfish ease I sought in writing it.

I had little time to brood on such things nor even on the loss
of Shelagh. The destruction of Hamburg was followed quickly by
an attack on Nuremburg, the city from which the image of the
ponderous jollity and splendid songs of the Mastersingers had
been all but obliterated in English minds by newsreels and films
showing Hitler ranting to the vociferous applause of the annual
Nazi rallies. These had grown bigger, the yell of "Heil Hitler"
more strident, the whole atmosphere more sinister in each year of
the crescendo of German war preparations. It was impossible to

feel any qualms about an attempt to destroy the town which seemed the epitome of the obscene triumphs of this evil man. Nuremburg was never a lucky target for Bomber Command and I do not remember any convincing result of this attack.

Then came the moon period in which I had planned to have some leave, part at least with Shelagh, but any such idea was scotched by a directive from Command that all experienced crews were to remain available. From our Group Headquarters came the instruction to practise intensively a method of bombing which we had already tentatively used. This combined visual aiming at target indicators with a timed run from a conspicuous point close to the target. It would be particularly useful if, towards the end of an attack, the target was covered with smoke. We were to practise using a height of six thousand feet, far below our normal bombing altitude. It wasn't difficult to guess that some very special target was in view.

The attack which took place on 17th August, with the moon only just past the full and in clear weather, was on Peenemunde which, as we discovered later, was the station for the research and development of the V1 pilotless aircraft and the V2 rocket-propelled bomb.

"Secret weapons" which would win the war for Germany had been part of Hitler's propaganda for some time and British sources had been energetic in ridiculing such stories. General knowledge that weapons such as the V1 and V2 were in an advanced state of preparation would undoubtedly have caused some alarm, and even we who were to attack them at their roots were not told what it was that we had so urgently to destroy.

The attack was a considerable success and, although it did not prevent the production and use of the V-weapons, this and later attacks on launching sites and storage depots considerably delayed the timing and reduced the scale of the attacks. The plan had been to launch no less than six thousand V1 bombs every day from the early summer of 1944 and if this had gone forward it is hard to see that the invasion of Normandy in June could have been mounted.

Attacking a target so deep in enemy territory in bright moonlight was bound to result in heavy losses and I saw so many aircraft shot down over the target and on the return trip that I was not surprised to hear that the tally was forty bombers lost. No. 5 Group had the honourable position of being the last to attack and we, therefore, bore the brunt of the fighter reaction which had been effectively delayed by a "spoof" attack on Berlin. But by the time we were over the target the German fighters had arrived and they were active throughout our long moonlit journey back. To avoid the German radar on this trip our instructions were to go low over Denmark and it was heartening to be flying at tree-top height over this occupied territory and to see the lights go on in the bedroom windows of farmhouses and figures waving as we passed.

Seventeen out of one hundred and twenty-six of No. 5 Group Lancasters failed to return, a percentage which could not possibly be sustained. Worst hit of all was my own squadron, of which four out of twelve were lost, a shattering blow. In spite of the dreadful losses among friends and crews, it was marvellous that morale showed no sign of cracking and I had the real satisfaction that we had tried, and to some degree succeeded, in our mission to inhibit whatever was going on at Peenemunde.

After Peenemunde, Berlin, known to aircrew simply as the Big City. It was only the end of August and the nights were still of summer quality and barely long enough for us to reach the enemy capital and clear his coast before first light.

There was always something special about attacking the Big City, partly I suppose connected with revenge for the blitz on London, partly that it was almost the most distant and certainly the best defended of all German towns. The feelings were partly of apprehension, partly of determination fuelled by the picture of Hitler himself cowering there below in his bunker.

Berlin is a very large city and its industries are scattered about the outer built-up perimeter, as is the case with London. When we arrived in the area that August night there was thin cloud, perhaps seven-tenths, over the city. It was scattered enough to be able to see something of the ground below but the huge quantity of searchlights playing on the cloudbase provided a brilliant white background against which, in a slow, unmanoeuvrable, black bomber, you felt you were sharply silhouetted, a sitting duck for the fighters patrolling above.

Through the gaps in the cloud layer there were the usual flashes of anti-aircraft guns, producing a scintillating barrage of bursting shells all around us. As we flew in I saw some target indicators descending slowly to ground level and was immediately conscious that they were very scattered. Some must have been several miles apart and there was no recognisable concentration. Equally the flashes of high-explosive bombs and the silver strips of incendiaries were soon spread over a wide area.

Uncertain how to bomb, I had the ghastly experience of seeing a Lancaster spinning out of control within a few yards of my starboard wing. The great aeroplane was still getting some lift from its wings so that its plunge earthwards was relatively slow, but as it passed us a wing came off. The hulk must have fallen into the built up area of Berlin, presumably with its load of bombs on board. And the crew? The gunners reported having seen two parachutes and, preoccupied as one was with one's own predicament, it was impossible not to think for a moment of those men, floating down, slowly, slowly, perhaps only to fall into the fires which were just taking hold, perhaps to be torn in pieces at the hands of a furious mob . . .

After we had bombed as best we could and thankfully turned for home, I was at last able to weave a bit. This probably had little effect on our safety but I knew it gave the crew some relief from the strain of the feeling that we were doing nothing in the way of evasive action, simply waiting to be picked on by a fighter. As we cleared the city I looked back to see that many of the silver lines of magnesium incendiaries had turned to red, but they were scattered over an immense area. Concentrating on my task of getting my aircraft and crew safely over the five hundred miles that lay between us and safety I had a hard task not to think about Joseph Bato's book and his drawings and his captions . . .

The reports in the press and BBC of this and another attack a few days later were most enthusiastic, implying really significant damage to the enemy capital. I was disposed to think otherwise and I well knew that losses of 58 aircraft on a single raid were far above the acceptable rate.

After this attack I received a telephone call from Group that the AOC wanted to see me and I was to report to his HQ immediately. No, they could not tell me on the telephone what it was about.

I motored over to Grantham in a state of some excitement. Now that the nights were longer it seemed likely that precision attacks on isolated objectives might be more frequent and I thought I might be picked to lead the next one. I had not been allowed to take part in an attempt in June to destroy the Zeppelin works at Friederichshaven in which the participants, short of daylight to return home, had had to land in North Africa. One result of that trip had been that many aircraft returned heavily laden with some pretty lethal Algerian wine. This, at a time when the supply of wine in England was virtually non-existent, was consumed all too quickly with dire results to all but the strongest stomachs.

In the event I was disappointed. There was no such plan as I had envisaged and instead I was told that expansion of the Group had led to a need of experienced officers as Station Commanders. The AOC gave it as his opinion that I had done enough Operations for the time and would now be better employed in a supervisory capacity. I was to be promoted to Group Captain and posted to Woodhall Spa as Station Commander with effect from a week's time. Meanwhile no more Operations.

To leave the squadron with whom I had shared the vicissitudes of the last six strenuous months and from whom I had received so much loyalty and, I think, affection, was a wrench indeed. Having to abandon the privilege of being the leader of such a band of brothers, even if I was a mite older than the rest, was hard. We had resisted the strains and pains of the inevitable losses, each and every day we had faced an unknown tomorrow, yet we had lived in some comfort and had lots of fun, epitomised in the wry humour of the bomber saying "There's always bloody something". But orders were orders and I had to go, well knowing that such gap as I left would very soon be more than adequately filled.

I handed over my command with a fairly heavy heart. Of the hopes and ideals which had been germinating in my mind since early in the war and which had budded that day at Swinderby Mess when I pored over the photographs of the Renault works, almost none had blossomed. Only at Peenemunde had I seen a comparable result to that at Renault. The two efforts at Skoda had been failures, one for me a near-disaster. I had, of course, taken my full part in the general task of Bomber Command as I had applied to do. It was nearly a year since I had left Training Command.

Before I left I wrote a memorandum to higher authority in the hope that what experience I had gained on my tour might be of some use. My concerns were twofold. I felt that more deceptions could be practised to bewilder and mislead the enemy defences. In particular I suggested the ruse of mounting "spoof" operations by crews under instruction. As part of the course at the Operational Training Units every pupil crew did an individual sortie over occupied France which was very lightly defended. I suggested that these exercises be co-ordinated and a fairly large number of training aircraft be despatched towards Germany to simulate a real attack. This should result in the enemy controllers making fighters airborne too early and in the wrong place, wasting their time and reducing the number available to meet the real attack an hour or so later. This tactic was adopted and was often successful.

My other contention was that Berlin was too large, too well-defended, too far away and its industry too widely dispersed to be a profitable target in the present imperfect state of the bomber's art. I believed that persistent raids on Berlin would produce only scattered damage to the city with little loss of industrial production and high, possibly unacceptable, casualties to ourselves. The comparative accuracy now attainable on shorter range targets would produce better results and allow more expansion of the Command in time to support the expected invasion of the Continent in 1944.

As for the moral effects, Germany was a huge country. To leave Berlin alone except for an occasional token raid to prevent the redeployment of the defences, would imply to the Germans that Hitler and his crew of ruling scalliwags were able to lurk safely in the capital leaving the rest of the country to suffer the rigours of our attacks. The temptation to attack Berlin heavily for prestige reasons or as revenge for the blitz on London was natural but it would be a gross strategical and tactical error.

I fear that this lecture addressed to my seniors was distinctly unpopular and, since the dictatorial Sir Arthur Harris was, as I feared, already fully determined on the "Battle of Berlin" I'm quite sure that no subordinate would have dared show him such a flat contradiction of his own ideas.

Alas, the Battle of Berlin formed the main thrust of Bomber Command effort that winter, resulting in the loss of over one thousand heavy bombers and what the historian Liddell Hart called the Command's "heavy defeat in the direct offensive against Germany".

8

"Ed" Murrow Flies to Berlin

A Moral Dilemma

Woodhall Spa was a station similar to Fiskerton except that the Officer's Mess and living quarters were in a requisitioned hotel which had once been a private house of a curious "art nouveau" sort of splendour. There was a proper bar, not allowed in standard RAF messes, and I had a comfortable and well-furnished flat with bedroom, bathroom and sitting room. Although as Station Commander I had complete responsibility for administration, organisation and discipline, I was only expected to exercise general supervision over the single operational squadron. I had to be careful not to seem to interfere in the Squadron Commander's sphere. I was lucky in that the Squadron Commander was an officer for whom I had the greatest admiration, both as an operational pilot and as a man.

Soon after I took over we had as a visitor, the American radio commentator, Edward, "Ed", Murrow, already famous for his broadcasts from London in the blitz. From 1939 onwards all America, no less than Britain, was agog for Ed's attractive, slightly gravelly, voice announcing "This is London", and giving vivid and sympathetic accounts of wartime scenes which, with the defeat of France, became increasingly strange and fascinating to peacetime America. I believe that the gradual diversion of American opinion from an almost universal determination to maintain neutrality to a realisation that American intervention on the side of Britain was acceptable can be traced at least in part to the broadcasts of Ed Murrow with their vivid depiction of

Britain's lonely determination to overcome the Nazi horror. When Japan attacked Pearl Harbour and Hitler declared war on the United States the acceptance of Roosevelt's decision that the defeat of Germany should take precedence over the war in the Far East, owed much to the sympathy and understanding stirred by Ed's quiet evocation of beleaguered Britain as America's necessary comrade in arms.

Ed Murrow came to Woodhall with permission to fly on an operation to Berlin and, while journalists as a tribe were not always popular with the RAF, Ed, with his quiet unobtrusive charm and deep interest in our affairs, quickly made his way into all our hearts.

Our operations were normally laid on by soon after nine o'clock in the morning and if, as often happened, the weather was impossible, the cancellation might come at any time up to ten minutes before the planned take-off time. This led to fairly harrowing days as all the manifold steps towards the operation had to be taken at their appointed times, only to be unravelled when the "scrub" order came through. Even when the weather forecast held little prospect of "working" you dared not skimp any of the preparations.

Ed stayed with us for two weeks of this very trying routine while the weather stayed in its most frustrating mood. In that time, very much of which he spent in my company, we became friends. He and I seemed able to discuss just about anything and, different as were our countries and our backgrounds, we were very close. He would sit in my office or accompany me to the Operations Block in the mornings, listening in to the daily round of orders and counter-orders. He would drink our nasty coffee without comment and his marvellous humour and powerful insights soon showed us why he was already one of the world's most famous journalists. It was no surprise to me that, with the advent of television, he became one of the world's most powerful men.

When at last the weather allowed a trip to Berlin to go forward and I stood by the runway to wave off the aircraft carrying Ed and flown by "Jock" Abercrombie, 619 Squadron

Commander, I hoped with immense fervour that that aircraft would come back..

It did and Ed made two brilliant broadcasts of his experience, parts of which he recorded on the aircraft, completing his account of the trip with the simple words "we touched down very gently, ran along to the end of the runway and turned left. Jock, the finest pilot in Bomber Command, said to the control tower 'D-Dog clear of runway'". Although I do not think Ed had flown in Bomber Command with anyone else, I would not quarrel with his assessment. "Jock" Abercrombie was an outstanding pilot and a splendid man but alas, like many of the best, he did not complete this, his second tour of bomber operations.

After Ed left us we kept in touch and, until he left England, whenever I went to London he would always take time off to meet me, busy and sought after as he was. We sometimes went to parties together and it was typical of him that, unlike other journalists, he never sought out the rich, the useful or the famous. He would simply stand in a corner of the room, often chatting with me, and the rich and the famous would never fail to seek him out.

After the war we corresponded but I hadn't seen him for a couple of years when I heard that single-handed he had toppled the odious but immensely powerful Senator McCarthy who had so deeply damaged America's image in the liberal world. Like many others I was desolate when Ed's incessant chain-smoking took its toll and he died of lung cancer. He was, I think, the only person I have known of whom I can say with certain truth that "take him for all in all, I shall not look upon his like again".

Apart from this interlude and several visits from Martha Gellhorn, then Mrs Ernest Hemingway, covering the war for *Collier's* magazine, who provided a marvellously transatlantic stimulus when my spirits flagged and often had a bottle of whisky when no one else had, the first months of my time at Woodhall were pretty miserable. I had no faith in the attacks on Berlin, and it was one of the least rewarding tasks of my RAF life to be continually despatching these young men on missions which I thought reminiscent of the Charge of the Light Brigade in military significance.

I don't like telling lies but I lied to them daily. In my job I dared not show any sign that I did not share authority's enthusiasm for the attacks on the Big City. I had to live the lie that I thought the Battle of Berlin crucial to the war, that I believed that we could paralyse the Nazi capital to the extent that the enemy war machine would crumble, that the effort and the dreadful losses on this distant, difficult and heavily defended target were truly worthwhile. I tried to convince myself that, in my relatively junior capacity, with no access to the information on which war strategy must be based, I had no right to differ from the plans which were made by people much more experienced than myself. But I did not succeed.

"Their's not to reason why" the poem said, but that was nearly a hundred years ago. It would have been the worse for the gallant six hundred if they had reasoned why, if they had known that they were the victims of a gross and palpable blunder by their higher command. But in our century, in our war, it was impossible, in England at any rate, that some participants in war should not reason.

I am prepared to believe that in that cold and dreary winter the Battle of Berlin, and the false hints about its success, may have raised the country's spirits. Hopes for a second front in 1943, egged on by violent and often rude demands from the Russians, had been unfulfilled. The victories in Africa were splendid but past. Progress in Italy was hideously slow. The Russians continually complained that they alone bore the burden of the war. The prize of the destruction of Berlin was tempting indeed. The optimistic reports on the wireless, and indeed Ed's broadcasts, provided something of a tonic to everyone. I had not told even him of my reservations about Berlin but in my heart I absolutely knew that the prize was simply not within our grasp. The shocking weather of that winter, in which no bomber or reconnaissance aircraft caught a glimpse of the ground near Berlin for weeks at a time, made for vague but ultimately deceitful claims of results. There was a widespread feeling that London was being avenged.

Then the function of Woodhall Spa was suddenly changed. "Jock" Abercrombie's squadron was moved to our nearby parent station at Coningsby and from there No. 617, the Dambusters as they were subsequently dubbed by a film, was installed at Woodhall. This squadron, formed at Scampton for special duties when I was at Fiskerton, had been through a bad patch since the success of the famous attack on the Mohne and Eder Dams in the spring. That night the squadron had lost nearly half its strength and Guy Gibson, a well-earned VC on his breast, was taken off Operations.

After an interval of rest, nothing had gone right for 617. Several operations had been only partially successful and shortly before they came to Woodhall a low-level attack on the Dortmund-Ems Canal had been disastrous. Heavy losses on this target had included their new Squadron Commander and Ralph Allsebrook, an outstanding young pilot who had been a tower of strength in my early days at 49 Squadron. The canal was intact.

To Woodhall, to command and revive 617, came the young Group Captain Leonard Cheshire, accepting a downgrading to Wing Commander to allow him to take the post. Very soon a sense of purpose emerged as new tasks, new bombs, new equipment and new methods were introduced. Although I was not allowed to fly with them, I took part in the introduction of these various novelties and I hope smoothed the way with some of them. The only contretemps I ever had with Cheshire was when he confided to me his intention to take a Lancaster and on Christmas Day drop parcels of goodies on the Prisoner of War Camp in Poland where his brother was incarcerated. The idea was spectacular and I felt perhaps derived from Fighter Command's dropping of a new artificial leg for Douglas Bader when he was a prisoner. But whereas that exploit was carried out as a mercy mission agreed by the Germans, Cheshire's was to be done as a surprise gesture. Cheshire's prestige and personality were already such that I am sure all concerned in the spectacular plan would have supported him with enthusiasm.

I knew, however, that in the context of the war this was a supremely stupid idea. The Germans would make propaganda of an "attack" on Christmas Day, there was some chance, remote perhaps but real, that the aircraft and crew would be lost to no purpose, it would entail airmen working on Christmas Day and the chances of the weather being kind enough to ensure finding a pinpoint target in distant Poland were not all that high. So I told Cheshire that he must abandon the idea which he most loyally did and no more was heard of it until various inaccurate accounts of the episode were published after the war.

It was from Woodhall that Cheshire, ably seconded by the old hands, "Micky" Martin, Dave Shannon, Joe Macarthy and Les Munro, experimented successfully in the method of marking targets by dropping target indicators from very low heights.

"Higher Authority" subsequently claimed part of the credit for inventing the low marking method while allowing Cheshire credit for pioneering it. The fact is, however, that the first outstanding success was the destruction of the Gnome-Rhône aero-engine factory at Limoges in February 1944 when the instructions from Group were that markers should not fly below one thousand feet. Cheshire, with my agreement, ignored this and the results were spectacular. I had the job of admitting the truth to the Air Officer Commanding, Air Vice-Marshal Cochrane, the next morning. As a noted disciplinarian he was a bit taken aback that orders so specific should have been disregarded but, with his clear and subtle mind, he forgave the lapse and, adopting the method, gave Cheshire his full support in obtaining lighter and more manoeuvrable aircraft, Mosquitoes and Mustangs, to replace the ponderous Lancaster for the job of low-level marking. As the months went on the method was adapted with modifications and improvements until it became the standard practice in No. 5 Group and was used in all of its most successful attacks thereafter. It is no exaggeration to say that there was, thus, introduced a new dimension in the search for real pinpoint accuracy in bombing.

The introduction of a huge new bomb and of a new and much improved bombsight, both used only by 617 Squadron, made this a fascinating period of great significance in the search for accurate bombing methods. There were attacks of varying success on the sinister "ski-sites" which were springing up along the coast of the Pas de Calais, all pointing towards London, and on other factories and installations in France. These were real pinpoint targets where a fifty-yard error would be too much. Practice on these sites, even before the Limoges operation, had shown low-level marking to be practicable and often superior to the very considerable accuracy obtainable with the short-range "Oboe" electronic device.

This time at Woodhall Spa was very rewarding for me. Although it was frustrating that I could not fly in these operations, I was old enough to accept that an efficient war machine must take little notice of individual preferences. What mattered was that we were making real progress towards rendering superfluous the bludgeon-type attack which had been the only possible method in the past. It seemed that we were on track to making the bomber a war winning weapon, a rapier able to attack and destroy significant targets with a high proportion of bombs doing damage of military significance. My small part in the beginning of this revolution was enormously significant to me.

Inevitably there were failures. An attempt to attack the Antheor railway viaduct in the South of France, in the hope of causing a bottleneck for the German defences against allied attack on that coast and impeding any attempt to reinforce German defences in France from the south, did not succeed. No allowance had been made by Intelligence for the great stepping up of the defences of this obviously important target which had already been attacked without success three or four times. The Germans, no less than ourselves, were fully aware of its significance and had doubled and redoubled the defences with the result that the attack was a failure and very nearly a disaster.

Deeply immersed as I was in these absorbing operations it came as something of a shock to me when I was sent for by Group and Air Vice-Marshal Cochrane. He told me that he now wanted me for a new job and I was to leave Woodhall at very short notice. Under Wing Commander (as he was then) Cheshire, I believe that 617 Squadron was probably the finest fighting unit ever to serve with Bomber Command. To have had a part in its development was a privilege and an immensely satisfying experience. I had been at last involved in operations of a sort in which I passionately believed, whereas in my own flying I had to confess to my inmost self that only the attack on Peenemunde had come into that category. And that had been at the cost of devastating my squadron.

I found it difficult to see what more important job there could be than the one I was doing but the Air Marshal was obdurate. He told me that the pressure on the supply of Lancasters and crews had been accentuated by the losses over Berlin and by the heavy damage which was often sustained by many of the aircraft which came home. It had, therefore, been decided that all crew training on large four engined types was to be carried out on Halifaxes and Stirlings, the more effective Lancasters being kept entirely for first line squadrons. Crews would, therefore, arrive in the Group fully trained for operations except that they had never flown in a Lancaster.

Cochrane quite rightly, did not believe that new crews would be given proper training and supervision in the stressful atmosphere of an operational squadron and had decided, therefore, to set up a special school within the Group at which crews would be converted to fly Lancasters. He was very loath to spare the Lancasters from operational duties and was going to set the school a near-impossible target in order that crews were made fully ready to fly and operate Lancasters in double-quick time. If this project was successful he hoped that squadrons would not have to use their operational aircraft for any further training. Top priority was going to be attached to the new school and I could choose a proportion of the core staff I would need.

Syerston, where the "Lancaster Finishing School" was to be situated, was a large station which would normally be commanded by a much more senior officer than myself. Cochrane, however, gave me to understand that because I had extensive experience of training under war conditions and, after a recent tour of bomber operations, had practical knowledge of the requirements, he had chosen me for what he warned would be a very demanding assignment. I had to pack my bags quickly and make the best of it.

My disappointment was naturally acute at being removed from the operational scene in the months when the whole country was holding its breath in the half-knowledge of the huge preparations going forward for the invasion of the continent. Security was excellent and even I knew no detail of what was going on. American forces, American aircraft were everywhere. Everyone knew that it was virtually certain that this summer would see the great enterprise go forward. In March, while I was en route for Syerston, 5 Group made its first attack on a French railway yard and by April Bomber Command's operations were nearly all aimed at weakening and disorganising German defences in northern France.

Compared to the great concept of preparing for the invasion, our task at the Lancaster Finishing School was humdrum, but the demand for new crews had never been greater. The losses on Berlin had to be made up and the intensity of operations in the better weather was at its height. Losses on French targets were low at first but more crews were finishing their tours and, as the Germans reinforced their fighters in France, losses rose again.

At Syerston I had an excellent team of experienced instructors who soon showed that they understood the reality of the problems. Never, I am sure, have four-engined aircraft been flown so intensively but we tried and tried not to let the quality of our teaching get submerged by the demand for immediate results. A main difficulty in such a unit was the servicing and repair of aircraft and in this section I had a Senior Engineer Officer who inspired everyone, worked very long hours and had a prodigious capacity for scrounging or making up any spares which were holding up the effort.

Within the first weeks I had proof of his exceptional ability to make bricks without straw. I had long known that there was a widespread failure in training crews both in dinghy drill, the procedure when a damaged aircraft had to be ditched at sea, and in the baling-out procedure, when an aircraft had to be abandoned at height. Although operational squadrons were supposed to train and practise these drills, I knew that this was regarded as a chore and more honoured in the breach than the observance. Crews on operational squadrons not unreasonably thought that, since they were flying against the enemy, their training was complete and when not actually fighting they had a right to leisure. There was also an element of lethargy, the insidious idea that "it won't happen to me" and "it'll be all right on the night". But the fact remained that a large number of crews were inefficient in these vital procedures which, when the emergency came, had to be carried out without a second's delay. In addition, having only flown few hours in Lancasters by night, they did not have the absolute instinctive certainty of knowing every knob and gadget of their aircraft in the pitch dark.

To plug these gaps we found a couple of Lancaster fuselages which had been written off after accidents and the engineers fitted them up for practice ditching and baling out drills. Since virtually all operations took place at night, these dummy fuselages were completely blacked-out so that, by constant practises which did not use up flying hours, every crew member knew with his eyes shut the exact position of every single instrument and control, every nook and cranny of the aircraft which on operations he might have to use or which might hinder his movement in emergency. Such knowledge was normally built up in a good many hours of actual flying experience on the type, but for these tyros who were to be thrown straight into the battle, that was a delay which could not be accepted.

To my desk at Syerston came quite good Intelligence reports and operational summaries so that, although I was more than fully occupied with the absorbing task of building my new unit where the minor but time consuming incidents and problems were endless, I did have knowledge of events beyond the station. I knew by the reports the part our Group was playing in the great events which were slowly unfolding. From the photographs I saw it was obvious that, contrary to the belief of Air Marshal Harris and the warnings of politicians and sources inside France, it had become possible to attack the railway targets in France at night with very great accuracy. Because of the much bigger bomb loads of the British heavies, we were doing more damage than the Americans in spite of their longer experience of attacking pinpoint targets. The success of 5 Group in these months was largely due to the new method of low marking introduced by Cheshire. What had seemed a special attribute of a single squadron, inspired by the genius of a single man, now enabled the whole Group to attack their targets in France without the awful loss of life to our erstwhile allies which would have been inevitable if the railway targets, all in or near built up areas, had been inaccurately attacked.

The enormous damage done to the whole railway network vital to the German defence of occupied France naturally caused the enemy to move his fighter squadrons westward and losses, small at first, mounted significantly. Some of those targets which crews had been wont to think of as a "piece of cake" proved unexpectedly expensive, but not until June did casualties reach the numbers experienced on German targets. They were high enough, however, with the intensity of operations, to convince us at Syerston that there had been no exaggeration when we were warned of the importance and magnitude of our task.

It was only sensible with these developments to switch attacks from time to time to the homeland of Hitler's Germany in order to ensure that a reasonable proportion of his fighters remained far from France. Prominent among these attacks was an onslaught by No. 5 Group on Munich, a target which, in spite of its associations with Hitler and the Nazis and its importance as a city, had so far escaped serious damage. After this attack it was claimed that "most of Munich's important public buildings, business property, public utilities and transport facilities had been destroyed". This was achieved without disastrous losses by only two hundred and fifty aircraft – one quarter of the number that was in the thousand-bomber attacks of 1942, which achieved far less spectacular results. After this attack Cheshire was awarded a Victoria Cross which was rightly stated as having been earned by four years of outstanding personal achievement. The long and four years of outstanding personal achievement. The long and splendid citation, however, stated that this was "exemplified by his conduct in an attack on Munich in April 1944".

In May many and wild were the guesses about when and where the invasion would happen as it became more and more obvious that it could not be long delayed. At Syerston there were occasional warnings that our aircraft might be needed for some extra effort comparable with the thousand bomber raids of 1942. Without interfering with our training programme, we made what preparation we could to be fit to take our part in that wonderful operation now known as D-day and I joined the senior instructors in forming a crew "just in case". It came to nothing, which I'm sure was sound policy, but we were disappointed.

As May drew to a close, attacks in support of the forthcoming invasion were stepped up and targets included gun batteries, radar installations, ammunition and fuel dumps and concentrations of troops and armour. Accuracy was all-important. Attacks on Germany were reduced and the single effort by our Group on a German town, Brunswick, failed, largely due to weather. There were high losses. But all-in-all the Bomber weapon was now being used as an arm of the great body of power attacking Hitler's fortress of Europe. This, I learnt later, was in spite of the doubts of the C-in-C himself who is on record as having believed that railways are "extraordinarily difficult and unrewarding targets". He opposed, to almost the last ditch, the transfer of ultimate responsibility for Bomber Command's operations from himself to the Supreme Allied Commander. To give him his due, however, when he was overruled he accepted the position with complete loyalty and directed the operations he was required to undertake with all his normal skill and determination.

There is no doubt that, without the spectacular improvement in bombing accuracy achieved that spring by which the whole railway system in western France was almost totally dislocated and enormous damage was done to the German static defences, the invasion of Normandy might well not have succeeded. The Germans had planned to move reserve divisions to wherever the

eight trains a day to effect the moves with all speed. In the event
they were hard put to achieve six trains a day. It took reserve
divisions as long to get from eastern France to the front as it had
taken them to get from Poland to eastern France.

The consolidation of the first landings in Normandy was
nothing like secure for quite a time after D-day. If the Germans
had been able to use their reserves, as they had planned, the
disaster which might have overtaken the allied forces in
Normandy doesn't bear thinking about. There could have been no
Dunkirk-type rescue operations from Arromanches and Omaha.

In June, after the foothold in Normandy was established,
attacks on transportation and military targets continued at even
greater intensity and practically all bombing effort was
concentrated on pinpoint targets in furtherance of the invasion.
There were failures of course. Nothing in war ever goes
completely according to plan but it was wholly easy to be proud
that Bomber Command had played an immense and, in fact, an
essential part in the great enterprise which, with our Russian
allies, was going to bring all this horror to an end. It was galling
for me that I had only an indirect share in that operation.

I never served on the Staff and was not immune from the
inherent antipathy that exists between personnel on flying duties
and Staff Officers. These latter were assumed to think that we,
who were flying, were a harum scarum lot who needed continual
supervision, guidance and detailed direction. On the other hand
aircrew thought that there were far too many Staff Officers, that
they led idle and sheltered lives, made no substantial contribution
to our efforts and often actively hindered them. With experience
I modified this extreme view but it is a fact that Staffs do tend to
proliferate.

I was not altogether surprised, therefore, when in September
of 1944 I was told that my station of Syerston was to be
upgraded to the status of a "Base" which would be commanded
by an Air Commodore. He would have a Staff whose function
under his direction would be to control and supervise exactly the
same work as was being done before this new layer of command
existed. The Air Commodore designated to take over was an old

acquaintance of mine, a first war pilot of distinction, for whom I had much liking as a person but little respect as a wartime officer. Since I would have to hand over my living quarters, offices and most of my real responsibilities to him, my position on the station would obviously become anomalous. In any case I felt that my work at the Lancaster Finishing School was done and I could legitimately hope for a move.

The development of the new target-marking techniques had led in April to the return to 5 Group of the two Lancaster squadrons which had been detached in 1942 to form part of the Pathfinder Group under Air Vice-Marshal Don Bennett. With these squadrons under direct control by Air Vice-Marshal Cochrane, No. 5 Group had become free to develop its own methods and use its own target-marking techniques, normally operating as a separate identity under the overall command of the High Wycombe headquarters of Air Marshal Harris.

Cochrane, with whom I had had a good deal of personal contact at various times, saw the anomaly of my position at Syerston and, since I happened to discover that he wished to make a change in the command of one of the Pathfinder squadrons, I asked for the job and was accepted. Because Bennett retained a measure of responsibility for operating procedures on Pathfinders, and in particular controlled the award of the coveted Pathfinder badge, I had to do a short course of instruction in Pathfinder methods and procedures before being approved by him to command a Pathfinder squadron. This caused no trouble, but I was surprised, in fact shocked, at the depth of his hostility to the operating methods of 5 Group which, he told me at my final interview, he believed could "lose the war". It was not in my interest to quarrel with him, and except for this one incident I liked him and had immense admiration for his technical abilities, so I made no comment.

One of the features which mitigate the horror of war is the spirit of comradeship and devotion to a national purpose which inspires participants. Among the less attractive offshoots of this in our war was the determination of individual commanders to win the war on their own and the jealousy and obstruction which this selfish tunnel vision engendered.

Such a rift existed between the very able officers who commanded No. 5 Group, in which I served, and No. 8 (Pathfinder) Group to which, as OC 97 Squadron, I was also to owe some allegiance. The rift originated partly in the different backgrounds of the two officers. Cochrane, of 5 Group, with aristocratic forbears and a long service in the Air Force, had a full respect for service discipline and tradition. Bennett, the younger, an Australian with only a few years' service before the war, enormous technical knowledge and ability, and civilian fame as a commercial pilot, had a less than complete respect for service traditions and a meteoric promotion to Air Vice-Marshal on the formation of the Pathfinder Force.

Such personal differences were a minor blot on my new job. The spectacular success of the operations in support of the invasion of Normandy made it a wonderfully exciting assignment to find myself in a position to take an active part in what seemed must be the final blows that would destroy the Nazi canker in Europe.

The first attacks on England by the so-called Vl weapons, known to us as flying bombs, came soon after the landings in Normandy. The German Staffs had wanted these to be used against the south coast ports from which the D-day landings were mounted, but apparently Hitler had insisted on a further attack on London, believing the effect on morale might be decisive. If the original plan to launch six thousand of the weapons in a single day had been achieved, there would certainly have been most grievous effects. As it was, Peenemunde and the subsequent bombing of launching sites delayed the start and reduced the scale of the attacks, and the foothold in Normandy was looking fairly secure when the first weapons came over. Re-organisation of our defences ensured that guns and fighters were soon taking a toll of these flying bombs. Nevertheless Vls were reaching London in considerable numbers, and against the even less accurate V2 rockets there was no defence.

I had had no leave while at Syerston and had not seen my wife for over six months. When I told her of my impending move she laughingly suggested that the reason I would not come south was that I was frightened of the flying bombs. She, in spite of her responsibilities as the mother of two fine children, was totally unafraid of bombing and had often during the blitz deliberately spent days and nights in London to see what was going on. One night at the height of an attack she and a friend, intending to go to the Cafe de Paris, had reached Coventry Street to find the place half destroyed and bodies being brought out on stretchers.

Now she said she wanted to see the flying bombs and, with a slight feeling of guilt, I agreed to come to London for a couple of days, making the proviso that we stay at the Ritz because the walls were thick.

We did the conventional London things, went to a theatre, restaurants and night clubs and were very conscious that the capital, which had so splendidly weathered the blitz of 1940-41 and successive waves of bombing since, was thoroughly jittery. Elation at the success of the invasion was not unnaturally tempered with distress that, after having survived its long ordeal, now, with victory seemingly on the horizon, Londoners should again be in the front line.

At this time the defences had moved out of London and were deployed in the depths of Kent. The fighters and light flak were taking a heavy toll of the horrid things but, when a Vl got through those defences, it flew unmolested at a low height over the city until the moment when its engine cut out. Then it nosedived into the ground and its large explosive charge, equal to the heaviest bombs the Germans had used, detonated, often causing damage and casualties.

Some, at least, of the effect on morale of the V1s was due to the fact that the air raid sirens were so frequent that it was impossible to tell which was an alert and which an all-clear. I was surprised once when, walking into St James's Street from the hotel, I found that venerable thoroughfare completely deserted with not a vehicle nor a pedestrian in sight. Reflecting on the grace of some, at least, of its architecture when free from the ugliness of traffic, I suddenly realised the reason. The quiet which I was relishing was suddenly broken by an increasingly loud "phut, phut" from an easterly direction. Over the elegant bow front of White's Club came this horribly alien "thing", a nightmare object out of Jules Verne or H.G. Wells. It seemed little above rooftop height and nobody could do anything about it except hide. It would go on phut, phutting until it ran out of fuel and spread death and destruction where it fell. Unable to pray, I willed it to go on, at least past the Ritz, although I was conscious of the selfishness of my wish since, unless it fell into the Serpentine, it was merely a question of which building it destroyed and whose wife was killed. It was an eerie feeling, one of the worst of the war. The V2 rockets were also in use at the time but these gave no warning of their approach although they made an even louder bang. From my short experience of these weapons, which were totally indiscriminate, it was not difficult to understand that many Londoners were not averse to the idea of revenge.

I took command of No. 97 (Pathfinder) Squadron at Coningsby with the highest of hopes and soon acquired a highly skilled crew, all of whom had done a considerable number of operations. We trained together or, to be realistic, they trained me, in the methods and skills needed for the job we were to do which was, of course, different from my previous experience in a main force squadron. Their high skills and keenness soon inculcated into me what was necessary and within a week we were able to declare ourselves operational.

A development which warned me that at thirty-six you are not as adaptable as you were at twenty-six was the change in the lighting of aerodromes. In 1943 German "intruders", night fighters with carte blanche to wander at will over England and especially at the times of bombers returning from an attack, were common. The lighting of airfields had then been pretty sparse, just enough to make landing safe and give enough guidance to taxi to dispersal. By 1944 the intruders had become rare and aerodrome lighting was stepped up to help reduce the accident rate. Paradoxically to me, used only to the old conditions, this new galaxy of light was bewildering and I found difficulty at first in dealing with it. On my first night flight I wasn't far off having a minor accident through simply not realising where I was on the aerodrome. By luck all went well and I was ready for my first Pathfinder Operation.

It happened that this was a "daylight", a rare occurrence for our Group even now that fighter escort was available on a large scale quite far into Germany. Our target was an oil refinery in the Ruhr Valley, our task being to "back up" the famed accuracy of the primary marking by "Oboe" Mosquitoes of 8 Group. On this occasion the Oboe marking was scattered and it was impossible to assess with any certainty which markers were accurate. The technique by which a "master bomber" gave instructions to the rest of the force by radio telephony had been revolutionised by the introduction of VHF so that communication, which with the old sets had been less than reliable, was now supposed to be "loud and clear". Loud and clear it was on this occasion, but unfortunately someone had left his transmitter on, which meant that speech on his intercommunication set was broadcast to the whole force. So instead of the master bomber's comments we were treated to several crucial minutes of undisciplined backchat by a crew who were manifestly more interested in getting out of the area than in contributing to the operation. This, occuring when we were over the target and with the extreme clarity of the new equipment, was, together with my first experience of heavy, concentrated and accurate flak in clear daylight, was a very muddling and distressing experience.

The Oboe markers were so scattered that I do not believe the operation would have been successful in any case but this radio error contributed a lot of extra frustration. The barrage seemed to me heavier than any I had known over the Ruhr at night. I knew that some of it must have been close because of the foul smell and taste of cordite which penetrated into my lungs, hungry for the oxygen which I needed to inhale. When we got home the aircraft was full of holes and had to go to a maintenance unit for rebuild. We were lucky that our engines were not seriously hit.

While over the Ruhr I saw the launch of a V2 rocket, a long plume of white smoke rising vertically with increasing velocity until it was lost to view above us. This was an extraordinary experience in those days, a preview of what is now commonplace on television showing space launches from Cape Canaveral. "The bastards," I remember thinking, "the bastards. They haven't the remotest idea where it is going to fall, or whom it will kill, nor whether it will do them the slightest good." Then I wondered how many below were thinking the same about me and my fellows. Then I stopped thinking and concentrated on getting home.

The attack was said to have caused some damage to the installation but my guess was that it wasn't much. I was glad to have had the experience of a daylight operation but it reinforced my belief that our real function in the new era of bombing was the location and marking of significant targets by night.

The immunity of transport targets, railways, roads, bridges, canals, to the bombing potential of the early part of the war was well-known. The impossibility of bombing by day without fighter escort, the inaccuracy of bombing by night and the low weight of bomb loads practicable had shown that attacks on transport targets in the first years of the war were at best futile and at worst extremely expensive in terms of aircraft losses.

In those early days the BBC's audience in our embattled island longed to hear that some price was being extracted from Hitler for the vast conquests he had made in Europe. The calm, confident voice of the announcer telling the world that our bombers had once more attacked the marshalling yards at Hamm, north of the Ruhr, brought some comfort to millions of homes despondent at our lonely and impotent stance against continuous and seemingly inevitable disaster. But however often repeated, the attacks came to nothing and many aircraft and valuable crews were lost. The marshalling yards at Hamm became something of a sick joke in the RAF, a symbol of the impossibility of seriously damaging transport targets.

The Dortmund-Ems Canal, the vital artery between the heavy industries of the Ruhr and the shipbuilding yards of North

Germany, was another such target. At least one VC was awarded in a heroic low-level attack when nearly all the aircraft were lost and eventually, although the long-term loss of the canal route would have been a severe blow to Germany, the planners had to admit that it was impossible to put it out of action.

In 1943 a new attempt was made by 617 Squadron, partly reconstituted after their heavy losses on the Dams raid, but this, too, was disastrous. It resulted in heavy losses and no real damage.

By 1944, however, it was possible to achieve the accuracy required with a large weight of bombs and destroy the banks of the canal or other important transport targets without inviting huge losses in the attack.

I kept no diary at this time but I did record some of my impressions and thoughts and this is what I wrote at the start of my tour of operations with No. 97 Pathfinder Squadron:

> The thing I do not understand is the use of air power in this Battle of Germany, which is said to be beginning. Since I have been at Coningsby we have been given to understand that it is a period of building up for the great assault on the Reich. But there has been no sign of a co-ordinated plan, no indication of a really ferocious assault by our whole strength on the two obvious targets, oil and transportation. We have certainly breached the Dortmund-Ems and Ems-Weser canals but these seem to have been isolated attacks. Other Groups attack railway yards, etc, sometimes but there is no appearance of a concentrated plan such as was so successful in destroying the French railways before D-day. In Germany we couldn't do that but we could do something like it. But last night we went to Munich. I suppose such destruction has a part in the pattern of the war but I feel the important thing now is for Tommy Atkins and GI Joe to stand together in Unter den Linden and everything, above all the personal ambitions of commanders who want to win the war on their own, must be subordinated to that."

Weather, decoys, mistakes and ill-luck were formidable enemies for us when they were added to stiff, although now much more variable, German defences. Our results were sometimes foiled or minimised by one or other of those factors but on the whole the first months of my tour with 97 Squadron brought good results with low losses.

After some successful sorties in the flare force my crew, who were of the highest quality in navigation, radio navigation, and bomb aiming by all methods, could be recategorised in the place of honour as Primary Blind Markers. These crews provided the four aircraft who were the first to arrive in the target area and who, by accurate navigation and with the radio aids available, dropped the first target indicators about ten minutes before the bombing was timed to start. These markers enabled the low-marking force of Mosquitoes, who were unable to carry weighty navigation equipment, to reach the target area on time and give them a reasonably accurate indication of where they should search for the exact marking point. This they were to find and mark within a period of about ten minutes during which the area would be kept brightly illuminated by the flare force of about eighteen Lancasters who also checked their positions by the Primary Blind Markers Target Indicators.

We were on the detail as Primary Blind Markers on the night of 21st December when our target was the synthetic oil plant at Politz, deep in Czechoslovakia. In the morning fog on the aerodrome at Coningsby was thick and the forecasters gave little hope of it lifting. We went ahead with preparations and, as the day progressed, the visibility got worse and was certainly no more than one hundred yards. Buildings and lights which you knew were only two hundred yards away were totally obscured. I am sure that many besides myself were not relishing the prospect of lumbering a heavily laden Lancaster into the air under those conditions.

I was surprised that by briefing time there was no cancellation and I could not but be conscious of a certain amount of incredulity as crew members looked out of the windows at the fog. I could feel the atmosphere in the room willing me to say "If the weather doesn't improve it'll be a scrub", but all I could come up with was "We shall have to take extra care taxying and we'll take off at longer intervals than normal. Met gives us little chance of getting back here so it looks like diversions to wherever the weather's fit."

So it proved. I knew it wasn't really difficult to take off in that very low visibility but I admit that as I ran up the engine I had qualms. I was the first to go, following the normal procedures. Brakes hard on, the whole aircraft shaking and vibrating as the engines neared full revs. Then brakes off, concentrate on the instruments to keep straight with just half an eye on the runway lights flashing by with increasing speed as the tail came up. The rumbling and thumping of the undercarriage gradually lessening until it stopped and we were airborne. "Wheels up", then a little more speed. Still a wall of fog. "Flaps up". Still dirty brown fog. Then a little light, fog now flying past in wisps. Still climbing carefully on full throttle until at last freedom in the clean air. Visibility unlimited but the carpet of fog below also unlimited. Throttle back a bit, coarser pitch for steady climb and turning eastwards towards the enemy with the sinking sun an unearthly red glow behind us in the west.

The weather over the target was satisfactory and the results were quite good. Unlike most pilots I didn't use the automatic pilot, then a fairly new invention which I thought inclined to wander slightly. I also thought that if you let "George" fly you were likely to relax concentration, especially if you were tired. This I thought dangerous and did not quite trust my reactions, once relaxed, to come quickly enough to full alert in an emergency. So when we crossed the English coast on return I had been flying manually for nine hours, after, of course, a normal day's activities before take-off.

The rest of the squadron had, as expected, been diverted to Scotland but our instructions were to land at an aerodrome near our base where, surely, I thought, the weather was unlikely to be any better than at Coningsby.

The navigator, checking in his books, solved the mystery. "Metheringham has FIDO," he announced. "Oh," I said. "Oh," and I meant it.

Bad weather landings were a problem which had then by no means been solved and "FIDO" was one of the ideas being tried out. I forget what the acronym stood for in full but the essentials were F for Fog and D for Dispersal. FIDO was a device by which the fog on a runway was dispersed by heat. Pipes were laid along the sides of the runway feeding paraffin burners at intervals along the whole length. When the burners were switched on large quantities of paraffin were burnt and the heat generated would, after a time, clear the fog along the runway allowing a landing to be made visually. The only "blind" landing equipment at the time was a German device, "Lorenz", which was effective in aligning you onto the runway but gave no help in the final landing.

The huge expense of FIDO was reckoned to be worthwhile if only a few aircraft and their crews were saved. It was only used in emergency and no crew had experience of it until they came to need it. Need it we did on that night.

It was pitch-black everywhere when my navigator told me that our FIDO base should be five miles straight ahead. We were flying at three thousand feet above the fog with no high ground nearby. As he spoke I began to see a dull red glow ahead.

"We'll fly over it and have a look," I said.

As we got closer the glow turned a deeper red and became diffused over a wide area and I realised that any light there might be on the ground was, at our height, merely highlighting a thick, black, oily cloud which had merged with the fog. As we reached the area of the glow I had expected to be able to pick out lines of fire which would show the position of the runway. There was nothing, nothing but a wide area of horrid deep red glow, conjuring up thoughts of the fires of hell. What was worrying was that it was much wider than any possible area of the airfield, let alone the runway. As we flew over it I called flying control who replied instantly with the clear, controlled voice of a WAAF radio operator giving us "Permission to land". "Ha, ha," I thought. "Ha, bloody ha." There was no sign of any line of light, only this wide area in which the black cloud lay heavily on a widespread, formless fire.

"No future in that," I said and told the navigator to give me courses to take us to about five miles from the airfield on the alignment of the runway. I would then go fairly slowly down into the fog and try to approach down to about six hundred feet and see if I could make some sense of what I could see. I knew that after my long day and night my judgement might not be of the best but I could only try to think and act rationally.

The navigator, working on "Gee", that marvellously accurate navigational aid, gave me the course to turn onto the runway bearing and I put on some flap and throttled back to fly as slowly as I thought safe. The Lancaster was fairly docile at low speed but no large aircraft will pick up height quickly if you get too slow.

As we approached the glow again the only difference was that it was more intense, the area wider and the black fog with its filthy smell of dirty paraffin was denser. We got nothing out of that run so I said, hoping I didn't sound as frightened as I felt, "Same again, navigator, except that this time we'll go right down on Lorenz and make sure." We climbed away and, turning, got only too good a view of what bore no relation whatever to the friendly FIDO I had read about. Instead of two straight lines of bright yellow flame with clear air between them and the runway showing up like a dark river, as the book said, there was nothing but this wide area of formless glow. The worrying thing was that the glow was so very wide when it should have been fore and aft following the line of the runway.

"Petrol's getting low, skipper," said the Flight Engineer. About twenty minutes, I should say."

"That's plenty," I said with a great deal more confidence than I felt. One more run and then we'll land. Same drill, navigator but this time we"ll go down and smell the bloody runway." "Provided its there," I added to myself.

We made the same type of approach, accurately calculated by the navigator with his Gee, and I checked our position central to the runway by Lorenz. When we were down to two hundred feet on the altimeter which isn't pleasant when you can't see the ground, I put on a little more throttle to be safe, and at last I could discern two lanes of fire and a gap between them which still wasn't very definite because of the volume of light to the side. But it was something like what one imagined of FIDO at last. It was too late to put the wheels and flaps down to land so I had to repeat the exercise but this time at least I thought I knew that the runway was there and should be visible from about two hundred and fifty feet. If I saw it in time, landing was quite feasible although I should have to put wheels and flaps down before I could be sure, which with petrol getting really short wasn't ideal.

When finally I touched down the heat and smell were horrible and the windscreens were filthy. A swing or a tyre burst would have been very awkward. However we pulled up and flying control told us to stay where we were until they could get a vehicle out to tow us in. There was no question of taxying. It was an unutterable relief to switch off the engines and feel my responsibility for the seven others was over.

The mystery of our difficulties was solved when we were told that an aircraft which had been supposed to land an hour before us had missed his approach and, tearing through a wood alongside the aerodrome had crashed, killing all the crew. The aircraft had caught fire, spreading its fuel over a wide area, so that by the time we arrived the whole wood was ablaze, quite beyond the power of any local fire brigade to control. That fire eventually gave out more flames and smoke than FIDO and the two had merged to produce the hideous area of flame and smoky fog which had so bewildered me. The fog was too thick to get home by car so we dossed down at Metheringham with the foul paraffin smell in our nostrils until dawn.

December 1944 and January 1945 were frustrating months with long spells of fog. The weather had been so bad during the German counter-stroke in the Ardennes that the Coningsby squadrons were often standing by for days and nights at a time in readiness to operate in support of the military. When the weather relented a little there were attacks on the German rear and communications which helped to bring the short-lived, but for a time dangerous, offensive to a halt.

By February the dust had settled on the Battle of the Bulge, as the Ardennes episode was popularly known. It was thought that shortages of fuel and equipment had contributed much to the failure of what might have been a major German success and now it seemed clear that, failing the emergence of some secret weapon greater than the Vl and V2, Germany was bound to lose the war. As yet only a handful of her enemies stood on German soil in the west and not many more in the east, but one could believe that the end, if not yet in sight, might not be far off. Hitler's defiance and the rumours that he was going to organise guerrilla war in the mountains of the south-east had to be taken seriously, but clearly every effort still had to be bent on the defeat of the German armed forces. It still seemed to me obvious that Bomber Command's part in that effort should be to continue and step up the attacks on oil and communications.

On the morning of 2nd February the front line ran roughly along the German border with France and Belgium, except that a salient into Germany at Aachen was in allied hands. Progress now seemed to depend on the crossings of the Meuse and Roer rivers and on the difficult task of clearing the Germans out of Holland with its maze of waterways. Then would come the crossing of the Rhine and Germany would be at the mercy of the Allied armies.

With this rough assessment of the situation in my mind, and knowing that I was due to fly that night, I made my way as usual to the Operations Block. As the Staff stood up to say good morning the teleprinter started the staccato clackety-clack which heralded the reception of the night's operation order.

"What's the target?" I asked.

"They've only just telephoned and I haven't looked it up," said the Senior Intelligence Officer, "but its a fish."

He dived for the codebook. The target code used names of fishes; trout, salmon, roach and so on, to signify German towns. When the code gave the name of a fish it meant that the target was a city.

"Karlsruhe," announced the Intelligence Officer and repeated "Karlsruhe." He started to rummage in his files for the target map and Intelligence information.

"Karlsruhe," I repeated, looking at the large map of Europe on which the approximate front line was marked, together with the defended areas in Germany and the "bomb line", to the west of which we did not bomb for fear of hitting our own troops.

The only information we could distil out of the Intelligence Manuals was that Karlsruhe was "An important centre of communications with some light industry". The town was a few miles on the east side of the Rhine and not more than twenty-five miles from the Allied front line. I looked back at the files and found that railway repair shops had been successfully bombed by the US Air Force in September and that not long afterwards Bomber Command had attacked "the city, the administrative centre of Baden". Reconnaissance had shown the administrative hub in ruins and factories with "severe damage".

The bomb load for main force aircraft was to be the normal for a town target, a "cookie" and a mass of incendiaries for each aircraft. The marking plan was normal and seemed to present no difficulties. We were to destroy what remained of Karlsruhe.

During the day I found time to sit alone in my office for quarter of an hour and I jotted down some thoughts about the night's work, the completion of the destruction of Karlsruhe.

The first, and overriding, thought was that I was utterly dedicated to the defeat of Germany. I believed wholeheartedly in the edict of the Casablanca Conference that the Allied war aim was to obtain "unconditional surrender". I know that with hindsight many have criticised that aim on the grounds that it prolonged the war. Perhaps that was true. But at the time I had no hesitation in accepting it. I had no sympathy with those who were trying to make a distinction between Hitler's Nazis and the mass of the German people. News of the attempt on Hitler's life had reached the British Press but I had no faith in any "political" solution to the war without a total defeat of the German military machine. I knew that Hitler had been joined by the military caste in spreading the story that there had been no military defeat in the First World War. The German armed forces were encouraged to believe that they had been betrayed by communist-inspired civilians. Surely, I thought, we don't want that said again. This is an army business and our job is basically to help the armies to beat hell out of the German armed forces.

If I had no qualms about unconditional surrender I did have doubts about the methods by which defeat should be inflicted, although I understood well enough the danger of forming opinions without access to top grade information. It seemed to me that at that time it was paramount that the victory should be obtained by the defeat of the German armed forces. A defeat of Germany through the collapse of civilian morale would be a rotten outcome, and might easily result in the German General Staff starting another canard about the invincibility of German arms if properly supported by the civilian government.

So I could not but ask myself what could be the real objective in completing the destruction of Karlsruhe.

The Intelligence Manual had talked about "light industry" but, surely, so near the front that was hardly a factor now? Looking at the map I could not see that essential road, river or railway transport would be badly affected for very long by the destruction of the town. The North-South autobahn was well outside the town and would survive. Experience had shown that railways were only seriously disrupted by continual bombardment of many connecting facilities. Large quantities of blast and incendiary bombs were not weapons for destroying railway facilities. For that you needed heavy-cased high explosives such as had been used throughout the attacks on the French railways. The Rhine river was some distance from the town and with the allied armies so close it was unlikely that that part of the river was being used for serious transport purposes.

There might, of course, be a tactical reason for the attack. Perhaps it was the allied intention to cross the river in this sector. Or perhaps to deceive the enemy into thinking that was the intention, so drawing his defences away from the real intended crossing point. It was even possible that German ingenuity, technical skill and scientific brilliance might have some devilish new weapon and that Karlsruhe was its home. That seemed a bit far fetched to me but I knew so little about remaining German capabilities that how could I judge? My log book was strewn with the names of German cities, why then should I be balking at this one?

I briefed as I was told and I flew as I was told. As Primary Blind Markers we found the area without difficulty, placed our target indicators accurately and dropped the secondary load of six one-thousand pound bombs in the town. The casualties they caused may have been considerable, or, of course, they just might have dropped harmlessly in an open space. There was no way of telling. After the raid, Karlsruhe was fairly high up in the list of badly-damaged German cities. The subsequent course of the US offensive did not indicate that the attack on Karlsruhe had any tactical significance.

13th February 1945 dawned, a day like any other. We had not operated the previous night so, weather permitting, we would be "on". The weather seemed fair.

At Coningsby the two Squadron Commanders were not allowed both to fly on the same night, and on 13th February it was not my turn. My part in the night's work would be to make out the flying roster for my squadron with details of the duties each crew was to perform, to settle the petrol, target indicator and flare loads and prepare the information and instructions I would give to the crews at briefing. I had to be on hand all day in case of changes to the orders, problems with the crews or snags of any sort affecting the squadron. These were a Squadron Commander's normal duties whether he was flying or not.

Since the night of Karlsruhe we had reverted to attacks on the canals and on distant oil targets with what seemed to have been considerable success. Losses had been relatively light and we were at last hearing that an incipient shortage of petrol, and particularly of aviation fuel, was beginning to affect the whole of the enemy war machine.

When I went to the Operations Block that morning I felt at once from the attitude of the Senior Intelligence Officer that the night's work was something a little out of the ordinary.

"What's the excitement," I asked.

"The whole Command's on it," he spluttered "in two waves. A couple of hours apart."

"Come on," I said, "what's so special? What's the target?"

"Its Dresden," he said. "Never been bombed before. The biggest city left in Germany. Two waves. The whole bloody Command."

"All right," I said, "But why so worked up?"

"Well, sir . . . its the plan . . . "

"Go on," I said, "what's the plan?"

"Well, sir, its this you see. The first wave is just 5 Group, so of course we mark. That means in effect we're marking for the whole Command. The place will be well alight before the second wave gets there. Won't Bennett be biting his nails? Nothing much for him to do. His boys are only marking for the second wave."

The personal dislike and rivalry between Bennett of the Pathfinder Group and our late AOC, Cochrane, had been well-known, and Bennett's attitude towards 5 Group hadn't changed with Cochrane's recent promotion and departure to Transport Command. However, I always made a point of showing no cognizance that this jealousy even existed. I did not relax my strong faith in our methods of marking from very low heights of which Bennett was so critical. Nevertheless, I felt that Bomber Command owed an enormous debt to Bennett and that we as a Pathfinder squadron, although detached from his command, were still bound to him by a considerable degree of loyalty. It was a stretched situation, but I felt it fair and wise on this day to conceal the pride I felt that we had been chosen to carry out the initial finding and marking of this distant target for the whole Command, a task which would normally have been given to Bennett and No. 8 Group.

At the flight planning conference, when station and Squadron Commanders were tied in by telephone to the Group Commander and operational details such as route-marking techniques and communications were discussed and finally confirmed, we heard more of the importance of the target and the reasons it had been chosen. First, as a transportation centre it was, we were told, the hub of the supply systems for the defence of the Reich against the Soviet armies massed on the Polish frontier.

Dresden had never yet been bombed by the RAF and it was suggested that its destruction might even prove to be the last straw which would stimulate rebellion against Hitler. But primarily it was a target in support of our great Russian ally. They had asked for western help by the bombing of this and other east German cities through which had to pass practically all supplies and reinforcements for the German armies opposing the Soviet thrusts. We were told that the Prime Minister himself, negotiating at Yalta with his Soviet colleague, had expressed the hope that Bomber Command would be able to accede to their requests.

It is quite difficult now, after forty years in which the behaviour of Soviet Russia was increasingly hostile to the West, forty years of suspicion, spying, diplomatic chicanery and open attempts to discredit and even dislodge Western Governments, to conjure up the spirit of the time when respect and even affection for the Russian people was a big feature of British life. But in 1944 and 1945 the tide of sympathy and admiration for our Russian allies flowed very strongly indeed. They had undergone awful hardships at the hands of the Nazi invaders and after a whole year of unmitigated disaster, in which they had lost huge tracts of their most valuable lands, they had fought back with amazing effort and were now chasing the hated Nazis back to Germany. This had inspired the British people who felt that their own wartime adversities were as nothing compared to what the Russians had undergone.

I had personal experience of this when I was at Syerston. I had then taken part in a meeting at Nottingham to raise funds for Mrs Churchill's Red Cross "Aid for Russia" Fund. Mrs Churchill herself presided, Guy Gibson of the Dams spoke, and a famous singer entertained. The large hall was crammed and the enthusiasm and receipts were tremendous. This at a time of some hardship and considerable poverty in our own country.

So, while I had had some misgivings over the attack on Karlsruhe, I had fewer about Dresden. There was considerable attraction in the idea of striking a blow to help the Russians, who had complained so often and so bitterly that they were bearing the whole burden of the war and that the West was indifferent to their suffering and to the appalling destruction the German invaders had inflicted on their land.

Many Soviet demands on the West had been unreasonable and their gratitude for the help they had been given was not exactly overwhelming. Being land animals, the Russians had failed, or pretended to fail, to understand the huge danger of throwing large forces onto a well defended coast without adequate supply and back-up. They had continually demanded that France be invaded in 1943 and never seemed to have considered the appalling setback which would have resulted from a hurried or botched attempt being hurled back into the sea, as it almost certainly would have been.

All this was little stressed by the media and we in Britain, who had known what it was to fight alone, had deep and genuine sympathy with the Russian's ordeal, which had been worse than ours. For nearly three years they had had a foul and ruthless enemy in their homeland, destroying their cities, pillaging, raping their women and deporting their citizens to work as slaves in the Reich.

We had fumed at our inability to give them more help in their crisis, we had watched with bated breath the defence of Stalingrad and applauded with massive unanimity the huge surrender of German forces there. Stalin was seen as our friend and was ennobled in British folklore by the bestowal of a nickname, "Uncle Joe". The Russians were indeed "our gallant allies" and the alternative sobriquet of "those red bastards" was totally forgotten.

I could see two substantial effects for the Red Army of a big attack on Dresden. First it would help the Russian offensive if the supplies and reserves for the German armies facing them which, from the map, must be largely dependent on facilities at Dresden, were disorganised. Secondly, the Germans would be taking some of the medicine they had so successfully administered to the French in 1940 when terrified civilians and refugees with handcarts and perambulators carrying their most precious possessions poured onto the roads. Those French civilians were oblivious – how could they be otherwise – that their desperate struggles to get away, anywhere away from the horror of their burning homes and the raping and pillaging enemy, was a huge handicap to their own armies trying to defend them. If this happened on the roads in the rear of the German front line it might easily trigger a major collapse of resistance to the triumphantly advancing Soviet forces.

So we forgot the icy reception allied aircraft had received when they landed at Russian airfields, we tried to dismiss the ugly rumours about Russian behaviour in failing to support the Polish uprising in Warsaw and went to Dresden with a will.

The result of that night's work is well-known and there is no point in my enlarging on it here. The damage wrought by the firestorm raised in the first place by 5 Group was immense and when the second wave of bombers arrived they had difficulty in finding any specific aiming points in the holocaust they saw below them. But they bombed just the same.

On the following day the Air Ministry issued a communiqué describing the object of the raid, telling of a "terrific concentration of fires" and categorising it as "one of the more powerful blows promised by the Allied leaders at Yalta". After attacks on the ruins by the US Air Force in daylight, the State Department issued the statement that it had been in response to Soviet requests for increased aerial support and was cleared in advance with Soviet authorities."

The best approximation of the numbers killed in Dresden seems to be 135,000 but there are other estimates as high as 200,000. The higher estimates may include a large number of deaths among the foreign labourers who had been flung into cattle trucks and forcibly imported into Germany from occupied territories to work as slaves for the Nazi military machine. These wretches, alive or dead, were often not properly recorded and the Germans treated them as expendable.

Although it happened that I did not fly in the Dresden raid, I was an active member of the team which brought about the destruction of the city and I do not pretend that my responsibility is any the less because I remained on the ground.

On the night after Dresden I was free to fly and, with a favourable weather forecast, it was certain that the Command would be out in strength again. Our target was a large oil installation at a place called Rositz, about fifty miles west of Dresden. It was a longish trip to find a small target but with the navigational aids and skills available to us we had shown that, provided the weather was reasonable, such places could be found, marked and bombed by the methods we had devised. The casualties on long-distance targets were now less than of old since there was relatively little heavy flak and fighter activity was falling off. This was generally attributed to the beginning of a shortage of petrol in the Reich and it was heartening to be attacking an important source of the precious fuel with the feeling that if we cut off another major source of supply the shortage might become critical.

For that night, however, we were told to expect considerable fighter reaction because the enemy was known to have concentrated his forces in the area. On our side there would be an elaborate and highly complex web of spoof, feint and manoeuvre using radar, electronics and "window", the aluminium-coated strips which, when freely scattered, completely confused the enemy radar screens. It was hoped that the real targets, of which there were now three or even more in a single night, could be concealed from the enemy until the last possible moment.

After I had made sure that the squadron's preparations were going ahead smoothly and had checked that there were no snags on my own aircraft, I went as I normally did, back to the Intelligence Block to get a picture of the plans for the night. As I had expected, with our target being in the same area as on the previous night and so far into Germany, the deceptions and tactics to divide and deceive the enemy's already overstretched forces were of double importance and interest.

First there was a minelaying effort in the Baltic and this was magnified to look on Radar screens as if Berlin might be the main target and it could be expected that some fighters would be drawn to the north. Then some Mosquitoes, dropping large quantities of "window", would make a feint attack on the Ruhr at Duisberg and on the Rhineland town of Mainz. This should get some fighters airborne early in the night so that they would not be available when the main forces emerged from the jamming screen on the way towards Saxony where the targets lay. The main target for the other Groups was Chemnitz, about twenty miles or so from Rositz.

With other things to do it was a little time before I went back to the Intelligence Block for my final check before briefing and noticed that there was another route marked to the south of the route I had seen before.

"What's this?" I asked and was told that it was a second attack on Chemnitz, planned, as had happened on Dresden, to take effect two hours after the first. It was only then that I realised that Chemnitz, which I had never heard of, was a town. I suppose that since we had attacked an oil plant at Politz and now were on Rositz I had come to associate the suffix "itz" with oil. But Chemnitz was a fairly large town.

So the other Groups were to attack and destroy Chemnitz as the whole Command, led by ourselves, had destroyed Dresden. German resistance, not yet crumbling, was clearly being maintained only by the most enormous efforts of will, courage and discipline. Soon, surely, it would crack. Was this then the moment to destroy another German town?

I told myself that the targets of other Groups were none of my business. I must absolutely not let any random thoughts distract my attention from the job in hand which was important and not easy.

It was satisfying to be told later that reconnaissance had shown the attack on Rositz to have been an outstanding success and that after that night's attack it was unlikely that it would produce another drop of oil for Hitler's Reich.

On 16th March, I awoke with the thought that I was due to fly on operations that night. A smell of victory was in the air.

Although it was disappointing that there had been no great Russian advance in the east after our operations on Dresden and Chemnitz, the fighting there was very fierce. In the west, the Allies had a bridgehead over the Rhine due to the fortunate and brilliant capture of the Remagen Bridge by the Americans. One bridge could not, however, sustain a major advance east of the river. The cautious delay in essaying the difficult task of moving huge numbers of men, and the necessary heavy equipment, over the wide and fast flowing river may have been justified. The Anglo-American armies stood along almost the whole length of the western bank.

Attacks on German positions east of the Rhine soon made it clear that all was being prepared for a crossing operation in which no risks were to be taken. Germany had not collapsed and her will to resist was still alive, but the feeling that it was now only a matter of time, and not a very long time at that, was unmistakable.

We had been off the night before and my routine visit to the Met Office told me that although there would be cloud about, the weather was likely to be reasonable fair to the east. I was pretty sure that we would be working.

Evidence had begun to accumulate that a real shortage of oil products was making itself felt in Hitler's Germany. Great as was the enemy's talent for organisation, if he became really short of oil nothing could save him. With the Romanian fields in the hands of the Russians, if oil did not flow smoothly from the synthetic plants and refineries to the storage units and from storage to the distribution centres, then within hours fighters would not fly, tanks would not roll, front line troops would not be fed. The whole huge complex machine of warfare could not subsist for more than a very few days without a safe, regular supply of oil. Intelligence was now showing that important activities in Germany, for instance flying training and even fighter patrols, were being curtailed or cancelled to conserve oil.

We and the Americans had attacked and damaged many of the big installations and surely if half-a-dozen more major sources could be destroyed the enemy's collapse would be inevitable. The

American Flying Fortresses which operated at a far greater height than the Lancaster's ceiling of about twenty thousand feet, were less vulnerable than us to the heavy flak defences of the Ruhr where oil was still being produced. In Bomber Command we had shown that we could find, mark and heavily damage oil targets far to the east. Seeing a good weather report I expected that morning that we would be attacking one of the installations in east Germany or Czechoslovakia.

Refreshed by a good night's sleep I had more than usual energy and dealt with the backlog of administrative work and organisational problems which cluttered my desk. Then the telephone rang and the Intelligence Officer asked me if I would please come over. This meant that orders for the night were coming in so I shovelled my in-tray over to my long-suffering and unfailingly helpful adjutant and made for the Operations Room.

Partly for exercise and partly from a curious instinct to put off for a few minutes my entry into the world of the night's operation, I left my car at the office block and walked. I knew that as soon as I entered the Operations Room I was bound, hand and foot, to my operational duties. I was inevitably the hub around which revolved the organisation of the squadron necessary to ensure that our aircraft could put down markers or release flares over pinpoint targets at times accurate to within seconds. There would be plenty to do in addition to flying, such as an air test on my own aircraft, but I could not resist pretending to myself for a few short minutes that I was still a free agent.

There was always an element of excitement on opening the door of the "Ops" Room and finding out the target allotted to us and it would be dishonest not to admit that this was heightened when one was flying oneself. On that morning I saw at once that we were not going to Czechoslovakia. There were two tracks pinned out in red tape on the wall map. They were some way apart but both pointed at first as if leading to the far east of Germany. However, at around 11 degrees east both turned abruptly south. Each track then led to a red blob on the map, the symbol for a defended area. The easterly blob was large, signifying a big city with defences over a wide area. Its position was familiar, but the other, to the west and a little to the north was much smaller. Peering at the map I saw that the first target was Nuremberg, but I had to look closer to read the name of the second. It was Würzburg.

"5 Group on Würzburg on our own," the Intelligence Officer told me. "The rest of the Command on Nuremberg. Maximum effort for everyone."

"Würzburg," I repeated. The name struck some obscure chord in my mind but I couldn't remember why. "What goes on in Würzburg?" I asked.

"Nothing very much according to the book," said the Intelligence Officer. "No big factories. Bit of a railway junction."

"Würzburg," I repeated to myself, trying to remember why the name was familiar. A cinema organ? Something about a famous staircase and a painted ceiling? Then I remembered that it was the code name for the standard German radar scanners which reported our movements to the enemy fighter controllers. There had been some consternation when the "Würzburg" was first introduced as it seemed to be much more efficient than the equipment it had replaced. This had made the name "Würzburg" unpopular with crews but as far as I knew no one had ever suggested there was any connection between the radar equipment and the small town in Bavaria which we were now to attack.

"H-hour for 8 Group on Nuremberg is the same as ours on Würzburg," said the Intelligence Officer.

I went on with the usual arrangements for an operation in which all of the squadron aircraft were to take part. My crew and another would be the Primary Blind Markers, first on the target, dropping target indicators on the aiming point by means of our sophisticated blind bombing equipment. This should bring the low marking Mosquitoes close to the point they were to mark with their target indicators. It also acted as a check to the flare forces who, starting two minutes after we had marked, were to keep the area brightly illuminated for seven or eight minutes, time for the Mosquitoes to find their exact marking point and drop target indicators as the aiming point for the bombing force.

Our Group had perfected an elaborate method of bombing towns whereby squadrons approached the target on slightly different courses and aircraft used slightly different settings on their bomb sights and waited a different number of seconds before releasing their bombs, while all used the same aiming point. This ensured that bombs were evenly distributed over the target area and was conducive, with the huge numbers of incendiaries used, to the production of a firestorm which, as at Dresden and Hamburg, would completely gut a considerable built-up area. This was the treatment we were to mete out to Würzburg.

Take-off time was early since the weather was likely to be less favourable late in the night but, since everyone in the squadron was fully competent in their jobs, we were not pushed for time. After I had done the air test on my aircraft I felt I needed a short break before the flight planning conference so I went to my quarters where I would be available by telephone if I were needed. Lying on my bed I asked my batman to bring me a cup of what then passed for coffee.

"Feeling all right, sir?" he asked somewhat anxiously. By some sort of bush telegraph he always knew when I was operating, and it was unheard of for me to be in my quarters at this time.

"Yes, thanks, I'm OK," I said. " I just thought I needed half an hour's quiet."

Sipping the glutinous mixture he brought, I could see in the sparsely-furnished bedroom the bookshelf which carried the few books I took around with me. Lying on its side, since it was too tall for the shelf, was the book of drawings of the London blitz which had given rise to my letter to Shelagh. Dear Shelagh. It was eighteen months since she had been killed and, although I had moved on, I often thought of her and of the strange short happiness we had had together.

I began, inevitably, to think about that letter. I had destroyed the original but I knew that there was a draft of it somewhere among the miscellaneous untidiness of my papers and I remembered well enough the confusion in my mind when I wrote it. At that time I had been able to overcome my doubts because of the implacable necessity to be absolutely certain that I did nothing to impede allied victory. I had always been able to reassure myself that, in a war as awful as this, in which the whole future of the world was at stake, it was ridiculous for such as myself, with no knowledge of industry, no knowledge of Germany, no knowledge of science, no inside knowledge of the strategic situation, to set myself up, even in my own mind, as the arbiter of how the war should be run, what should be attacked and when and how. For those whose moral sense was absolute it might be easy to accept that defeat would be preferable to doing what you knew to be wrong, although I suspected that in practice few confronted the starkness of that choice. But I always came back to the knowledge that I would do anything, yes anything, to avoid defeat by the Nazis. But even in those, now, far-off-days I had sometimes felt that there were other methods which could be used, other targets which could be attacked, than those which our leaders had chosen. But I never flinched from the certainty that it was always essential that for middle leadership, people like me with some responsibility and influence, to give complete loyalty to the orders we were given and to the commanders who gave them, and I could not flatter myself that my inexpert instincts, without back-up of research or Intelligence, were superior to the considered judgements of the top war leaders whose experience and knowledge were light years greater than mine.

The position on 16th March 1945 was very different from that in the summer of 1943 when we were still unable to land in France. Now the Western allies were at or across the Rhine and the Russians at or across the Oder. It was impossible not to believe that the war was, to all intents and purposes, won. The only question left was when and how the ultimate collapse would come.

What I had to face for myself was the decision that tonight, when the weather seemed reasonably fair, Bomber Command's task was to destroy two towns: Nuremburg, which had often been attacked but was always a difficult target; and Würzburg, which most people in England had never heard of.

Nuremburg made me think wryly of an occasion in 1943 when I had been instructed that journalists from the *The Sunday Times* should watch the progress of an operation from Fiskerton. In my preliminary talks with them they were not allowed to know the target, but they saw the Operation Order (which did not quote it) and watched the general preparations. They came to the runway with me to see the take off and I had to look after them until debriefing at which they listened to some of the crew reports which, as usual, described big fires around the target indicators. Eventually I said goodbye to them and went to bed even later and more tired than usual.

Early the next morning I was awoken by the "scrambler" telephone by my bed. The personal assistant to the AOC, a nice young WAAF officer with whom I was friends, said, surreptitiously warning me of "trouble", that Air Marshal Cochrane wanted to speak to me most urgently.

I braced my sleepy mind as best I could and said "Good Morning, sir." I was already on good terms with the AOC stemming from mutual respect in Training Command so I was surprised to hear the anger in his voice as he said, "Johnson, what the devil have you been telling those journalists?"

"I was told they were to see the operation, sir," I said, "and that's what I did. They came to briefing and debriefing and", (looking at my bedside clock which said eight thirty) "they left here about five o'clock."

"I don't care what time they left," snapped the AOC, "Have you seen the papers?"

"No, sir," said I, rather pathetically. "I'm still in bed".

"Well when you do get up," he said, his rudeness quite out of character, "just have a look at the papers. Let me tell you the raid was a disaster. Every bomb fell on a decoy site in the woods and *The Sunday Times* has a headline that you told them "Nuremburg is destroyed."

"I didn't . . . ," I started, but he interrupted me.

"Next time you talk to journalists," he said acidly, "you'd better be a sight more careful what you say." He rang off, leaving me totally bewildered, looking at the silent instrument in my hand.

After a good deal of heart-searching I realised what had happened. Of course I hadn't said anything like "Nuremburg is destroyed". Crew reports, always optimistic, would never justify such a statement without good clear photographs, only available long after debriefing. But the clever journalists had seen the Operation Order which said that the object was "to destroy an enemy city". Then, before they left they had asked me whether I thought the raid had been a success. 'Yes, I think so," I said, thinking of the considerable fires which the crews had all reported. "As far as I can tell I think it was very successful." What they made of that, and I couldn't really complain, certainly taught me to be cagey to a degree in my future dealings with the press.

The name of Nuremburg also brought memories of the disastrous trip of nearly a year before when nearly one hundred bombers were lost, but Würzburg most people never knew existed. So tonight it was Nuremburg and Würzburg. Nuremburg, I thought, was perhaps all very well. It was the town of Hans Sachs and the Mastersingers, yes, but also it was a foul nest of the Nazis. It had been the scene of those ghastly annual Nazi Party rallies before the war. I remembered the horror of Hitler's voice on the wireless and the obscene chanting applause that greeted his threats to helpless Poland and Czechoslovakia. I thought with horror of the thousands of Germans in Nazi uniforms filling the huge Nuremburg Stadium and their ecstatic yells of "Sieg Heil, Sieg Heil," in answer to Hitler's sinister, near-hysterical blustering. No tears for Nuremberg, maybe. But Würzburg?

I didn't know what the other Groups might do to Nuremberg. They had their own methods. But I knew quite well what we, weather permitting, would do to Würzburg. A huge weight of incendiary bombs, supported by high explosives "to keep their heads down", would be distributed as evenly as possible all over the town. It was probable that the heat raised by the fires would be so great that it would generate winds of gale force and more which would carry the flames into every nook and cranny of the town. Casualties were bound to be high because the roofs of shelters and cellars would collapse with the heat and a weight of rubble they could not carry.

My target indicators, which would draw the marker Mosquitoes to the area, would be the first harbingers of the calamity on its way to the town. Many citizens would be lulled to false security by being inured to many air raid warnings which had merely denoted bombers passing on their way to greater targets. Some would stay in bed with their families and, realising their danger too late, they would either be incinerated in their beds or caught in the streets by the firestorm. The cautious who had reached the cellars might or might not emerge. I had a morbid vision of a deep shelter half collapsed with its exit almost blocked, packed with men, women and children struggling to get to the entrance which only opened on a vast conflagration above. Perhaps some of the high explosive bombs with delay fuses which I and others would carry might then explode and make rescue even more improbable.

I was thirty-six years of age, quite old enough to think for myself, and I knew I was being morbid, merely compounding and not really confronting the personal position I had to grapple with. I was being ordered to lead my squadron to be the spearhead of a large force of bombers on a mission of a type which had continually been rejected by the British people and their rulers as inhuman, criminally infringing the rather shadowy concepts known as the Laws of War.

I had heard only a few days before that an MP, Mr Stokes, who had long been something of a thorn in the side of the Government, had asked the Air Minister in Parliament whether "terror bombing" was the policy of the RAF. The Minister had conveniently left the House when the question came up but a deputy answered Mr Stokes with a flat and emphatic negative. The reply stated:

It does not do the Hon. Member justice to come here to this House and suggest that there are a lot of Air Marshals or pilots or anyone else sitting in a room trying to think how many German women and children they can kill.

If that was so, what was I doing, lying on my bed looking up at the shelf where lay the Bato book about the London blitz from which the extracts in my letter to Shelagh had been taken?

I knew little or nothing of the International Conventions and Agreements which were supposed to constitute the Laws of War but I did know that a Law is little use without an authority to enforce it. In this case the only authority was moral feeling. Heaven knew that the Germans had broken every law in the book during their victorious attacks on France, Poland, the Low Countries, Yugoslavia and Russia. The long drawn-out blitz on London and the sporadic attacks on English towns had been terror bombing in the fullest sense of the word. Atrocious German behaviour in the conquest and occupation of Western Europe was well vouched for by survivors and escapees, but the stories which were gradually filtering out of Eastern Europe and the Soviet Union were even more horrendous. The atrocities which were alleged against Jews, civilians, women, children and prisoners were positively mediaeval in their horror. The Germans had totally ignored any so-called Laws of War in country after country, in the air and on the seas. The only check on their behaviour could have been moral indignation in their own country which, although we knew of a few dissidents, was, so far as we knew, so small as to have no effect. So the German nation had no absolute right to demand that the West waged war with the highest degree of humanitarianism.

I had always believed that the work of Bomber Command, for which I had specifically volunteered, was a necessary factor in planning the overthrow of Nazi Germany. The Command accepted its heavy losses in the belief that, by weakening the enemy's base, casualties in the inevitable land fighting would be much reduced. About our attacks on great German cities in 1943 I had accepted that it was the total industrial potential which we were attacking and that German ability to make war would be greatly affected by undermining the welfare and morale of the citizens and the destruction of facilities, including housing. Numerous meetings of the war leaders of Britain and the United States seemed to have agreed and approved the bombing directives by which these activities were guided. The communiqués announcing our attacks had always regaled the public with the information that this or that industry, factory or warlike facility had been heavily damaged or destroyed.

Such criticism as there had previously been in England had come from quarters unable or unwilling to suggest new or alternative policies to win the war and they had cut little ice with the general public and went unnoticed in Bomber Command. Since Dresden, however, informed critical comment had been much more free and had penetrated via neutral sources through to Britain. Since it stemmed largely from German propaganda efforts led by the notorious Goebbels, the attempt to make capital out of the loss of life and the destruction of churches and other splendid buildings had at first made no great impression but by the beginning of March it was too vociferous to be ignored and had produced misgivings in many quarters.

Lying uneasily on my bed that afternoon, I still believed that the destruction of Dresden was a potent blow in assisting our Russian allies who had borne so much of the burden of the war and suffered so appallingly from German atrocities in their homeland. But I was finding it difficult to justify the deliberate destruction of a small city whose military value to the enemy seemed negligible. Of those whom we would kill, there would naturally be some prominent in the Nazi hierarchy and few who were not involved in some way in the Nazi search for victory. But the majority would likely be the young and the old, many of them refugees from other disasters, non-combatants in the truest sense. I found I simply could not shut my eyes to this, nor could I convince myself that "success" in our attack would make the slightest contribution to bringing the war to an end nor to saving casualties among our armies on the Continent.

So I tried to be honest in confronting my problem. What should, and could, I do? I could take myself and my crew off the detail. It would look odd but nobody could question my decision. There was another Primary Blind Marker crew available who would be delighted to go in our place. But it seemed to me that that would be the ultimate in cowardice. The only difference would be that I did not risk my neck, which wasn't a very uplifting thought. It made no difference to my personal responsibility whether I flew or not. I would accept or try to modify the plan of attack at the flight planning conference, elaborate it in detail as necessary and give detailed orders to my squadron. By my position I was an essential cog in the machinery which was to carry out the destruction of Würzburg. I have already said that my responsibility for Dresden was no less than that of the other Squadron Commander who had actually flown on the raid.

I had an impulse to look at the book of drawings of the London Blitz and as I was taking it down the telephone rang. "Would I come over to the Ops Room? No, not urgent, but as soon as I conveniently could."

I looked at the faded grey-blue cover of the book and saw the scribble in pencil across the dust cover, 5/-. On the spine was the original price, 12/6. So not many people had bought it. Wondering whether the Germans had published such a book, I put the slightly tattered volume back on the shelf.

I could see that I was trapped. I was sure that what we were to do was not only wrong but stupid. Wrong because the pain and grief we should cause was unnecessary, and stupid because it was pointless. I had no instinct to over-dramatise the sufferings of the innocent. I didn't see any German as innocent. Maybe they all deserved punishment for the horror the German people had brought on the world. But punishment wasn't my job. I had to believe that the top brass, civil and military, thought this the best way to win the war, but this time I couldn't say to myself that "Oh well they know best". I simply could not see that the destruction of Würzburg would further the allied cause or accelerate our victory. I knew in my heart that I wanted to have none of this operation. But twist and turn as I could I saw no way out.

I considered whether a braver man than I, with the courage of his convictions, would not only refuse to fly, which as it was within my competence to decide, didn't entail flouting authority, but would refuse to give the necessary orders to the squadron.

If I did that it would, I supposed, be mutiny and I should be put under arrest and relieved of my Command. My second-in-command would take over and the Operation would go ahead as planned. Later I would be court-martialled and possibly shot, almost certainly dismissed from the service. My squadron, who I think genuinely looked up to me, would be indescribably shocked and their morale badly shaken. My personal action, however "right" it might be, would have little effect and the only result would be that my wife and children would get no pension.

There was also a nagging feeling that the only reason for refusing to go on operations in Bomber Command was LMF, lack of moral fibre, gobbledegook for cowardice. If I refused to fly that would certainly be suggested as the real underlying reason.

In the course of my time in Bomber Command I had had to deal with more than one case of pilots or other aircrew who felt unable to continue on Operations. The tales they told were various but usually the assertion was that they had lost confidence in themselves and were unwilling to jeopardise the rest of the crew. The real reason was that they couldn't bring themselves to face the music any more. Since to publicise these cases by formal disciplinary action was the sure way to encourage others, my policy had usually been to try to shuffle them as rapidly as possible off the station via the "trick cyclist" (psychoanalyst), who could produce some medical grounds. It wasn't the pleasantest of tasks. You always remembered that these men were volunteers who had failed, not conscripts who had revolted.

But I had never heard of a case of an aircrew member refusing duty on the moral grounds that he was unwilling to take part in an Operation which entailed killing women and children. Wondering, somewhat wryly, how I would have dealt with such a case, I went back to the Operations Room where the problems were soluble.

The flight planning conference was a 5 Group institution which had been initiated by AVM Cochrane, with the intent, I think, of knitting the Group together as a coherent unit. It was a slight misnomer to call it "flight planning" because the flight plan had already been made and circulated and this was merely a last chance to discuss or modify the plan with all Stations linked to the Group by scrambler telephone. The AOC presided with the Group specialists around him and Station Commanders, with their Squadron Commanders available, could make comments and suggestions and ask questions.

AVM Constantine, who had replaced Cochrane, was a younger man who had been a well-known rugger player before the war. He started the conference with a conventional pep talk, emphasising that the war was not over and the task of Bomber Command was as important as ever.

I had taken part in many such conferences but I remember thinking that seldom had destruction been so carefully prepared. It seemed impossible that any house would be spared or any individual escape. With a strongish wind at ground level the fires would spread very rapidly.

The technical details over, the AOC summed up. He was, I think, conscious of the shadow of his distinguished predecessor and wished to impress us with his determination to be a worthy successor. He said that he expected all commanders to impress on crews the necessity of strict observance of the plan and the importance of the target. Were there any questions?

My mouth was dry and my heart was sick but I felt I must say something. I was Station Commander of Coningsby as well as commanding the squadron, so it was my right to speak. All I said was to the effect that my Intelligence hadn't much information about Würzburg except that it was a residential town with some light industry. Was there any special reason for the attack?

The pause was palpable. When he answered the AOC did not conceal his irritation.

"I've said its an important railway centre," he said, (it wasn't), "and also there are thousands of houses totally undamaged sheltering tens of thousands of Germans. I hope that will not be the case tomorrow, which will be another nail in the enemy's coffin." With that the conference closed.

The raid on Würzburg was carried out according to plan. My markers were dropped correctly and my six one-thousand pound bombs fell in the town. The Mosquitoes had little difficulty in finding their aiming point and the bombing was reasonably accurate. It was a night of quite bright moonlight, such a night as would have kept us on the ground a year before. There was a layer of thin scattered cloud below us against which we must have been starkly silhouetted, perfect targets for fighters patrolling above. As it was, the German controllers seem to have guessed Nuremburg as the target when the leading aircraft of both waves turned south for their final run in to the targets. The Nuremburg force, flying under the same conditions as ourselves, suffered considerable losses. I could see that the flak and searchlights over Nuremberg were as intensive as ever and, while flying to and over Würzburg, was conscious of combats and casualties clearly visible fifty miles away, reminiscent of the disastrous return from Peenemunde in 1943. I had to wait near the target for a time to do a communications job while the bombing proceeded and I could see for myself that the fires in Würzburg were rapidly gaining control. Realising that the casualties of the other groups on Nuremberg were going to be quite heavy and that it might yet be our turn, I was thankful to set course for home.

9

The End of the War

Operations "Thunderclap" and "Exodus"

In the last three weeks of the war we had little to do and my
squadron had no part in the last astonishing advance of the allied
armies nor in the final devastating collapse of Nazi Germany. It
was galling to be idle in the days of victory after the long years
of deprivation and often of defeat. I think all in the squadron felt
cheated that we were not allowed a share in what was perhaps the
greatest triumph of arms in all the long history of war.

We did desultory training and practice in our art but this for
crews who were already known to be the most highly skilled in
the force was pretty meaningless. I tried arranging competitions
but there was no zest in the effort and everybody, including
myself, thought it was just a waste of petrol.

There was a feeling that we were cast aside, discarded. The
Battle of Britain was still rightly seen as a turning point in
history. Victory in the Battle of the Atlantic was remembered
with pride by a maritime nation. The Army with its vast air
support was now sealing the defeat of Germany in the west as it
had in North Africa. But we were urged by the Staff to occupy
ourselves with training. For what? It wasn't an easy time as
victory followed victory in the news bulletins.

At some time in 1945 there was talk of a revival of
"Operation Thunderclap" which had been mooted and abandoned
in the summer of 1944. This was a plan, the knowledge of which
was confined to Squadron Commanders, for a huge attack on
Berlin by the massed forces of Bomber Command and the US Air

Force. All were to attack in daylight as a single unit, every available aircraft and crew being pressed into service. Well over two thousand heavy bombers would have been available and it was estimated that the bomber stream would extend over sixty miles. The city would be subjected to a torrent of bombs on a scale never before known in warfare. The total effect would eclipse any previously experience and would probably have been more destructive and certainly more terrifying than the explosions of the atom bombs on Hiroshima and Nagasaki.

Bomber Command was to provide the leading aircraft and the targets were to be marked initially by the Pathfinder squadrons of 5 Group. I was to have had the honour, if honour it was, of flying the leading aircraft of the whole immense cavalcade. I admit that I had no particular relish for the privilege.

Whether, had it been carried out, "Thunderclap" would have provoked the surrender of Nazi Germany as the second atom bomb did of Japan, is a matter of debate. Hitler would probably have survived in his deep bunker but the death roll in Berlin would have been horrifying, exceeding that of Dresden where more were killed than in either of the atomic attacks on Japan. Probably the mad Führer would have continued to exhort his wretched dupes to resistance, in fact I suspected that the operation would have actually contributed to the crazy dreams of *Götterdämmerung*, the final destruction of the Reich by its own people, which were already known to be festering in Hitler's morbid mind.

My chances of survival in the conspicuous position as leader, a prime target for the still appreciable defences, were not over-good. Apart from that I thought the plan senseless, almost evilly senseless, savouring more of revenge than of military significance. I suppose it might have provoked surrender a mite quicker than the armies could achieve it, but it would have been the wrong surrender, the defeat of the German people and not of the armed forces. The operation would, I thought, have almost fatally stained the honour of the two great nations of the West. When victory was already assured it seemed to me that to try and knock a few days off German resistance by such means would hand the moral leadership of the world to the Soviet Union. But since the plan for a time seemed to have the approval of the highest authorities there was no prospect of any comment from me carrying any weight. Mine not to reason why, mine but to do and die. Self-pity? Self-dramatisation? I suppose so, but for the sake of truth I record it.

I was thankful when the plan was abandoned but it had cost me a day or two brooding over the old arguments. If it really stopped the war and saved some thousands of British, American, Russian and even, on balance, German casualties, would it have been justified? The German lives lost would include many women and probably children, although I imagine most children had left Berlin and were those women so innocent? Would it be a great crime to let some of them die if it saved thousands of young men who would otherwise find early graves or awful disabilities? What of the rules of war? Can there really be any rules of war? And if there are and one side breaks them all, does the other side have to stick to them? Luckily I had only a day or so to torture myself with these doubts before the whole crazy scheme was abandoned. Würzburg lay uncomfortably at the back of my mind.

By May Russian guns were firing on Berlin and advanced units seemed to be in the city. Fighting seemed to have virtually ceased in the West. We had continued with our desultory training and begun to think about the continuing war in the Far East. I knew I would not be allowed to take the squadron there if we went as it was rumoured we might. I was inclined to encourage these speculations which gave crews some kind of objective to fasten on to, suspended as we seemed to be in a no man's land of our own while the final blows were administered and surrenders were being accepted. Then, in the first week in May we received an Operation Order, couched in similar terms to those many which had passed through our teleprinter ordering the destruction of this or that target. This day, however, the objective was simple and peaceable "code-named Exodus". We were the first squadrons selected to repatriate some of the thousands of British and Commonwealth prisoners-of-war who were assembled at Brussels.

The aerodrome there was said to be serviceable for Lancasters "with extreme caution". A wave of enthusiasm passed through the whole squadron. Here was work which we, and no one else, could do on the scale needed. We were back in the real world where we could be of real use and we went about our preparations with a zest equal to or exceeding that of the days of war.

The Met Office forecast fine weather with just a chance of a shower over the sea. It was strange to be crossing the coast in daylight and without a load of bombs. The motors of my aircraft were beautifully synchronised with no vestige of irregularity and the atmosphere was so still that, travelling at two hundred miles per hour over the sea, there was no sensation of movement. We might have been in a punt on a lake on a drowsy summer afternoon. There had been many such days in that cloudless May of five years before when the wretched suicide, whose bones were now being sought in the charred rubble of Berlin, was striding to his greatest victory over poor demoralised France.

I don't know who certified that the aerodrome at Brussels was fit for bombers but it was worth the risk to get the ex-prisoners home. Landing first, I warned the others that "extreme caution" was right. The runway was narrow with bomb holes only crudely filled. There were no taxi tracks and the grass surface was pockmarked with moonlike craters so it was necessary for each aircraft to taxi back down the runway before the next one could land, making our arrival a slow business.

Unfortunately one of my squadron suffered a tyre burst, and had to be towed off the runway, wasting valuable time. We had brought servicing personnel with some equipment and spare wheels but there would be a good deal of improvisation needed with some help from the local Spitfire squadron there before the lame duck could fly again.

We parked our aircraft, wingtip to wingtip, off the runway, waiting for the landings to finish before we could take passengers on board. It was very hot and the crews lounged about in the shade of the wings, eating sandwiches and drinking from thermos flasks of tea.

There was a tent from which the movement of ex-prisoners was controlled. They wore the most astonishing motley of clothes and, although they looked fairly clean themselves, some of the clothes weren't very good. They were quiet and docile, waiting their turn in the queue where a rather officious officer was mobilising them into parties of twenty-six for each aeroplane, the maximum a Lancaster could take. They would be pretty uncomfortable, sitting on spars and huddled in corners, but who cared? Some of them hadn't seen England for six years.

Curiously they didn't wait like servicemen usually wait, with songs and mouth organs and an accepted humourist making not very funny jokes. They showed none of the impatience you might have expected from those who had had a raw deal and were now a privileged elite, free at last.

Many had had a kind of freedom for quite some time since the Germans, driven westwards from Poland by the Red Army, had opened the doors of camps in the east before the Russians reached them. Some of the stories emanating from this curious circumstance of freed prisoners, still officially enemies, at large in Germany were quite extraordinary. "A" had clubbed three guards and ridden to Brussels on a German tank. "B" had six gold watches and a Mercedes car which he had sold for £20 in Belgian francs. "C" had walked from Silesia to Hamburg and halfway back again. "D" had seen a hundred of his comrades die by the roadside. "E" still had scars on his back from being beaten for trying to escape but now had the warder's little finger pickled in his pocket. And so on and so on. Many of the tales were romantic, some quite fantastic, some were true, many exaggerated, some probably plain fabricated.

These stories ran round the aerodrome at Brussels like quicksilver on a plate, but the curious thing was that it didn't seem to be so much the ex-prisoners who told the stories. Nearly all were hearsay. Among the prisoners it seemed that the British facility for talking with strangers had died with the blitz and there was much silence, waiting. In some ways the aerodrome might have been a pre-war railway carriage.

Every bomber aircrew member has speculated about being a prisoner-of-war. Capture by the enemy happens to soldiers and sailors but to no category of the fighting services was the possibility so permanently vivid as it was to bomber crews. In some ways it helped. When losses were high and it looked like being his turn next, an airman would say of his friend who had not come back, "well, perhaps he baled out, perhaps he's a prisoner". Almost no one in Bomber Command was ever reported "Killed in Action". Casualties were at first "Missing", then "Missing, believed Killed", but there was always a tiny, lingering hope that they might be at large or prisoners.

Many of the flotsam floating through Brussels aerodrome were RAF aircrew who had been shot down, perhaps in the very type of aircraft which would take them home. It was even recorded that a man shot down in "C. Charley" of 97 Squadron was taken home in a new "C. Charley" of his old squadron.

You would have expected much fraternisation and swapping of stories, "What was it like?", "How did you get back?", ex-prisoners eagerly asking about home and what the food was like. But no. The tradition of the English railway carriage was stronger than ever and a good deal of silence reigned.

The long queues waited patiently and the aircrew chewed their sandwiches and emptied their tea flasks in the shade. Someone told the story of "old George" who had collected a wristwatch by going through pockets in a pile of miscellaneous garments which the passengers-to-be had been forced, against their wills, to discard. It was a dirty, smelly collection ranging from Wehrmacht uniforms to filthy women's fur coats, from ancient British flying kit to curious shaggy sheepskins which had probably had half a dozen owners since they were stolen by German invaders in the Ukraine. Many of the ex-prisoners were very upset at having to discard these curious garments and it is a measure of a prisoner's tragedy that they seemed to have a real and not only a sentimental value to their "owners".

When the landings were complete, returnees in squads of twenty-six were marshalled to the aeroplanes which were to transport them and the crews would get up off the grass, rather self-conscious, and pretend not to look while their passengers awkwardly mounted into the Lancaster. They would brief them, distant but polite, as to the rather complex seating arrangements and distribute the special rations for the journey which consisted of a few sweets and what the Government chose to call "Bags, airsickness". Then the aircrew would revert to their professional selves, start the engines and away, taking off in quite rapid succession, climbing and turning gently so as not to upset the passengers whose stomachs had mostly undergone such awful vicissitudes in the last month or so.

I saw my own aircraft off flown by another crew, since I had to stay to see that the unserviceable machine was properly fixed up and I had no wish to delay the homeward trip for twenty-six men whose one thought was of touching down in England.

It was going to be some time before the wheel change could be effected and the slight damage to the undercarriage repaired so I went over to the mess where I met an old acquaintance from fighter days and a troupe of Belgian girls, miraculously well dressed and made up in spite of the "five years hard" of German occupation. This was my first glimpse of that curious, half-hysterical world of victory and "liberation", with its welter of fun, black market, scandal and corruption.

Tale-telling and backbiting were already rife, mixed up with genuine feeling for the liberation forces, possibly a little bit stimulated by interest in their supply of cigarettes and coffee. I tried to concentrate on the splendid tales of everyone having a good time in Brussels, which had, of course, been cleared of Germans some time ago. I seemed to be classed as an honorary liberator and after a time I was singled out by a quiet but dazzlingly pretty girl who had gathered that I was a visiting Lancaster pilot.

She took me into a corner and told me how she and her family used to listen at night for the sound, however distant, of the British bombers. Often, she said, when they heard the hum of the stream of Lancasters and Halifaxes, the whole family would go down on their knees together and pray for the success of the mission against the "sales boches" and for the safe return of the crews.

She asked how long I would stay in Brussels and I explained that I must go home that day, but it would be some time, perhaps three hours, before my aircraft would be ready.

"Good," she said and I said it wasn't really good. Although I was enjoying myself the delay must be trying for the passengers I was to take to England, since so many of their comrades were already home.

"I didn't mean that," she said seriously. "I meant that it is good you will be here for a little." Then she said she had to go home, but would I please meet her in one hour's time, outside the mess. "It must be outside," she emphasised. I was mystified but intrigued, and, escorting her to the street, we synchronised our watches and agreed a time and place. It was all rather solemn and mysterious.

I went to see how the lame duck was progressing, and when I came back to the Mess it was quite tempting to join in the general drinking with the animated young fighter boys who were determined that everyone should have a good time, extending a welcome even to such a queer fish as an ageing Group Captain.

Their fun and their experiences were new and exciting to me who had not had so much as a glimpse of the fighter world for some years, so self-contained had the different branches of the Air Force become. In spite of what they obviously saw as my advanced age, they were soon treating me as nearly one of themselves. Confused and garbled as were some of their stories, especially those gleaned from prisoners-of-war, I was fascinated. Some nearly incredible tales had come hot from the mouths of men who had walked across hundreds of miles of enemy country, a gaggle of aliens with no official organisation, nominally still prisoners-of-war with German officers and guards, but in truth already conquerors in a demoralised country whose administration had fallen to bits. There were extraordinary tales of escapes and recaptures, terrible hardships on the march with only scraps of rumoured news and often fewer scraps of food. They told tales of how British NCOs had replaced German officers as effective commanders and how, speaking no German, they had managed to bully German authorities into giving them a modicum of food and shelter at the expense of the locals who had little enough for themselves. Some of them had broken through what was left of German lines and, bringing German prisoners with them, were taken prisoner by allied front-line troops who could not recognise their curious attire. Tales were multiplying when the time came for my rendezvous and I said goodbye, sustained by a battery of invitations to come back and stay a week with them when I could fly all their fighters and drink as much as I liked.

My pretty girl was punctual, walking towards me with a parcel under her arm.

"Champagne," she said, thrusting it onto me. "Quite good, papa says and he knows wine. I wanted you, one of those . . . up there," she gestured vaguely at the sky, "to have something from us. To show we knew . . . and were grateful. Will you please take it to your aeroplane and hide it. They . . . ," looking towards the mess, "they mustn't know. They're good to us. But this is different."

"Put it inside your tunic," she said, "but, first, please . . . " she was suddenly shy while I started to mumble thanks. Then she interrupted me.

"Please . . ." she said, "please . . . will you kiss me, once"

I put down the bottle and, not at all unwilling, took her in my arms. She returned my kisses with an ardent, passionate desire which was almost ferocious.

After a while she drew away, breathing quickly and still holding me, she looked at my face as if to make sure she would never forget it.

"Thank you", she said. "When I have children I shall tell them that I was kissed by . . . one of those . . . " again the gesture to the sky. She picked up the parcel and gave it back to me.

"Oh, thank you, thank you," she said and was gone.

I walked back to the aeroplane trying to conceal the precious bottle under my tunic. It was all of four years since I had tasted champagne. I could not help but be excited by her passionate kisses, but above this hovered another, stronger emotion, of humility at the sincerity of her gratitude.

When at last we got away the homeward flight was even more peaceful than the outward and the world seemed poised, breathless, waiting for a miracle which just might really happen, the miracle of peace.

A little thought conjured up the spectres of Japan, the European frontiers, the displaced persons in their millions, the hunger and disease, all the awful things that one knew could, almost certainly would, still have to happen because of the war. For God's sake, I thought, stop thinking. Just for one evening stop thinking and be one of the millions of men who haven't got to kill each other any more, haven't got to hate anyone any more and will soon be back at their homes. Think of the millions of women who will go to their beds tonight clutching their pillows in thankfulness and desire, saying, its all right, he's going to come back after all, one night soon, not so long now, and he'll be here, with me, and it'll be like it was before. He and I.

The few little clouds in the west were pink at the edges as we flew across a sea so smooth we might have been suspended becalmed above a mirror. There was no other aeroplane in the sky, all would have landed by now and their crews gone about their partying. It was a shame that I had had to keep my own crew so late through no fault of theirs but they remembered the ordeals our passengers had endured and had no grumbles.

I thought of the Belgian girl and the warmth and sincerity of her words and, yes, the passion of her kisses. I couldn't question a word she had said nor forget the sentimental picture of the little family on their knees, praying. Would she one day discover that I was no better than the enemy, that I had killed women and children, destroyed hospitals and churches? Not deliberately, of course, as the Nazi press must have told her in its lying propaganda. Perhaps she would one day regret the bottle of champagne and wipe my kisses from her mouth?

Ah well . . .

I told the wireless operator to tune his set to the 9 o'clock news and put it on the intercom, although we could not broadcast it to our passengers.

News was of the German collapse on all fronts, of the Russian advance to Berlin and speculation about Hitler's suicide or death. The smooth unemotional descriptions of chaos and disorder jarred on me and dispelled my tranquillity. I told the wireless operator to switch off and give our estimated time of arrival to the station in Oxfordshire where we were to drop our passengers. Even then it would be two hours or more before we could be back at our own base.

That week saw the final collapse of Germany and the formal surrenders, first of forces to Field-Marshal Montgomery and then of the German Reich to General Eisenhower. The British people were given a formal holiday for "Victory in Europe Day", VE Day. The end of the ordeal which had been the greatest and the most dangerous in the long history of the British people would undoubtedly provoke the greatest, most spontaneous celebration ever known in Britain.

I had to tell my squadron, however, that there could be no immediate high jinks for us. There were still large numbers of ex-prisoners stranded in Germany where local transport had broken down and the army's resources were stretched to the limit. On VE Day we were to go to Rheine in northern Germany where ex-prisoners were assembled. The aerodrome, much smaller than that at Brussels, was said to be only just fit for Lancasters lightly loaded. There was no one who did not willingly give up his participation in the celebrations for those who had not seen their homes for so long.

Again the day was calm and clear and the line of our flight took us across Holland and the heartrending sight of the island of Walcheren, almost totally flooded by deed of the RAF.

Months before, Antwerp, with its marvellous harbour and vast docks, had been chosen as a chief supply port for the allied armies in their final thrust into Germany. It had been an appalling setback to find it unusable because of impregnable German batteries on the Island of Walcheren at the mouth of the estuary. It would have been suicide for a ship to try to enter Antwerp with those batteries in position. Also a considerable minesweeping operation would be necessary before the port could be used and that could not be undertaken under enemy guns.

The only solution, ghastly as it must have been to impose it on the Dutch, was to break the dykes and flood the island, thereby confining the German garrisons to a narrow strip and cutting them off from any hope of supply or succour. It was a hard choice but the Dutch, who had already lost so much, accepted it loyally and, as we flew back from Rheine we could see the results of the work of our own Group. The whole island was under water, farmhouses standing proud, but otherwise water, water, water, and salt water at that, flooding over the rich farmland. After the flooding the German garrisons were quickly dislodged but the delay in achieving the use of Antwerp probably prolonged the war into 1945 and cost many lives.

The depredations of the sea on Walcheren were bad enough but there were also huge areas on the mainland where the dykes had been deliberately breached by the Germans, even after they knew the war was lost. They gained nothing but the lasting hate of the Dutch. At least we in Bomber Command made some atonement by dropping food to areas where the population was totally cut off by the floods and very near to starvation.

The aerodrome at Rheine was much less suitable for Lancasters than that at Brussels and since there was virtually nowhere to park I had to keep some incoming aircraft in the air while those who had loaded up took off.

This time we were to take our passengers to an aerodrome in the south of England which had been fitted up as a centre for documenting ex-prisoners-of-war and equipping them with some of the necessities of life before despatching them to their homes. I and my crew said goodbye to each of them as they climbed down the ladder and stood on English soil, some of them for the first time in five years. They were tired and still numbed by their freedom. Many were emaciated from lack of proper food. It was queer that not one of those that I brought back said "Thank You" to the crew who had given up the day of celebration to bring

them back, but we all realised what they had been through and
no-one minded.

I had had to stay until the last to make sure all was properly
finished and it was quite late by the time we got back to base.
I and my crew had been in our aircraft without stopping
the engines for well over ten hours, and I still had some
arrangements to make at the squadron. Thankfully, I was now
able to give virtually everyone a couple of days leave.

For myself, tired as I was at the end of that day, I felt rather
urgently that I needed to share the reality of peace, which I had
hardly grasped as yet. So, late as it was, I took my bottle of
Brussels champagne and drove to Skegness.

Knowing of the trip to Rheine, my hostess wasn't really
expecting me. I was rather exhilarated, waving my bottle of
champagne and talking about celebration when she took me off
my guard by being completely serious.

"Celebrating, yes," she said, "but first we ought really to be
on our knees, thanking God its all over and you're alive and
safe."

She wasn't a religious person, but it was said with such
simple sincerity that, for the second time in the dawn of peace
I was made to feel humble and a little sad that I understood but
could not quite share the emotions of two very different girls
who had perhaps come nearer the meaning of life than I had.

I had been hoping to be able to take some leave and see
something of my children with whom my contacts in the war
years had been fragmentary, although better, I told myself, than
those who had been abroad for almost the duration of the war.
But it was not to be. The order came that the squadron was to
prepare and train to form part of what was called "Tiger Force",
the squadrons of Bomber Command who were to proceed to the
Far East to ensure that Britain had some part in the final defeat of
Japan.

Tiger Force was to be commanded by Air Marshal
Sir H.P. Lloyd, a formidable but very popular character known
throughout the service as Hew Pew. With an MC and DFC from
the first war, he had performed spectacularly in the fiasco in

Greece. A better man for the job could not have been selected and when he visited 97 Squadron he enthused us all with his vision of the mission.

One of my immediate jobs was to weed out from the squadron those of the ground staff who were near their already announced date of demobilisation and would not be available to go overseas. This also applied to aircrew with the rider that those who had nearly completed their quota of operational trips would also be excluded or excused, (depending on how they felt). There would be few exemptions from these rules and, although "Hew Pew" tried to get me exempted the application was firmly and rapidly turned down.

We had one interesting assignment in this difficult and unsettled period. This was to take as many as possible of our ground crews on a so-called "Inspection Flight" in which we flew a pre-arranged course round the British Zone of occupied Germany to show both ground and air crews some of the results of five years work of Bomber Command.

The course took us over most of the towns and targets which I knew only as concentrations of searchlights and flak areas. It was a fine clear day and we flew at about four thousand feet, a good height for an overall view, and we saw as we passed something of what had happened to, amongst others, Hamburg, Lübeck, Hanover, the Ruhr towns, Cologne, Aachen and Düsseldorf and so south to Stuttgart, Nuremburg and Munich. Was I cowardly in attempting deliberately to avoid Würzburg? Alas, the small and distant oil targets we had worked so hard on were all in the Russian-occupied territory, over which, (the shape of things to come), allied flights were already totally prohibited.

The general devastation was almost unbelievable. In town after town hardly a building seemed to be intact, hardly a house seemed to be habitable. All that showed from the air were rows and rows of empty boxes, walls enclosing nothing. There were spaces with piles of rubble which might have been factories or warehouses. There seemed to be no traffic on the streets, no movement on the railways. We crossed the Rhine more than once and saw no bridge intact. All were collapsed and sunken in the great river on which no barge could move because of the obstruction of the twisted wrecks of what had been bridges. We saw the great dual pontoon bridge at Wesel which had been and was the main artery for allied forces east of the Rhine. Here there was movement, service transport going to and fro on occupation business. In Wesel itself the desolation was complete and not even the walls of the houses stood.

In the Ruhr towns I was conscious chiefly of two things. First the silence. Of course at four thousand feet with four engines running one couldn't have heard anything anyway, but the silence, the atmosphere of desolation, managed to project itself upwards from the ruined towns where nothing moved so that in the noisy aircraft I felt the silence in the streets which had once been busy with traffic and talk and the noises of industry. The other feature was the number of high factory chimneys standing erect and undamaged among the ruined buildings. They had apparently been immune from the blast bombs and the fires and still stood, silent and useless like demobilised sentries, not a single one emitting the smallest whiff of smoke. Their considerable numbers were the best emphasis that the whole area was, for the time at least, dead, dead, dead.

I wondered to myself whether this truly dreadful sight represented a degree of overkill, whether such destruction had really been necessary to stop the production of arms for the Nazis in the greatest industrial complex in Europe.

Then I remembered that when the Ruhr was encircled by allied forces, the German people were still obeying Hitler's frenzied calls for resistance to the last man. He still demanded that all in his Reich should, as he later did for himself, accept death rather than surrender.

In the Ruhr pocket was a large force of over 300,000 men, under the command of Field-Marshal Model, the Nazi General whose career, of all Hitler's Generals, had been most fostered by his passionate devotion to the Führer. Had he and his armies been able to obey Hitler's command there would have been great casualties on either side before the Ruhr capitulated. But as it was these forces could not be supplied with fuel or ammunition because of the total desolation in the area. They could neither try to fight their way out nor establish a coherent Fortress Ruhr and their resistance crumbled within days. In a capitulation greater than that of Stalingrad, 325,000 men surrendered with virtually no allied casualties. Here, at least, was some reward, if an unplanned and unexpected one, for Bomber Command's long years of effort and its substantial losses.

From the desolation of Germany I flew home with no feeling of triumph or even satisfaction in victory. Even my crew and the ground crew we carried, young men all, were silent and subdued when we landed at our home field. I think we were all stunned by a new comprehension of the horror of war.

I did not know when I landed that this would be my last flight with 97 Squadron and my last flight in a Lancaster.

After the inspection flight I had, once again, been intending to take a few days leave but this time my intention was thwarted by an urgent summons to report to Bomber Command HQ for interview with the Commander in Chief. This was my first personal encounter with the formidable "Bert", "Butch" or "Bomber" Harris as he was variously known. The first nickname came from his pre-war intimates in the regular RAF, the second was bestowed on him by many of the aircrew in his wartime Command, the third grew gradually through use by the press, politicians and ultimately, in the time of his deep unpopularity, by the general public.

For my interview he showed little of the aggressive, not to say bullying, technique for which he was well-known. He did, though, not conceal his contempt for, and dissatisfaction with, the staff at Air Ministry through whom he received instructions and directives.

He told me that the United States had a large unit in Germany, the US Strategic Bombing Survey, which was investigating the results of bombing. There was a staff of about fifteen hundred which had started operations well before the war finished, already fully equipped and prepared for its task. No corresponding organisation existed or was planned for Britain and his frequent representations that one was needed urgently had been met with a stony silence.

He was naturally concerned that the American results would be published to the glory of the US Air Force and the detriment of Bomber Command. Consequently, he had instituted a small unit from within his Headquarters which would be able to carry out at least a skeleton survey of the results of British bombing before too much of the evidence disappeared. This unit was now in position in Germany. It had a Group Captain in command with three Operational Research experts, a photographer and an interpreter, supported by a full back-up of administrative personnel, office and domestic staff and transport. They had support in Germany from the Bomber Command Liaison Unit at General Eisenhower's Headquarters which had been in position from the start of the Normandy campaign.

Unfortunately, the officer commanding the unit had been killed in a motor accident and, after what the Air Marshal said had been a careful trawl round the Groups, I had been recommended to him as a replacement. We then had a quarter of an hour's talk about the work of the unit during which time I was introduced to the Head of the Bomber Command Operational Research Section, a civilian academic who wore, rather awkwardly, the uniform of a Group Captain.

I was then fairly abruptly dismissed and told to make myself known to the Senior Air Staff Officer, whom I already knew, and other heads of departments, reporting back to the C-in-C at five minutes to one for luncheon.

The journeys through the lanes of Buckinghamshire to and from his official residence, on which I was driven by the Great Man in his Bentley, was one of the more alarming experiences of my three years in Bomber Command. The luncheon, however, with the C-in-C's wife as an excellent hostess and no-one else present, was an unmitigated pleasure. The Air Marshal emerged as a thoroughly civilised, if very opinionated, man and I really enjoyed more than an hours conversation on many subjects outside bombing. Nevertheless, I left the Headquarters without any definite indication of my future.

That was changed soon enough. After breakfast the next day I received the message that I was posted to HQ Bomber Command, for duty with the Bomber Command Bombing Research Unit. I was told that I was to report to High Wycombe in five days time, ready to fly to Germany the next day. The Command courier which plied three times a week between Bomber Command and Frankfurt, would take me and the very small amount of baggage I was allowed. I could not have asked for a more interesting and challenging posting, assuming that I had to relinquish command of my squadron.

On the day before I was to leave I was asked to come to the big room at Coningsby which was used for lectures and station meetings. I was surprised to find the whole squadron assembled there to bid me farewell. People made embarrassingly pleasant speeches and I was presented with a pair of fine silver candelabra and a beautiful bell-shaped inkwell inscribed "with best wishes from all members of your squadron". I was particularly touched that the inscription included the words "all" and "your". This seemed to emphasise that there had been a closer, more personal relationship between us than was normal in such a large unit as a Lancaster squadron. I left 97 with a heavy heart, feeling that this was the end of my flying life. With the exception of my two tours as a Station Commander, on both of which I had been able to keep my hand in, I had been on active flying duties throughout the war.

10

Investigating in Germany

Control Council Law No. 10

The transport aircraft which flew me to Frankfurt, chugging slowly across Belgium, was an elderly Anson. The "Annie", designed long before the war as maid-of-all-work, had done long and splendid service as trainer, transport, submarine chaser, even bomber. It was sentimentally loved by RAF pilots, but by 1945 standards it was slow, cumbersome and inefficient. When we landed at Frankfurt and parked alongside large numbers of new and shiny American transports, poor Annie's shabby livery and old-fashioned lines proclaimed only too clearly the new British status as poor relation to our transatlantic cousins who once again had saved Europe.

To imbibe something of the techniques of life with the occupation forces I was to stay a night or two with the Bomber Command Unit attached to General Eisenhower's Headquarters which occupied the whole of the giant IG Farben Building, peacetime head office of the world's largest chemical company. The Supreme Headquarters Allied Expeditionary Force was no more loved by regimental soldiers than any other big Headquarters has ever been and its acronym, SHAEF, was often alleged to stand for "Some Have Army Experience First". I have to say I never had any complaints about my treatment in the American Zone of Germany.

On the way to the quarters of the Bomber Command Unit, now surely totally redundant, our car was imperiously ordered to the side of the road and, with sirens shrieking and eight or ten outriders and escort cars, the Supreme Commander himself flashed past. Hitler could not have had a more ostentatiously arrogant progress. I was told that "Ike" did not like it but that such demonstrations were considered desirable as part of a policy of keeping the defeated Germans in their place. I found it distasteful but came to realise that, for the time at least, it was probably sensible.

After a couple of days at Frankfurt I travelled by a much damaged autobahn to join my own Unit at Essen. Our living and working quarters were in a comfortable house just outside the town on a hill which overlooked an attractive lake. When I arrived in the early evening I sat out in a well-kept garden having a drink with the staff who were to be my companions for the next months. There was an excellent show of hybrid tea roses and the only difference from a similar garden in a prosperous English suburb was that it showed no sign of wartime deprivation. Also that a procession of fireflies, glowing more brightly as the colours of the roses faded in the warm dusk, circulated round the rosebeds. It was very restful and peaceful.

The officers of the Bomber Command Bombing Research Unit consisted of myself, three academics from the Operational Research Section at Bomber Command, looking slightly uncomfortable in their hastily assumed RAF uniforms, and an RAF administrative officer who had to make arrangements for accommodation, rations and suchlike. There was a back-up of interpreters, photographers, driver/mechanics, cooks, clerks and typists, all necessary since we had to operate as a self-contained unit. We made no contribution to the immediate and colossal tasks of the occupation authorities, who could not be expected to understand the importance of what we were doing. We were, consequently, low down in their priorities and the Administrative Officer often had difficulty in prising accommodation, rations and various sorts of passes out of bureaucratic and self-important Control Commission officers. I came to understand why the acronym of the original title Allied Military Government of Occupied Territories (AMGOT) had been assumed to stand for "Ancient Military Gentlemen on Tour".

However, the Military Government had to struggle with huge problems of near-starvation among the Germans, of housing and feeding the occupation forces and looking after the many thousands of "displaced persons", forcibly imported by the Nazis as slave labour, who were sloshing about free but homeless and destitute in a foreign land. DPs (Displaced Persons) were entitled to priority over their late oppressors and they made urgent and difficult demands on the limited food, accommodation and transport available to the British authorities for distribution. With such colossal responsibilities on their hands it was understandable that outsiders were unpopular. Nevertheless, seen from the perspective of the time, an assessment of the efficacy of the bombing weapon was not without importance.

Attached to my unit was a well-known artist, Paul Maze, whose friendship with the great in both France and Britain had given him access to many situations closed to the general run of people. He had been a friend of Winston Churchill before the war and had been one of the "pleasant but deeply anxious company" with whom, in August 1939, the future Prime Minister "passed some sunshine days in the old chateau where King Henry of Navarre had slept the night before the Battle of Ivry". Sir Winston recorded that he "found painting hard" in the uncertainty of the time and that he knew "that if war came – and who could doubt its coming? – a major burden would fall upon him".

Paul Maze, whose son had served with distinction in Bomber Command, had also become close to Air Marshal Harris, which accounted for his presence among us. I was somewhat hostile to this at first but in the event, since he was trilingual in French, German and English, and had wide experience of affairs and people, he became a most valuable addition to our party and a stimulating participant in all our discussions.

The day after my arrival in Essen we were to start an investigation into the effects of the bombing on one of the most important targets of Bomber Command, Krupps of Essen. At the start of the war Krupps was probably the world's greatest manufacturer of armaments and associated products. The nominal head of the firm, Alfred Krupp von Bohlen, was under arrest and likely to be charged as a Nazi war criminal, so I had to make arrangements with the Managing Director, who was the most senior executive available, to get the information we needed. First, however, it had been arranged that we should have an overall view of the works followed by a tour of the Krupps complex and its offshoots. The firm's senior guide had been instructed to show us everything we wished to see.

Next morning Herr Singer arrived punctually. He was driven by a uniformed chauffeur in the largest Mercedes model, in which he had clearly conducted many such tours. I caught him looking with some disdain at the shabby camouflaged Humber Snipe which was my official car. I admit I had a sneaking urge to go in, and perhaps later to drive, the Mercedes but I did not propose to accept hospitality from Krupps so I told Herr Singer to dismiss his fine polished limousine and come with me in the lead car which the others would follow. Herr Singer's disapproval was, in the manner of servants of the great whose dignity is upset, only just veiled.

Driving through Essen I had my first close-up view of a bombed German city. As we progressed slowly down the pitted and cratered roads and streets leading to the centre of the town, the full horror of what I had seen from the air three weeks before came through to me. Every street, virtually every building, was gutted, the empty window frames showing the bare and blackened interiors, with twisted and charred remains of beds and furniture often hanging over into the streets. There were very few people about and almost all were old. Dressed mostly in black, they walked slowly, their heads bowed. The pall of their defeat was all around them and they seemed as desolate as their ruined houses. Where on earth, I wondered, did they live? Not, surely, in these gaunt skeletons which served no purpose except to mark the streets. I soon discovered that most German houses have cellars and that much of the population had long been spending the nights underground. Many families had been evacuated, leaving the breadwinner to fend for himself. Thousands of workers had lived this way for up to three years.

There was virtually no traffic on the roads except for British service vehicles, all going at the same snail's pace as ourselves because of the heavily pitted roads. The lack of movement added to the desolation of the silence all around. No shops were open but occasionally we saw a queue patiently waiting before the skeleton of what had been a bakery. Seeing my questioning look Herr Singer shrugged his shoulders.

"They hope for a little bread," he said. "The ration is not always available. It is worse now than it ever was." This was the first of many times that I was to be confronted with the implication that the troubles of the German people were the fault of either deliberate action or gross inefficiency by the occupation forces. Herr Singer himself was clearly indifferent to the plight of these drab figures whose world had collapsed around them.

He spoke good English and while he directed our driver to the factory he regaled us with some of what was obviously his standard patter for distinguished or useful visitors to Krupps. He aimed to show that Krupps was much more than just a firm, it was an institution which, for him, outshone all others in the Ruhr and Rhineland. He told us that he had been showing celebrities and customers around Krupps for many years. Krupps was his world. Governments might come and go, but he clearly believed that the greater and, for him, totally beneficent institution of Krupps would last for ever. In the course of the time I spent in his company, he never showed a vestige of suspicion that his fierce devotion to Krupps might not be shared by the rest of the world.

He directed my driver to the main factory gate and we drove slowly under his guidance round a scene of desolation which would have been impossible to imagine if it had not lain there before my eyes. It seemed that every building, every shed, even every wall was ruined. From time to time I stopped the car, got out and walked through the wreckage. What was most eerie was the silence in a place which must for so long have thrummed with the clank of steel and the noise of machinery and was now a succession of roofless ruins occupied by heaps of twisted metal rusting in the damp air. Occasionally we saw a few workmen picking about in a desultory way among the rubble but they seemed to have no direction or objective and it was difficult to see what they could have achieved if they had. A few great chimneys stood undamaged but useless, grotesque fingers starkly pointing to the sky whence had fallen the wrath which had destroyed their function. I remembered how, when I had flown over this scene a month before, the chimneys had seemed then to project their silence even to us flying noisily overhead.

"This," said Herr Singer, "was the locomotive shop, where railway engines were built." The desolation of the big shed was complete. Only the shape of a once fine locomotive, half buried by rubble, indicated the activity which once had ruled there.

"Many countries," said Herr Singer, "countries in Africa, Asia, South America and of course in Europe, depended on Krupps that their railways could run and their trade continue. Now . . . ," he shrugged a questioning shoulder. In his view it seemed that the allied bombing had deliberately deprived those faraway people of an essential pillar which had sustained their innocent lives. We moved on.

Herr Singer's knowledge of the great works was encyclopaedic and he delivered a stream of information far beyond anyone's capacity to absorb. "This is the main foundry, here the assembly shop for axles . . . " and so on. He knew the dates when each shop had been damaged although production, he said, had continued until towards the end of 1944 when a final raid had virtually put paid to the whole town. He never pointed specifically to where guns, ammunition, armour plate or tanks had been made or assembled but it was not difficult to pick out the remains of such among the general shambles. After a couple of hours of this I had had enough and told Herr Singer to start on the second part of his programme, which was to consist of touring the outside properties and activities directly connected with, or owned by, Krupps.

As we drove slowly through other parts of the town the all prevailing silence enveloped me as if I were muffled in a cloak of cotton wool, my senses unable to penetrate the curtain of quiet which dominated the world. Essen was a city, not so much of the dead as of the stunned. Although everything was still, consciousness of the blows which had paralysed the town was almost as vivid as the awful results around us.

We passed a large ruined building. "Here," said Herr Singer with great meaning, "was the Krupps hospital. It had been maintained by Krupps for the employees. It was one of the best in Germany with the most modern equipment and the best doctors and nurses. It was bombed in 1943 and many persons were killed." The building had obviously been hit several times before it was finally destroyed by fire. It was not far from the centre of Essen and quite close to the armament works.

We passed some tall ruins which had once been blocks of flats. All seemed to be completely gutted and I wondered how safe were the high walls which enclosed nothing and seemed dangerously ready to collapse. "These," said Herr Singer, "were the workers' flats. Built by Krupps for the workers. As good as any in Germany or America. Everything you could need and the men could walk to work. All families were very happy there. Very happy," he repeated unctuously. "Now," he went on as if he had read my mind, "it is said the walls may collapse and perhaps more people will be killed." This was a problem which many cities were living with and which would not go away for quite some time.

Next we came to an open space which, Herr Singer told me with pride, had been Krupps playing fields. The land had been bought and levelled by the firm and it had provided splendid sports facilities for the employees and their friends. Every evening and at week-ends these grounds were used for games of football, ("as in England, no?" said Herr Singer, currying our favour). Also for hockey, tennis and all sports. The employees would help with the maintenance but all was provided and paid for by Krupps. He sighed with nostalgia for the dear dead days.

I asked him whether Jews had been allowed to take part and whether the Nazi Party had used the ground for their rallies and drilling, but to these questions he proffered no real answer. The world of Krupps, he seemed to be saying, was happily sealed off from anything that went on elsewhere in Germany. The Nazis had never interfered with Krupps and as far as he knew there were no Jewish people in Essen. Not any more, I said to myself, not any more.

I subsequently asked many other German businessmen, whether they had been Nazis. The answer was nearly always the same as that which Herr Singer gave, that they had to pay a subscription but had not taken part in any Party activities and knew nothing of what went on within the Party. Who, then, I often asked myself, were the real Nazis? Who sustained this huge organisation which had permeated into every corner of German life, personal, commercial, artistic and industrial? Someone, apart from the top officials, now mostly in allied custody, must have kept the whole vast evil show on the road. It was extraordinary that I met so very few who participated or even admitted to having been among the more than three and a half million who had voted to make Hitler the leader of the biggest party in the Reichstag of 1933.

Towards the end of our tour of Essen I saw a crude temporary building erected among the ruins of what must have been a handsome brick-built complex covering a considerable area. "Here," announced Herr Singer, "was the Krupps school". It had been rebuilt since his own schooldays, but he had been educated by Krupps in an earlier building on the site and his children had attended this school. It was, he said, one of the best in Germany. There had been first class-teaching staff and recreation facilities, a large library and unlimited school books. "All examinations," he said, "were passed with flying colours. Now, all, all is kaput." It seemed to have been the work of the rascally allies again. I was, in the next months, to get heartily sick of the endless masochistic repetition of the favourite word "Kaput", signifying totally destroyed or useless. No one specifically blamed the allies but in no case did I ever find any responsibility attached to any German action.

I asked whether the Nazis had supervised and altered the curriculum and the teaching of Krupps school. Herr Singer answered that the school was controlled by a teacher of the highest qualifications from Heidelberg University. Of course education had changed. There had to be progress? In England surely the curriculum was different from what it had been in the days of Dickens? It was the policy of Krupps, he said, to keep up with the times. Heidelberg was a University of the highest repute, otherwise Krupps would not have selected one of its graduates as Head Master. It would have needed a more skilled cross-examiner than myself to have torn aside the veil of flannel with which Herr Singer surrounded the great firm which had dominated his life.

When we came to the shell of a large concert hall with the roof intact or replaced, Herr Singer told me that it now sheltered many of the thousands who had no roof or home. In former times Krupps had provided concerts of Beethoven, Bach and Brahms . . . the greatest musicians had played there . . . but now . . . there was no music in Essen. It was clear that in his view the British had made a deliberate assault on the three great "Bs" of German music.

Lastly, we were shown a middle-class housing estate, detached houses with gardens which were, said Herr Singer, the residences of Krupps managers. He himself had lived in one of the smaller ones but now all were burnt – kaput!

Herr Singer grew less and less attractive to me the longer I listened to him. His obsequious attitude to me as being, he wrongly thought, someone who might have influence in reviving the fortunes of his beloved Krupps, would have done credit to Uriah Heap himself. But he managed to combine this with an undercurrent of implication that what had happened in Essen was a modern equivalent of the ransacking of Rome by the Goths and Vandals. In his eyes, a high civilisation provided by a great firm which had given security and prosperity to a whole town had been torn down and destroyed.

I diagnosed that his attitude to the Nazi regime had been one of absolute acceptance. He may not have been active in the evil and violent activities of the Party but it seemed to me impossible that he was as ignorant of them as he professed. As long as an authority supported Krupps he would wholeheartedly support that authority. Since the future of Krupps, and consequently of himself, now seemed to depend on the British occupation regime, he had no difficulty in wiping his personal slate clean of any Nazi connection and handing to the British the signal honour of resuscitating Krupps. He firmly believed that no one in their senses would fail to do just that.

At the time I believed that it was the intention of the occupation authorities to do nothing of the kind since distrust of Krupps and their like was firmly embedded in British and allied minds. The idea of the almost total demilitarisation of Germany had not then been abandoned and the role of the German armaments industry in supporting the Nazis and fermenting the spirit of aggressive war was still in the forefront of British thinking.

In the end Herr Singer was right and I was wrong. A phoenix Krupps, supposedly under British supervision, soon rose from the ashes and ruins of the old. It was, and probably is, not the same as the original firm which was so often classified as the archetype of the "merchants of death", and which Herr Singer so blindly worshipped. But it was and is still Krupps.

By this time I had had a surfeit of looking at ruins and was heartily sick of Herr Uriah Heap Singer so I told him I was now ready to see Dr Hübener, the senior working Director, who had been told to make himself available.

From him I ascertained that the firm's records, meticulously maintained throughout the war, had survived pretty well intact. I gave him a detailed *frageboden*, a longish questionnaire the answers to which would help us, and checked that he would provide accommodation and such assistance as we might need to distil the information we wanted for our detailed report. I also arranged that later I would make a tour of the works with our photographer, for which we would need a guide who should not be Herr Singer. At this, for the first time, he smiled.

It was fortunate for us at this stage that senior German officials üand businessmen did not distinguish the functions of British officers. Nearly all of them clung to the idea that any Englishman in an official position might be able to influence their future and the co-operation we received at first was complete.

I did not flatter myself or them that this was for any reason except self-interest but it made a great difference to our work. Later in our tour, as German confidence started to return, things became very different and the information we sought was often difficult to obtain.

Before I left him I asked Dr Hübener a few personal questions, emphasising that his answers would not go further than myself. He obviously did not believe me.

At first he was at great pains to explain that any connection with politics or the Nazi Party was at the level of the Supervisory Board of which he was not a member. He professed to have taken no part in politics and said that, at his level of technical and business management, political issues did not affect the firm of Krupps. He had paid a subscription to the Party because it was not possible to avoid it, but he had never been involved in any Party activities. I was already becoming unwilling to take such declarations at their face value but that wasn't truly my business. All I really needed from this rather cringing individual, who had been one of the most powerful men in Essen, was the assurance that we would be shown all the records and accounts we needed. This he had given most willingly and this undertaking he honoured during the weeks we were at Krupps.

I spent a little over six months in Germany on damage research, during which time the unit prepared reports on several towns and made fairly detailed investigations into three very large firms in the heavily-bombed areas. Among the towns we saw were Hamburg, Dortmund and Hanover as well as Essen, and, in addition to our work on Krupps, we looked in some detail at the results of the Rheinmetall Borsig of Dusseldorf, an armament manufacturer comparable to Krupps, and the Bochumer Verein, a typical large steel works in the north of the Ruhr.

The hard slog of collecting, analysing and arranging the information we wanted out of the immense mass of statistics was the work of our three academics, and nobly they performed it. Throughout our investigations we were astonished by the meticulous and detailed figures which had been kept in German industry. There was something awesome about the volume of the material and the methodical way in which it was arranged and displayed.

At first we regarded the figures we were shown as being gospel truth, giving an objective picture of what had happened. After a time, however, we began to suspect that we were in the presence of a considerable confidence trick since it appeared that the true reliability of many of the figures and tables we were shown was pretty doubtful. In Nazi Germany the eye of the Führer hovered over every report and figure which related to the output of war material. Hitler himself had given the orders on which were based the high targets for production at every level, and woe betide those responsible if the targets were not met or surpassed. The result was that the targets normally were met and it was possible for nearly everyone to report that the dictate applying to him had been obeyed and the required production achieved. In our minds we were soon convinced that many miracles of production, especially the figures of recovery from bombing attacks, had been faked or upgraded. Krupps was not immune from these suspicions. The only thing totally undeniable was that all production at Krupps had ceased in October 1944 and had not yet restarted.

After Krupps and Essen we worked on the metal manufacturing firm of Rheinmetall Borsig just outside Düsseldorf. We stayed in our quarters in Essen although the daily commuting on terrible roads and with numerous badly signposted diversions was a chore, but it would have been much more trouble to try to arrange quarters in Düsseldorf. Rheinmetall had been one of the most important factories in Germany and here it was rather refreshing to meet a director who admitted his early conversion to the Nazi cause and his belief in Hitler. He had been no callow youth susceptible to Hitler's ranting when he joined the Nazis in the late 1920s.

"Of course there are no Nazis now," he cynically told me in such good English that I could dispense with an interpreter. He had believed when he joined the Nazis and threw the influence of his firm behind them that the industrial situation of Germany, owing to reparations and to the determination of the French to obstruct any recovery, was quite hopeless without radical change. Such change had proved impossible to the various combinations of parties who had ruled without purpose or vigour throughout the time of the Weimar Republic. Only the Nazi and the Communist Parties, at opposite ends of the political spectrum, had then, in his view, been capable of forming a strong government. If the large and powerful German Communist Party had come to power, as had been possible, he was convinced that Germany, under the thrall of the Soviet Union, might have survived but at a frightful cost. His own firm would have been nationalised and he would have been replaced by some inexperienced Communist official without knowledge or experience of the business. Living standards would have fallen even further and Soviet Russia would have become the arbiter of Europe. In his judgement, the Nazis had offered the only political base acceptable to industry and the only way of stemming the tide of communism which had threatened to engulf Europe and, he said with feeling, was still the greatest future danger to Britain and America. He neither denied nor regretted that he had belonged to Party. The regime had done much good in promoting public works, reducing unemployment and allowing industry to sweep away the stifling cobwebs of lethargy which had proliferated under the feeble governments of the Weimar republic. The breaking of the bonds of the Versailles Treaty and the decision to rearm in equality with other great nations was natural and inevitable. When I asked why this had not been achieved by negotiation he answered that the French would never have allowed any relaxation. There would have been endless talk and no action. Rearmament was necessary, not against France or Britain who were too prosperous and contented to threaten Germany, but against the menace from the East.

It was, of course, tragic that there had been war but Hitler's foreign policy had, he believed, stemmed from the refusal of the French to allow Germany her proper place in Europe. Like many Germans, at all levels, he thought it clever to play off the occupying powers against one another. In his opinion, the war had deranged the Führer who, after the first two years, had become incapable of rational decision. But by then it was too late to change.

When I asked him what he had thought about Nazi behaviour towards the Jews he said that he was convinced that after the First War the Jews had been an actively disruptive influence in Germany. He "knew" that they had been more responsible than the Allies for the awful raging inflation of 1922-23 when a new currency had to be introduced at the rate of a billion old marks for a single rentenmark and a barrowful of paper notes was needed to buy a newspaper. I didn't believe all this, by any means, but I wasn't in the business of arguing. He would have run rings round me since I had little knowledge and no experience in what he was talking about. His views have since been discredited by history, but I found his comparative honesty more attractive than the more usual attitude of most of the Germans I interviewed, that they had known nothing of Nazi activities.

When I asked him whether he had known of, or thought of setting up, any kind of opposition, he answered that for such as him that would not have been practicable. In any case, it would have been unpatriotic since there was no real alternative to the Nazi Government.

I never heard what became of him but I suspect he probably evaded the rather random Allied purges of known and active Nazis. He was an obvious survivor and, while probably a rascal of the first order, he had a certain perverted honesty which I found more attractive than the studied deviousness of Herr Singer and his like.

From Düsseldorf, while the team were working on Rheinmetall, I went to look at the results of tactical attacks which had been made on the small towns of Jülich and Düren on the Roer River. These were strong points which could have obstructed a projected advance and their destruction by Bomber Command had been requested by the military in November 1944.

The outcome, more than six months after the event, was horrifying. Approaching the area I drove very slowly because the road was even more pitted than most with craters made by rockets, anti-personnel bombs and cannon shelling from the air. I could see no town ahead of me although the riverside country was quite flat. Then I realised I was already in what had been a town. There was no town, not a building, not a street, not a human facility of any kind was left. It was not even a series of rubble heaps. It was merely rubble, rubble everywhere. An occasional cornerstone or girder of a building stood, stark and solitary, above ground level. There was a recognisable track where a road had been and the rubble had been flattened with a heavy roller. Elsewhere the effect was of a crude arena, a mottled surface, pinkish in colour since it was made mostly of crushed bricks. These "towns" had not been damaged in the same way as large areas of the great cities which had been burnt out. There you could see where there had been terraces and streets, buildings where people had lived, perhaps still were living in the cellars. You could discern roadways and pavements. There were passers by and bicycles, women and children, an occasionally car or lorry. In Jülich and Düren there were none of these things. There was not even a pattern as in archaeological remains of ancient cities. The only proof that there had been life in these dusty flattened arenas was an indefinable but persistent smell, the smell of death.

I wondered how it had been in those towns on that 15th November only a few months ago. The allied forces in terrifying strength had been no more than five miles away across the river Roer, which clearly had been designated as the next German defence line. The predicament of the families who had lived in these ill-fated towns defied imagination. There would have been virtually nowhere for them to flee to. Cologne, fifteen or twenty miles to the east, was on the west side of the Rhine and, with the disasters which had already overtaken that town, it can hardly have looked like a welcoming haven for refugees. Perhaps they had decided to stay put and hope that either the German line would hold or that the conquering Allies would be merciful. But what had the German Army demanded of them? That they keep out of the way of the defences? Or put up passive resistance? They could know nothing of the Allied Army Commander's call to Bomber Command to destroy the two towns. The answer to that call was all around me and it seemed impossible that anyone who had been there on 15th November could have seen 16th November. But perhaps there had been no one there except military. I hope there wasn't but it was several days before I could rid myself of the smell of death which hung about those flattened ruins.

As Officer Commanding the Research Unit I was in overall charge of, and ultimately responsible for, all its functions, including the preparation of the reports. I was inexperienced in the techniques of research and had had no academic training, so I had naturally to rely on the specialised staff to obtain the necessary information and to distil from it what had been the real effects of our bombing.

At Essen and Krupps I kept close to the academics in their work because I wanted to understand their methods. Even more I longed to know what effects the huge and costly effort of which I had been a small part had really had on the ultimate defeat of Germany.

At first the maze of figures seemed so complex that I began to despair of producing any of the tangible answers we needed. But after a week or so of hard slogging some definite indications began to appear and by the end of our stay in Essen we were able to produce a pretty coherent report.

It was clear at once that until the big raids of March 1943 the many attacks on Essen and Krupps had had no more than a minor nuisance effect and there had been no appreciable loss of production. This was no surprise. We knew that the thousand-bomber raid aimed at Essen in 1942 had been a failure and that realistically little or nothing had been achieved in attacks on Ruhr targets until the coming of three crucial developments.

The introduction of the Oboe marking system which gave very considerable accuracy on Ruhr targets, the formation of the Pathfinder Force and the availability in increasing numbers of really heavy bombers came together in March 1943 to make possible for the first time attacks on a scale and with accuracy enough to have serious effect. Oboe range was relatively short but the system covered all Ruhr and Rhineland targets.

The attacks which began in March 1943 became known as the Battle of the Ruhr and, including heavy raids on the Rhineland towns Cologne and Düsseldorf, that battle continued until the end of July. During that time there were two major raids on Essen/Krupps in March, two in April and one each in May and July. In making our assessment of this phase of the Bomber war we included attacks in March and April 1944, one in each month, because we took as our timescale the period of intense operations against German targets which concluded with the order to Bomber Command in April 1944 to switch to preparation for the coming invasion of Normandy.

In this period, March 1943-April 1944 we discovered a loss of about twenty per cent of total production at Krupps, far below what we had been led to expect by British Intelligence at the time. Had the reduction been in the really important areas of production, even that figure might have given us some satisfaction, but there were qualifying factors. It was not within our function to emphasise these in our report but, in discussion amongst ourselves, we could not fail to realise that the overall statistics did not tell the whole story.

The Krupps locomotive shop, the largest in Germany, produced nothing at all after the raid of 5th/6th March 1943. The same applied to the important department which produced fuses, key component of all bombs, shells and other explosives. In addition, no more large shells were produced at Krupps after July 1943. The abandonment of production in these three departments and a switch away from non-essential goods such as had been done in Britain two years before, would account for nearly all the total loss of production.

My first instinct on seeing the ruins of these three shops had been that this was a win for Bomber Command. No more railway engines from Krupps, no more fuses, no more heavy shells. But a little thought qualified that assessment. When Herr Singer wept for the citizens of Asia, Africa and South America bereft of Krupps locomotives, these were crocodile tears. It would have been impossible for Germany to export such items through the British blockade. With the production of factories in the occupied territories available to the conquering Nazis, locomotives were not going to be a shortage in Germany. The Nazis may even have been pleased to shut down Krupps loco shop and use the skilled labour elsewhere.

As for shells and fuses we knew from British experience that, vital as these items were, their manufacture was not a matter of specialised heavy plant and could be started and carried on at many locations at relatively short notice. It was most unlikely that the production of these two shops could not be more than made up elsewhere. There had been virtually no shift-working in Germany before 1943, and its introduction represented a huge potential available to replace lost production. Again, it may have been seen as preferable at Krupps that these shops should be abandoned and the labour thus freed used in repairing and reinforcing other shops. We found that the production of guns and turrets had been temporarily affected by raids but soon recovered and, thereafter, increased and went on increasing. The production of tank hulls continued to increase until late in 1944.

All-in-all, our researches at Essen were for me a truly melancholy calendar of discovery. The appalling devastation I saw all around me in the town and in Krupps itself had seemed to presage that Essen, probably the most formidable and important enemy which Bomber Command had challenged in its long and arduous war, had been defeated. Well, so it had, in the end. But that end had not come until March 1945 when the greater war had already been virtually won by other means. In the crucial period up to the autumn of 1944, by which time the defeat of Germany was not in real doubt, Essen and its great factory of Krupps had continued to make a contribution to the German war effort which, although it was made in hardship and with difficulty, was not substantially reduced. I had to face the fact that no German unit had gone short of the essentials for making war because of our efforts to destroy Essen and Krupps.

While these largely statistical facts were emerging from the mass of figures with which our researchers had been confronted, we also got a good deal of information from the harassed town authorities about the general effects of bombing on Essen. They told me that no less than eighty-eight per cent of the dwelling units in the town had been either destroyed or badly damaged. They could not tell accurately the number of casualties but said that between five and seven thousand people, including women and children, had been killed and somewhere between eleven and fifteen thousand seriously injured. Very great damage had been done to buildings and property by fire during the first phase, but living conditions in 1943 and until the autumn of 1944 were, through improvisation and the use of the ubiquitous cellars, difficult but not impossible. The high-explosive raids in late 1944 and early 1945 were the cause of most of the casualties, and with the reinforcement by large numbers of low-paid workers from the occupied territories, there had been no shortage of labour while the factory was working.

We had expected that there would have been major effects on production in big towns like Essen through disruption of utilities, electricity, telephones, water, gas and transport. We had not thought it likely that such effects would have been serious before March 1943, but it was surprising and disconcerting to be told that even thereafter such troubles had been "combatted fairly easily". Throughout 1943 and most of 1944 there had never been any serious breakdown in distribution, transport or essential services. Most foods were rationed, but the ration was always met and there was no serious shortage of food until towards the end of the war.

From 23rd October 1944 until the end of the bombing campaign the weight of bombs aimed at Essen was twice that of the whole of the previous five years of war. In this phase the bomb loads were predominantly of medium cased high explosives, whereas in the Battle of the Ruhr four thousand pound blast bombs had been used in conjunction with huge quantities of incendiaries. In the last phase, production at Krupps dropped by sixty per cent and stopped altogether in March 1945. Of the total casualties, sixty per cent were suffered after September 1944. From then on, general maintenance of all services had begun to crack. The important river and canal system was seriously affected; gas often stopped; and water and electricity were very intermittent. Road and rail transport gradually declined in efficiency until by March 1945 they were virtually non-existent. Attacks by fighter-bombers had been most effective on roads and railways.

I made careful enquiries about whether casualties and the enormous damage to property had affected morale or the performance of workers in industry. Answers to such questions were met with a certain amount of equivocation, largely I think, because all Germans at the time were at pains to distance themselves from close association with the Nazi Party. With some reading between the lines, I concluded that morale had remained unaffected and had even improved until the end of 1944. Even then it had been stimulated by the intense campaign mounted to emphasise the allied policy of unconditional surrender. Propaganda was able to convince the mass of people of the appalling consequences which would befall the German people if they were defeated. This had been materially helped by knowledge of the "Morgenthau Plan" for prohibiting nearly all industry in Germany and reducing the country to an almost totally agricultural economy. This Plan, although never agreed by the Western Allies, became known after the Quebec Summit meeting in September 1944. By emphasising the horrors that awaited the German people in the event of defeat, Goebbels was able to make very effective propaganda out of the supposed intent of the Allies to implement Morgenthau.

The well-informed Germans we interviewed, almost without exception, said that the workforce was very determined, had faith in the Government and were prepared to accept the increasingly severe conditions of their lives. Fourteen days leave was normally given to a head of household whose home was destroyed, time for him to make arrangements for his family or dependents. This was more than had been normal in Britain and I was told that in Germany the allowance was seldom accepted in full and almost never exceeded. This had also been the experience in England during the times of heavy bombing by the Luftwaffe.

I left Essen in a state of deep depression. It seemed that all that had been done in the long and often terrible summer of 1943 had been in vain. All the agonies and casualties, the numbers of the dead and missing aircrew, the huge war effort in providing us with aircraft and high technology aids to find our targets and protect us from the strong and determined defences, the long hours and uncomfortable lives of the devoted men and women of Bomber Command who backed us and believed in us, the civilian men, women and children we had killed in Germany by our rain of bombs, all this had been for nothing.

When we had finished our reports on the Ruhr area we were to go to Hamburg to investigate what had happened there, particularly in the great attacks of July/August 1943. With a day to spare before we left Essen, I decided to visit the famous Mohne Dam, target of possibly the greatest individual feat of bombing in the war. Under Guy Gibson, 617 Squadron were training at Scampton when I was first posted to 49 Squadron at Fiskerton, a satellite aerodrome of Scampton. I knew Gibson and others of the crews of 617 but, although it was not difficult to guess that a special operation was being planned, security was so tight that even I knew nothing of their epic mission until it was completed.

The attack took place in the second moon period after my arrival in Lincolnshire in 1943. On that 16th May, main force squadrons were stood down and I was taking a girl out to dinner at a pub not far from Scampton when we saw 617 aircraft taking off. It was a fine clear evening and I could truthfully tell my companion that I thought they were merely continuing the training they had been doing for some weeks. By the morning we knew differently.

When, with Paul Maze and three or four others of the unit, I reached the Mohne Lake the dam itself had been repaired, the new material showing up as a great "V" in the concrete where the massive structure had been breached. The level of the lake was still low, barely half the normal height, the line of which was clearly visible on the elegantly curved structure which held back the huge volume of water.

The day was hot so, leaving the cars under guard, I decided to take our picnic lunch to a clearing which I had seen in a wood from which we could look down on the still waters of the lake. I followed a well-worn path towards the place, which was perhaps a hundred feet above the level of the top of the dam.

I was leading the way as we climbed through the wood and I remember giving an involuntary cry at the sight which greeted me as I turned the last corner into the clearing. In the centre of the open space stood a large-calibre machine gun. It was pointing towards the lake, fully loaded with a long belt of live ammunition hanging down beside it. Large quantities of used cartridge cases were strewn about the ground all over the little clearing.

I hadn't thought of this being a gun position but of course it was a perfect place for firing at low-flying aircraft attacking the dam. The Barnes Wallis concept of the bouncing bomb which was used was entirely new and I'm sure the Germans were quite unprepared for it, but I suppose they had guarded against the fairly remote possibility of attack by torpedo bombers. No normal torpedoes, even in large numbers, would conceivably have broken the massive dam.

But German guns were no longer loaded and their empty cartridge cases had been cleared away so it was a shock to find this survivor standing unmanned but still ready to fire. I supposed that the crew must have abandoned their position when the dam was broken or perhaps one or more had been wounded by Gibson's gunners and the rest had fled. With the lake emptied, the power station wrecked and the whole area in chaos, no one had thought of recovering the gun and there it stood just as it had been when it had been abandoned during the night of 16th May 1943.

Full accounts of the Dams operation had not then been published but I knew something of the details since I knew most of the pilots and 617 Squadron had been under my command at Woodhall Spa. Looking at the dam from where I sat eating my unappetising sandwiches with the silent gun at my elbow, I could not help reconstructing the incredible scene of that moonlit night two years before as it might have appeared to the German who had manned the gun.

All gunners would have been alerted and ready for action before Guy Gibson started the first bombing run. They would not have seen him and hardly heard his engines as he settled his aircraft to its operational height over the lake but out of sight of the dam. Then as he turned into the straight for a run of about two miles all must have heard his engines and clutched their triggers. This would probably have been the first time they had fired at an enemy aircraft. I could imagine their astonishment when Gibson turned on the two small searchlights which, intersecting at the surface of the water, gave him the exact height of sixty feet, very low, actually below our gun position. The gunner would first have seen these two intersecting lights, then at a range of perhaps a mile, he might have begun to pick out the shape of the Lancaster. From where I was and he had been, it seemed at first impossible that he could have failed to hit the vulnerable aircraft as it flew straight and level towards the dam. But Gibson said that on his bombing run he was not hit.

Then I thought again from the gunners viewpoint. Two hundred and forty miles per hour, one mile in fifteen seconds, more than a hundred yards in a single second. A heavy machine gun which he had to depress, an angle he was almost certainly unused to. Only about three seconds to aim and fire with the deflection, vital factor in all shooting, changing from nil to full in those three seconds, Verey lights hanging over the lake diverting his attention for a moment, perhaps for one of those three seconds. All in all, it wasn't so surprising that he missed. I imagined him cursing himself as the Lancaster vanished over the dam and he heard the dull explosion of the mine deep down against the dam and saw the spray rising high in the air and the surface of the water agitated as if in a storm in the moonlight.

Then the waiting. He would have heard the aircraft still around, wondering why they didn't attack, not knowing that they needed a calm surface to aim. They had to wait, not pleasant over enemy territory. But then they came. The gunners got the second

one, putting his Lancaster on fire before he could aim so that he
pulled up and crashed beyond the dam and his mine produced a
huge explosion near the power station. Was it this gun that got
him, I wondered. But with the next attack and the next and the
next there were in each case two aircraft flying not far apart,
guns blazing, tracer for tracer, Verey lights above, the
converging searchlights below. And each time only those three
seconds to get their target. And then, after the fifth attack, a
ghastly rumbling noise and, when the spray cleared, a great crack
in the dam, widening, widening, until a huge wall of water was
rushing, swirling, through. Did our gunner see this or had he
been disabled or killed by the counter-fire? The abandoned gun
and the empty cartridge cases could not tell us the story of their
single night of action. Only the great V of new construction on
the dam wall and the still low level of the dam remained to
remind of that desperate night's work.

We had brought beer as well as wine with our sandwiches but
the picnic was less than hilarious. I doubt if anyone except a
Lancaster pilot who had seen the engagement from the angle of
the defences could really appreciate the immensity of the heroism
of those who carried out the famous raid. Nearly half the aircraft
which attacked that night did not come back and all who did not
come back were killed.

After our sombre lunch I stood below the huge structure on
the dry side and imagined the terrifying moment when it first
cracked and the first waters seeped through to become within
seconds a raging torrent.

Then we motored down the Ruhr valley, following the route
the floods had taken. Charmed by Paul Maze's fluent German,
people who had seen and survived what they called the
catastrophe, willingly described the horrors of that night when
houses and farm buildings, cars and machinery had been engulfed
and destroyed. People and animals were carried helplessly along,
some already dead, others to be hurled to death against anything
solid the torrent encountered. Marks of the depredations were
everywhere still; trees uprooted, makeshift pylons, improvised
bridges, roads reduced to cart-tracks. We were shown marks of

the heights to which the water had risen and local inhabitants, not in the least unfriendly, were ready and even pleased to tell us of their terrifying experiences. We returned, silent and depressed, to pack up and prepare for our move to Hamburg.

Towards the end of our time in Essen my administrative officer had reported that his requests for accommodation for the unit in Hamburg were being treated as frivolous. "There was," he said, "an undercurrent of "your lot were responsible for this mess so why the hell should you live here in comfort?" Eventually, I had to go personally to the Military Governor, of whom a less military figure it would be hard to imagine. By the standards of that time he was a strong Germanophile, having a good command of the language and much regard for his German co-operators in the struggle to revive the ruined city. The more belligerent among the British, mostly non-combatants who could not restrain the temptation to act the conquerors, were in the habit of referring to him as the under-burgomeister of Hamburg since they believed, wrongly, that he was unduly influenced by the chief German official, the Oberburgomeister. In fact, Dr Dunlop's exemplary tenure at Hamburg was rightly rewarded by a knighthood.

When I explained our circumstances he was most co-operative and by 24th July, the second anniversary of the first of the attacks which razed much of the city in 1943, my unit was installed in a fine house standing in its own grounds in Blankenese, a fashionable suburb which was relatively un-damaged. My bedroom was a beautifully proportioned and well-furnished room which had been occupied by a prominent Nazi. The fine windows gave a splendid view through a gap in the trees to the Elbe estuary and on the evening when I moved in I could see the lights and hear the siren of a large steamer moving slowly up-river towards the port. I reflected that it would have been about the time when, two years before, other sirens would have been giving the first raid warning.

It was in Hamburg that I was given first-hand accounts of the dreadful effects of a firestorm. We knew that enormous concentrations of fire were kindled by the raids of 1943 and particularly so in Hamburg, but if the full story was known to Intelligence at the time it was not communicated to the operational squadrons nor to the media. I had thought of what I had seen on the night of 24th July as a city fire on a big scale, greater than usual because of more accurate bombing due to the disorganisation of the defences by the first use of "window".

What had actually happened in Hamburg, and this I was told by a number of people who had been there at the time, was that hundreds, if not thousands, of fires were started simultaneously. The fire-fighting organisation, unable to work properly because of the big blast bombs mixed in with the thousands of incendiaries, was completely swamped. As the fires developed, enormous heat was generated, estimated at between 600 and 1,000 degrees Centigrade. This caused huge volumes of air to rise rapidly, setting up a giant bellows effect in which air from outside was sucked into the holocaust with such violence that hurricane force winds of more than one hundred miles per hour were recorded.

The ferocity of the fires was redoubled by the strength of the winds which broke windows and doors so that the flames gutted every house. Whole trees of two or three feet diameter were uprooted and hurled along streets in company with blazing beams and even helpless men and women. The tarmac underfoot melted and houses collapsed on every side. The predicament of those who had taken refuge in cellars or even air raid shelters in the middle of such a ghastly conflagration is hardly imaginable. I was repeatedly told of the strange sound, comparable to the roar of Niagara Falls, which was heard even above the crashes of bombs and falling masonry. This was the sound of the terrible hurricane which blazed through the streets to kindle and re-kindle fires fiercer than any man-made furnace.

When shelters were eventually dug out of the debris and opened up, almost no bodies were found but just little piles of charred ashes or small pools of glutinous liquid. In the streets the shapes of unrecognisable corpses were found glued to the tarmac, and men and women were crushed by falling roofs, scalded to death by boiling water from bursting pipes or incinerated after a more merciful death by asphyxiation or carbon monoxide poisoning.

As I heard these harrowing descriptions from individuals or read them in documents, I could not help thinking back to the calm atmosphere of flight planning in my operations room at the time of the Hamburg battle. I remembered that the operation order had told us that the "intention" was "to destroy an enemy city". We may not have known at the time exactly what that had meant but we certainly carried out our orders.

In the fourth raid on Hamburg I had flown into a huge thundercloud, the largest, dirtiest and most turbulent I had ever known. I knew at the time that this was no ordinary storm but I did not know that it was the result of an uprush of filthy smoke-laden air, heated by the gigantic fires which had raged in the city for three days. I was told that this storm, which had so alarmed me at twenty thousand feet, had poured down on the town an enormous quantity of dirty water, covering everyone and everything with black, oily filth. It apparently extinguished some of the still smouldering fires, but many would have preferred the fires.

After two years the whole district of Wansbek, one of the most thickly populated areas in the city, was still barricaded off and sealed even against those who hoped to find evidence of missing friends and relations. It had simply not been possible to find the resources for the effort needed to clear the rubble or to dig for the corpses which were known to be buried there. The number of casualties in Hamburg was never accurately known but it was generally believed that it was about fifty thousand killed and probably about the same number injured, many seriously. The plight of the survivors, injured or not, was appalling, since the hospitals were destroyed and food and medical supplies had to be improvised from elsewhere with local transport at a standstill.

The city had been virtually evacuated after the second attack but this was done without plan or resources. It was not so much an evacuation as a panic: people fleeing from the city without regard to their possessions or destination, with no purpose but to get away from the burning ruins. Apparently, most of those who had fled returned after a few weeks to resume their shattered lives as the city struggled bravely to revive.

In Hamburg more than a quarter of a million dwellings were totally destroyed, yet I was told that most of the dispossessed who made their way back had found somewhere to shelter. We were even more surprised than we had been in the Ruhr at the degree and speed with which some kind of partial recovery from these enormous disasters was effected and Speer himself admitted that, in warning Hitler of the likely effects of further such raids, he had underestimated the power of a determined people to recover. Remembering the proud patience with which Londoners survived their ordeal in 1940-41, I well understood the strong local patriotism of the Hamburgers under equal stress. Because of traditions inherited from Hanseatic League times, and of being Germany's premier international port with strong ties abroad, not least with England, many of those with whom I talked made a point of the internationalism of their city and of its culture and outlook. They claimed that Hamburg had always been less in thrall to the Nazis than the rest of Germany. Hitler, I was often told, never visited Hamburg if he could help it and his appearances there had been minimal throughout the era of Nazi power.

The cynical view of my Düsseldorf friend that "there are no Nazis now" was often in my thoughts in the many interviews I had with German business people and I was tempted to view this attitude among Hamburgers as just another ploy to distance themselves from war guilt. In retrospect I do believe there was substance in their boasts.

Albert Speer, who at the end of the war, as Germany's Minister for Armaments and Munitions, had almost total control over the production of war material and its allocation to the services, was often quoted as having said, and having told Hitler, that if six of the largest cities in Germany had been subjected to the same scale of disaster as Hamburg it would have been impossible to continue to prosecute the war.

That testimony is not negligible but Speer, like most Germans at the time, was addicted to giving the answers which he thought would either best please his interrogators or place himself in the most favourable light with the Allies. There were enough contradictions in his depositions to justify doubts about his reliability. He was in the custody of the US authorities with whom he enjoyed a period of interrogation and discussion which he subsequently described as "our university of bombing". In this he expressed his fervent belief that US bombing had been the chief danger to his production schedules. Interrogated by the British, however, he reiterated his belief that Germany would have surrendered if subjected to further attacks on the Hamburg scale. He did admit, however, that he had grossly underestimated the possibilities of recovery from even the fiercest disaster, an error which he shared with British Intelligence. We found, contrary to what we had been told during the war, that many Hamburg firms were working again, not with full efficiency but working, by October 1943.

I suspected Speer of hopes that he could manage to represent himself as having turned so totally against Hitler that he might escape being tried as a major war criminal. An idle hope since he could not possibly conceal his major part in the ruthless procurement and use of the forced labour imported from the occupied territories. I suspected that he even had ideas of being given a substantial job under the Western Allies in the rehabilitation of Germany. There were certainly enough contradictions in his various depositions to justify my doubts about his reliability.

After a few weeks in Hamburg I could not help being struck by the differing attitudes of my compatriots towards the Germans who had been their enemies and for whom, in various ways, they were now responsible. Some, as I have commented above, were still activated by the spirit of the war. They almost believed in the old saw that the only good German was a dead German. Field-Marshal Montgomery had promulgated, no doubt with the approval of the British Government, a strict order against any form of "fraternisation" with the ex-enemy and there was at first a good deal of support for the French and Russian view that the Germans should somehow be "made to pay for the war". Looking around it was difficult to see how this idea could be translated into any practical policy. The immediate problem was to keep a maximum of Germans alive while providing reasonable justice for their one-time victims. The rations available were below the normal subsistence level.

A section of the British employed in Germany were at first even inclined to regret that the Morgenthau Plan, for de-industrialising Germany and maintaining it indefinitely as an agricultural country, had been scrapped. The unfortunate leaking of this plan from the 1944 Quebec Conference at which Roosevelt and Churchill had seemed to give it a very guarded and qualified approval, had been pounced on by Goebbels and widely publicised in Germany. Nothing could have been more effective in encouraging resistance to the bitter end. The plan was never Allied policy, but knowledge of its existence certainly lengthened the duration of the fighting and cost many lives. The later area attacks by Bomber Command, especially that on Dresden, were convincingly held up by German propaganda as proof of Allied intentions to implement Morgenthau after unconditional surrender. No German patriot could have wished to surrender on these terms.

It is fair to say that no appreciable section of the British would have wanted to impose such a peace but there was a body of opinion which could not yet approve any friendly feelings towards the former enemy and believed that the occupation should not flinch from its task of de-Nazification, punishment of offenders and the prevention of any possibility of German power ever again being able to impose its will on Europe.

In gradually mounting opposition to these sentiments within the British occupation authorities stood the "builders-up", those who thought the ordinary German not a bad chap at heart and "more like us than the French". In spite of the strictness of the orders against fraternisation in any form, which forbade any communication or contact with Germans except at a strictly official level, surreptitious evasion of the order rapidly increased.

A bored soldier with little to do was unlikely not to be tempted by German girls and many of the girls, confronted with a shortage of young German males, were not unnaturally complaisant. Control Commission officials at all levels found it hard to resist the temptation to take advantage of the privileges of their position. In their laudable efforts to learn the language the "long haired dictionary" became a commonplace. There sprang up a flourishing black market in cigarettes, coffee and petrol coupons which helped Germans to evade regulations, obtain petrol and extra rations and revive the economy in their own free market way. It also enabled many of the British, not naturally dishonest, to achieve a lifestyle beyond the wildest dreams of those who would otherwise have been enduring the austerities of post-war Britain.

The increase in direct contacts led to the widespread acceptance of the view, assiduously if often unconsciously promulgated by Germans, that the Nazis had been a small clique who had managed by trickery to obtain power over the unwilling German nation. With a gigantic effort of wishful thinking, many Germans were able to believe that this relatively small number of active Nazis had been solely responsible for the atrocities in the occupied territories, for the employment of forced labour dragged from home to work in factories as virtual slaves, for the horrors of concentration camps and for the persecution and "final solution" applied to the Jews. It was apparently not difficult for them to make a mental transition from not having been actively involved in the worst of the horrors now revealed, to taking a position of not having had the slightest inkling that such things had gone on at all. Long exposure to the continual propaganda and genuine resentment against the Versailles Treaty made it easier for people to think it unfair of the Allies to hold the German people as a whole responsible either for the war or for the crimes of the Nazis.

In the British Occupation Zone there was much subtle flattery of the British as having been the only Europeans who had held out in 1940. The attitude to the Americans was often faintly derogatory. There was no overt criticism but it was implied that they were a less civilised and, therefore, less congenial nation to the equally civilised Germans than were the British. When later I spent some time in the American Zone of Occupation I was conscious of the opposite technique. The elevation of the French to a place of equality among the victors was regarded as a joke and was a favourite subject for gibes by the political humorists so popular in German night life, which, in all the misery of the immediate post-war years, never disappeared.

I was, of course, responsible for enforcing the unpopular "no fraternisation" order within my own unit, but as long as matters were not brought before me officially I took no action, although I observed the ban myself. My batman, a Southern Irishman who had been with me since 1942, was something of a character and, like many servicemen in Germany, he did not approve of Field-Marshal Montgomery's edict. I knew quite well that he had acquired a German girl friend but it was only when this behaviour was brought to my notice officially that I had to pull him up about it.

When I had him on the mat, he looked me straight in the face through the very strong spectacles which gave him a deceptive appearance of owl-like solemnity, and pointed out that he was a national of a neutral country and, while he was willing to fight for England when there was a war on, he didn't see why he should be denied his harmless pleasures when the war was over. His fighting had consisted of getting me my breakfast, making my bed, keeping my clothes clean and generally making me as comfortable as was practicable. However, I saw the force of his argument and laughed so much that my formal reprimand was as about as insincere as his promise to desist from his illegal practices.

I obeyed the order from my own preference, having no immediate urge or requirement to do otherwise. Of where I stood in principle I was unsure. I had a long history of suspicion and dislike of Germany and the Germans, stemming originally from the childish knowledge that they had killed my father. I knew there was no rationale in this, and I had long ceased to blame them for that specific action. I had realised before I was grown-up that for a submarine to sink a surface warship was a legitimate act of war, whereas when I was a child the grown-ups had managed to make me believe that my father's death had been the result of some sort of dastardly and cowardly conspiracy amounting to the murder of a blameless, even saintly, man. The gradual fading of such ridiculous notions did not ever, I think, totally erase the effect they had once had on my immature thoughts. Subconsciously the Germans were always the baddies in my mind and, as I had watched the progress of Hitler between the wars, I had little reason to think otherwise. In my fairly confused thinking in Hamburg in 1945 I had to add to the cynicism of "there are no Nazis now", the story of the German businessman who was asked what he would do if the Germans lost the war. Three times he replied that it was impossible that Germany should lose. Pressed to answer on a purely hypothetical basis he thought for a moment and replied, "I shall organise sympathy." I felt that he was not alone.

I had a strong distaste for being taken for a ride. I felt strongly about German guilt, and that meant the guilt of all Germans, not only for the war but for the crimes, the crimes against the Jews, the forced labour, the indiscriminate submarine war, the cruelty of their conquests, the indiscriminate attacks of the V1 pilotless aircraft and the V2 long-range rockets.

German guilt, yes. But what about my own?

Whatever I thought about that I was clear in my mind that Germany would have to be resuscitated and brought back into the company of nations. But in 1945 I thought yes, but not yet, not quite yet. There is too much stench of evil around, the stench of a whole nation which, if it did not commit, certainly connived at ghastly crimes. And enjoyed the spoils and proceeds and admired to little short of worship the man from whom the fleeting greatness of 1940-42 had sprung. All this could not be dissipated in a day.

When the work-plan for Hamburg was going satisfactorily forward I went to stay for a couple of days with the RAF at Celle, which had been a Luftwaffe fighter station. The buildings there were far better than existed at any RAF station in England

and the Officers' Mess was positively luxurious. There was a courtyard about forty feet square in which you couldn't see the floor for empty champagne bottles. The few full ones that had been left had not long survived but the cellar was otherwise well-stocked and the prices were frighteningly low. The Group Captain commanding, who was named Anderson, was especially addicted to an excellent Apricot Brandy which he pressed on all and sundry, especially me. I retain very pleasant, if somewhat hazy, memories of having christened him, much to the delight of his juniors, "Apricot Andy".

While I was at Celle I visited Hanover, which had been the target of two unsuccessful attacks in September 1943, in each of which a heavyweight of bombs fell just outside the city, no doubt making a lot of noise but doing little damage. I could imagine the state of mind of the citizens having twice escaped by a whisker and so knowing their town was high on the bombers' priority list. They would by then know of the disaster which had befallen Hamburg and be sure of the fate which awaited them. Sure enough, within a fortnight their sirens sounded again and this time there was no mistake . . .

I was astonished at the size and grandeur of the almost undamaged Palace of Herrenhausen, home of the Electors whose line inherited the British Crown. It must have seemed odd to our George I that none of his palaces in rich and powerful England exceeded in grandeur that in his relatively small and poor Electorate in Germany.

Not far from Celle was the notorious concentration camp of Belsen and, although there was a general ban on visitors, I was prevailed upon to go there with a special pass and get something of the whole fearful story at first hand.

My visit was some twelve weeks after the 12th April, the day when a German commander approached the British Army Commander in the area with a request for a truce so that fighting could be avoided around the Belsen camp. The truce was granted by the British authorities who were told that there were about fifty thousand men and women interned there: yes fifty thousand, of whom nearly all were virtually starving and many were dying of typhus. The camp was controlled by the SS, together with a body of Hungarian guards and a unit of the Wehrmacht. These were all to remain in position until the British had taken over when the Wehrmacht unit only would be returned to Germany.

The task, which the British Army had no choice but to accept, must have been one of the most horrendous ever undertaken by a military formation. Conditions were far worse than anyone could have imagined. There was no electricity, water or food and all the diseases associated with famine were raging. Most of the prisoners who were still alive were suffering from either typhus, typhoid, T.B. or gastro-enteritis. There were about ten thousand, yes ten thousand, typhus infected corpses lying unburied, many in an advanced state of decomposition. The daily death rate was said to be four to five hundred. There were no sanitary arrangements whatever, and the ground both inside and outside the huts, in which people lay three to a bed, was described as an "almost continuous carpet of human bodies, excreta, rags and filth". Cooking facilities were totally inadequate and the only containers for the swede soup which, with a morsel of bread constituted the sole daily ration, were some old dustbins.

Belsen had been a *Krankenlager*, a Sick Camp, to which men, women and children were sent when the Nazis wished to dispose of them because they could not work, were Jewish or were otherwise unacceptable to some Nazi official. The avowed purpose of the camp had been to dispose of the inmates. Virtually no-one ever left Belsen alive and the Army found no-one there who had survived more than eight months, the average span being about three or four. There were no artificial means of extermination; starvation and disease being the executioners. The register showed that seventeen thousand had died in March and that the average death rate had been about fifteen thousand a month. Many of the inmates could not move from their beds or the floor of their huts or even feed themselves. They had been reduced to the level of beasts and when food was brought to them they fought like wolves to get a mouthful.

The death rate had been accelerated by a daily roll-call at 03.00 hours whatever the weather. This often lasted six hours or more and was accompanied by beatings and flogging at the slightest provocation. Indiscriminate shooting was not uncommon.

This is not the place to analyse or extol the heroic work of the British units who managed in an incredibly short time to get the dead buried, the huts burnt, the survivors revived and deloused and some sort of order restored. When I was there it was still common to see inmates scrabbling in dustbins because they could not believe they would be fed again the next day. The SS guards had been put to work on burying the decomposing dead and on cleaning up the worst of the filth. If they objected to these jobs or to having to wait upon their erstwhile prisoners, it was not surprising that they were not always treated with exemplary kindness.

At first I was almost unable to believe that the horrors of Belsen had been intentionally inflicted. I wondered whether the starvation might not have been due to the difficulty of getting rations in what was already nearly a battle area. But no, that was simply not the case. The daily ration for months before the end had been three pints of swede soup per person and three or four ounces of bread. The photographs I was shown haunted me day and night for months: the piles of emaciated bodies thrown naked into ditches, one on top of another; the filthy huts, with three sleeping in each bed and the rest on the floor with excreta as pillow. When a band of German burgomeisters from towns in the British Zone were forced to see what had been perpetrated several were physically ill and others fainted. Belsen, I knew and they knew, was only one of many concentration camps established all over Germany and in Poland.

I went back to Hamburg thinking deeply, unable to get the pictures of Belsen out of my mind. I, like most Englishmen, had had enough of war and blood and hatred, but I devoutly hoped that Kramer, the Kommandant of Belsen, his female assistant who had the idea of making lampshades from human skin, and all their close associates, would be executed by hanging, which indeed they were.

After Belsen I could not help taking a fresh mental look at the frame of mind which was epitomised in the title (but not actually in the lyric) of Noel Coward's famous song, *Don't lets be beastly to the Germans*. I admit it became much less attractive. The more I thought about it, and willy-nilly I could not stop thinking about it, the more I felt that the magnanimous attitude of "giving the benefit of the doubt", the acceptance that the majority of Germans had neither known of nor connived in Nazi tyranny and brutality, simply would not bear examination.

There were at least twenty or thirty major concentration camps, including those in Austria and Poland, so the number of persons directly employed in the guarding, supervision and execution of prisoners must have been very considerable. Each of these had a circle of friends, acquaintances and relations, through some of whom at least some information must have penetrated outwards. To fill the camps many thousands of trains must have run, conveying Jews and other sufferers in horrible squalor to their fate. Large numbers must have seen such trains, or known railwaymen who worked them. Did none of these tell what they had seen? It was simply not credible that inhabitants of Celle and neighbouring villages had no inkling of what went on at Belsen. I arrived back at Hamburg in a very chastened and thoughtful frame of mind.

As we came towards the end of our investigations into what had happened in Hamburg, two unforeseen events changed our situation. The first was that I heard that the Air Staff had belatedly realised that they were no longer bound by Mr Churchill's refusal to allow a full scale investigation into the results of bombing. The Air Ministry now believed that an assessment of what had or had not been achieved by the bombing offensive would be a vital factor in the planning of the role of the Royal Air Force of the future and, with the approval of the new Government, a full-scale unit had been formed to investigate and report. The second was the use of atomic bombs against Hiroshima and Nagasaki and the abrupt end of the war with Japan.

The official British Bombing Survey Unit arrived in Germany and started work with a brief similar to ours. It was commanded by an officer senior to me and had far greater resources of men and equipment. Their results, with the backing of the Air Ministry, would obviously be the main source of information for future historians who would tell the tale of the war and for the strategists and planners who would need to understand the past in order to mark out a course for the future.

This immediately made the work of my unit, improvised on a shoestring by Bomber Command, look redundant. The new unit made it clear that they were not interested in our results, preferring to work from a blank page, asking their own questions and taking sole responsibility for conclusions. I could see that this was a natural enough decision, but I warned my counterpart of one snag he would have to contend with.

This was that the attitude of the Germans, from whom all information had to be obtained, had already changed from complete and willing co-operation to a certain reluctance to take part in an exercise which, to them, was a waste of time. I knew that their initial keenness to give us all possible information had been part of a general urge to mollify their conquerors at all costs while they were unsure of what the policy of the Occupation would be. Their one aim, then, had been to get started again and for that they were wholly dependent on the goodwill of the Allies. We had been able at first to take advantage of that goodwill in our search for information.

However, it was already clear that there was a widening rift between the Soviet Union and the West and that Britain and the United States were agreed that both should take an active and positive part in reviving Germany. In only a very few corners of the economy were they holding back the process, and the Germans were naturally more and more inclined to get on with the job on their own terms. These did not include spending the valuable time of key personnel in digging up a past they would rather forget or in preserving documents which no longer had any value to them. Especially it did not include filling up the elaborate questionnaires which were the basis of most investigations. The word *frageboden* had become something of a sick joke, and to produce one to a senior German industrialist or public man was now to invite openly sarcastic laughter. Although you did not get outright refusal to complete your *frageboden*, it would not now be done willingly, quickly or even necessarily accurately.

The second factor, the use against Japan of the atomic weapon, many thousand times more powerful than the biggest bomb a Lancaster could carry, was making it look likely that all previous bombing strategy and tactics had been rendered obsolete. In particular the type of bombing in which Bomber Command had specialised and the results of which we had been investigating, seemed obsolescent if not obsolete.

The combination of these two factors took most of the zest out of the continuing work of my unit and, although we went on with what we were doing, the enthusiasm with which we had originally addressed the task had gone.

I was the senior RAF officer stationed in Hamburg so one of my duties was to represent my unit and the RAF in general at a Thanksgiving Service for the Conclusion of the War held in the requisitioned Garrison Church. The war had not affected my lack of religious faith nor my suspicions of the religious establishment, but as the Service had been officially designated, I obviously had to attend.

My fears about the outbreak of hypocrisy likely to be displayed were well-founded. The clichés which lesser English divines have superimposed on the noble rhetoric of the St. James Bible and Cranmer's Book of Common Prayer were present in their expected profusion. The Service assumed that, notwithstanding setbacks on the way, God had always been on our side. We were, therefore, urged to "pour out our hearts in fervent thanksgiving for all thy loving kindness during the long days of battle", and to "thank thee for the deliverance from the hand of our enemies". We were to remember the "willing sacrifices made in Thy cause", to thank God for His "goodness in granting us victory" and for "hearing our humble petitions" and we asked that he remembered "His servants who laid down their lives for their friends". There was a psalm of praise, some fairly martial hymns and the National Anthem.

It was all quite unemotional and British and in no way caught or stirred the real feelings many of us had at the end of the war. I found myself disturbed by what seemed to me the blatant hypocrisy of the whole thing and I wondered how it affected true believers. Did they really think that a divine power had acted on our side? If so, at what stage did that power decide to intervene? And whose side was it on at the holocausts of Hamburg and Würzburg?

In September I had a short but hilarious leave. I had telephoned my hosts at the fighter base at Celle to accept an invitation to visit them again. On my arrival five or six young officers, all ten or even fifteen years my junior, had no difficulty in persuading me to go with them to a "leave centre" in the South of France. "Mary" Coningham, AOC of the 2nd Tactical Air Force, a master of the art of prising some personal fun out of the dreariness of war, had managed to persuade the American authorities to allot to the Royal Air Force a small hotel in Cannes as a leave centre. The British Government had neither the money nor the inclination to set up such facilities in France.

Before leaving in the inevitable Anson, we had a very festive evening in the Mess during which I was asked what cigarettes I was taking with me. When I said I didn't smoke there were hoots of ribald laughter and it was explained to my innocence that the amount of money we could take wouldn't get us anywhere and cigarettes were the only useful currency. In the morning the batman who packed for me put a large parcel wrapped up in a towel into my suitcase.

The leave centre turned out to be a small hotel opposite the tennis courts behind the Carlton Hotel in Cannes. Before the war my brother and I, in true "Mad Dogs and Englishmen" tradition, had often used those courts after lunch in the broiling August heat when everyone else was having a snoozing siesta.

The Americans had requisitioned the best accommodation from Cannes to Nice as the "United States Riviera Recreation Area", and used their own currency in their hotels and clubs.

French francs were useful but didn't buy you much. The main hotels at Cannes were reserved for American officers, those at Nice for "enlisted men" with the Negresco reserved for NCOs, while the Provençal at Juan-les-Pins was entirely occupied by the feminine element of the US services. I think entry there was fairly closely restricted.

Settled in at Cannes, I went over to Antibes to deliver a parcel which had been entrusted to me to give to Lady Orr-Lewis, an Englishwoman who had spent the war in her large villa there, apparently without excessive hardship. Her son was a pre-war acquaintance whom I had happened to meet at Hamburg. In exchange for giving her a parcel of "goodies", he had suggested that I should use the car he had left there if, of course, it still worked. I had the battery charged and it started up in a flash. It was a fine old Wolseley, big enough to transport all of us around and to include at times some of a bevy of young French girls, very much of the noblesse, to whom Lady Orr-Lewis introduced us. Petrol, of course, was unobtainable unless you had cigarettes or coffee which we had. The French girls, of the Nouailles clan, seemed to prefer us, or at any rate my transport, to the richer Americans, and we had a lot of fun with them.

Bathing was still prohibited as the beaches were still being cleared of mines, mainly by German prisoners. The French, with Gallic charm, had allotted the task of supervision to an array of coal-black Senegalese soldiers. It was fairly clear that the *herrenvolk* did not much appreciate these new masters and a good deal of persuasion was needed to make them exert themselves. Plenty of such persuasion was available.

The Orr-Lewis villa had a splendid bathing place, quite comparable with Eden Roc, which we could use, but high summer had passed and we found the water a bit cold for much swimming.

I liked the French girls and enjoyed practising my rusty French on them since their schools under the Vichy regime had taught German and they had almost no English. They produced a male cousin, apparently very rich and titled, who said that he was going to emigrate to Argentina just as soon as it was practicable since he saw no future in his own country. In reply to my question whether it was not up to him and his like to help in the resuscitation of France, he simply shrugged his shoulders. All he wanted was to get out. He was an unpleasing character although the girls seemed to like him. I wondered later whether perhaps he had been an over-zealous collaborator who might find it convenient to be abroad for a time. I think he was typical of the atmosphere of suspicion and distrust which pervaded France at a time when the scars of defeat and the shame of the collaborators and the Vichy regime were turning son against father and friend against friend. Perhaps, if he did manage to emigrate, his country may have been better off without our aristocratic acquaintance.

When, as my companions had warned me would happen, I ran short of French money, they offered to sell the cigarettes they had provided for me and I gave them the packet wrapped up in a towel. They brought back a wad of notes and a message from the buyer saying, "What did I want for the towel?"

Back in Hamburg, the expected orders to wind up the Unit and return to England soon arrived. It was disappointing not to be able to finish our work a little more tidily. I had been much impressed by the way the three young academics from Bomber Command Operational Research Section had gone about their task, distilling sensible reports out of the enormous masses of material and figures offered them by German thoroughness and passion for records. There was nothing to be ashamed about in what they produced, even if we suspected that some of the figures we had to use might not have been quite as reliable as we would have wished.

Perhaps the most surprising thing our figures told us was how little stretched the German economy had been even as late as 1943. In England, especially after Goering's "guns before butter" speech, the belief had proliferated that the Nazi regime was demanding considerable sacrifices from the German people in peacetime in order to accelerate rearmament. It surely followed that the enormous war effort must have entailed continuous maximum effort and rigid austerity for the long-suffering populace in order to support the huge demands of the armed forces. This had been the case in Britain from 1940, surely with the enormous tasks and wide deployment of German forces it must have been the same in Germany.

I think the basis of the thinking behind the Bomber Command area offensive was based on that assumption. We soon found that such ideas had no foundation whatever and that the further belief, encouraged by propaganda, that these hardships, exacerbated by the blockade, were far greater than what was being experienced in Britain, was just as untrue. The German economy was not stretched before 1943 and the real hardships undergone by the populace, except as a result of the bombing, did not appear until 1944 when the end of the war was already looming.

Our figures told us that, until well after the invasion of Normandy, the Germans had been able to make up for losses in production simply by taking up the considerable slack in the economy, which, until 1943 had operated more or less on peacetime lines. The slave labour force imported from occupied lands made up for its incompetence by its numbers. It was said that Eva Braun, Hitler's mistress, personally intervened when it was suggested that the production of cosmetics should be discontinued. We had no doubt that the Nazi system, far from being the efficient command economy most people in England believed it to be, was inefficient to a degree and riddled with corruption and exploitation on a vast scale.

The de-housing effect, the idea that if houses were destroyed people could not or would not work, had been proclaimed initially by Churchill's intimate friend and adviser, Lord Cherwell and had gained many advocates, not least Sir Arthur Harris and Bennett of the Pathfinders. We could not find any evidence to prove that even the vast scale of de-housing in many of the largest towns had had any direct effects. As in England, a period of leave was given to sufferers to allow them to make arrangements for their families or dependents. As happened in England, many workers and servicemen were back at work before the leave period had expired. No executive interviewed by myself or any of my staff spoke of appreciable loss of production due to absenteeism caused by "de-housing".

In Essen between five and seven thousand people were killed and between eleven and fifteen thousand injured, many seriously. In Hamburg the death-roll was probably fifty thousand and many more were injured but in neither of these towns, heavily damaged as they were, did we hear that casualties among the workforce had any dire effect on output. It was clear that until towards the end of the war, and even with the accelerated call-up of the forces for the Russian front, shortage of labour never became a real bottleneck in essential production.

Although some shops at Krupps, at the Bochumer Verein and at Rheinmetall were put permanently out of action, it seems nearly always to have been possible to transfer functions. There were exceptions but these were little more than isolated instances. On the whole it seems to have been possible to take up the slack within a reasonable time even in such cases as the Hamburg disaster and the breaking of the Mohne Dam which almost totally immobilised Dortmund for a fortnight.

Shift systems were hardly known in Germany until quite late in the war, nor was there before 1943 any substantial reduction in consumer goods nor much employment of women. By using these resources and adding a general increase in efficiency after the replacement of Todt as the Minister responsible for production by Speer, a large increase in production might have been possible.

Our research suggested that the reason this did not happen was partly the result of bombing. But we found no evidence that it would have been possible for the Nazis to use any large increase in weapons even if they had been produced. There was no pool of men of the necessary calibre available to form new fighting regiments, nor was there any indication that the Wehrmacht ever went short of weapons or essential supplies.

Neither I nor my academic staff were going to be able to report to the C-in-C that the terrific effort which had set out to destroy the German ability and will to continue to prosecute the war had achieved that objective. The crippling of German industry which he and others had foreseen as the result of the heavy area raids of 1943 simply did not come about. Our results, which included the towns of Essen, Hamburg and Hanover which were very heavily bombed in that time, suggested that total production at the end of that year was little, if at all, less than it had been at the beginning. Production of some vital items, for instance tanks, had actually increased.

It seemed to me that British Intelligence had been mesmerised by the damage to German towns into extrapolating the huge damage to housing into wild estimates of industrial decline, but it is quite certain that the results we unearthed were a severe disappointment not only to me but to everyone who saw them. The fact that in March 1945 practically all production stopped in a final holocaust did not affect the result of the war which by then was clearly lost to Germany. The head of the Operational Research Section at Bomber Command had been in close touch throughout our mission and was fully in agreement with the findings of the academic staff who worked under his supervision.

Winding up the Bombing Research Unit entailed a good deal of paperwork and a certain amount of conflict with the local bureaucracy. I was content to leave most of this to my young but competent administrative officer. So I took a few days leave at the RAF Leave Centre at Travemunde on the Baltic.

In peacetime this had been a fashionable country club and, in the hands of the Control Commission, offered rest and recreation for the occupying forces. The very moderate golf course had lacked recent maintenance and the prospect of losing your ball in the prevailing long grass was inversely proportional to the supply of balls. You were allowed a ration of, I think, two or three but, as elsewhere in Germany, there was a thriving black market operated in this case by young German boys who had plenty of spare time from their inadequate education facilities. They marked errant drives with great accuracy, pretending to help to look for the missing ball with no intention of recovering it until its owner had given up hope and moved on. The missing ball would then miraculously come to light and be offered to a following player for an outrageous sum, which could be substantially reduced by the exercise of a certain amount of threatening gestures.

I played a bit of golf but spent most of the time walking on the fine springy turf, every bit comparable to the fine English downland which we ploughed up for victory and which will never be the same again. Most days I would take a picnic and a bottle of wine to a place where I could be solitary and from which I could see over the silver grey Baltic to the shore of Mecklenberg. That was in Russian-occupied Germany and, therefore, as far out of bounds to us as if it were still ruled by Hitler. Not twenty miles away and within easy reach of the Kiel Canal, the Soviet Union was deploying power on a scale far beyond anything possible for any combination of European Powers. It was odd to contemplate this huge, secretive, mysterious and possibly hostile power brooding there across the Lübeck Bight and to know that no European power could dare to challenge its might.

Of course there were then no real European Powers in a military sense except for poor, tired, over-stretched Britain with a new and idealistic Labour Government likely to be only too willing to welcome and accept Russian assurances of peace and goodwill on their own terms. It was a sobering thought that came to me across that short stretch of sea: not only had the Americans won the war but now they, and only they, could accept real responsibility for the peace.

However, I wasn't then inclined to do too much worrying about the future. This was the first time I had really relaxed for ages, my wartime leaves having normally been occupied in the pursuit of more active pleasures. Now, for the time, there was nothing that I had to do, not much that I wanted to do and nobody immediately available that I wanted to do it with. There was time to think a bit about myself and come to terms with the past and, to some extent, with the future.

Service people in Germany at that time were much preoccupied with discussion, information and rumours about the forthcoming trials of the surviving Nazi chiefs who were to be indicted as war criminals in a spectacular court case in Nuremberg where so much of the Nazi evil had originated and festered. The lesser criminals were to be tried by military courts in the zones allotted to the occupying powers, now four in number with the French being given responsibility for a relatively small section of western Germany bordering on France.

Having been told that the RAF had at last decided, after extended prevarication, that I was superfluous to their peacetime needs, I had rather lost interest in the spate of documents, orders, records and general bumph which littered the desk of even such a non-mainstream and peripatetic unit as mine. However, in one of my solitary lunch picnics I had taken for light reading a pile of RAF and Control Commission documents overdue to reach the "Out" tray.

When you have been confronted for some years with a considerable bulk of staff-generated verbosity, you acquire, in fact it is necessary to acquire, a special skill in "non-reading". This entails being able to tell, without actually reading a document, letter, minute or order, if it will make any difference whether you read it or not. Without a reasonable development of this skill many an excellent officer has succumbed to mental paralysis brought on by over-exposure to official gobbledegook.

Halfway through my wine, and having put most of the papers aside for discard, I was pulled up sharp by an unobtrusive document headed: "Appendix II. Control Council Law No. 10." "Punishment of Persons Guilty of War Crimes, Crimes against Peace and Crimes against Humanity."

This, I realised, was the formal public document resulting from the determination of the Allies that those most responsible for the horrors of the Nazi regime should not go unpunished. It was one I was not tempted to put in the waste paper basket. Glass of good German wine in hand, I read the first paragraph:

In order to give effect to . . . and in order to establish a uniform basis . . ." and so on and so on . . . "the Control Council enacts as follows . . ."

Well, I thought, well. I wasn't all that sure exactly who the Control Council might be.

Article 1 of about ten lines was an easy victim to my non-reading skill but Article 2 was a good deal more meaningful and

I found myself reading and re-reading it with a curious fascination.

It started with the stark statement that:

> 1. Each of the following acts is recognised as a crime:
>   Crimes against peace. Initiation of invasions of other countries and wars of aggression . . . including but not limited to . . . participation in a common plan or conspiracy for . . . any of the foregoing.

That's all right, I thought. Nothing wrong with any of that. It may seem a bit odd that we have to make up the law first in order to have trials, but clearly in this case there isn't any alternative. Reading the small print I gathered that these formidable provisions weren't to apply to the international gala already taking shape at Nuremberg although the principles there would be the same. This document was to ensure that the smaller fry, who would be tried by each of the four victor countries, would get broadly the same treatment. We were gradually getting used to the concept of France as one of the four victor countries. Uniformity was the crux. I thought if I were a German I'd rather be tried in the British or American Zones than in the Russian or the French. Much the same rules were to be applied to the top brass in the dock at Nuremberg.

The real meat came in the next paragraph:

> War Crimes. Atrocities or offences against persons or property constituting violations of the laws or customs of war, including but not limited to, murder, ill-treatment or deportation to slave labour or for any other purpose, of civilian population from occupied territory, murder or ill-treatment of prisoners of war or persons on the seas, killing of hostages, plunder of public or private property . . .

All right so far, I thought. That describes a lot of German behaviour in the last five years. No doubt about that . . .

I went on to the last sentence in that paragraph. It read (completing the list of war crimes):

> ". . . wanton destruction of cities, towns or villages, or devastation not justified by military necessity."

I refilled my glass pretty thoughtfully before reading on. This was getting a bit near the knuckle. I thought of those dozens of Operation Orders I had read off the teleprinter in the Operations Blocks at Fiskerton, Woodhall Spa and Coningsby. These were couched with standard headings under which were specified all the relevant details of the planned Operation. The vital paragraph "D" laid down the overall intention of the raid. When I joined No. 49 Squadron paragraph "D" had normally specified the "intention" in such terms as "to do maximum damage to an enemy industrial centre", later came " to do maximum damage to an enemy industrial city" or "to do maximum damage to an enemy port". Later, as the strength of Bomber Command increased, the intention would be simply "to destroy an enemy city". I could shut my eyes and see dozens of such operation orders, each one clack-clacking out of the teleprinter to be translated into practice by the squadrons of Bomber Command of which mine was one. Those were our orders, not every night of course but on many nights: to destroy an enemy city.

Suddenly, looking into the clear yellow-green of my wine, I saw in it the face of the little fat Chancellor of the Exchequer who had visited my squadron at Fiskerton in 1943. I could see him quite clearly as he scanned the spectacular air photographs of a bombed town, Düsseldorf, with the rows and rows of empty boxes which had been houses and I could hear his chuckle. "Capital," he had said, "capital. This is really getting somewhere. I do congratulate you." I could remember my gasp as I looked over his shoulder at the photographs and the destruction they displayed. And now the Control Commission Law was spelling out that "Wanton destruction of cities, towns and villages or devastation not justified by military necessity was a war crime. So what was military necessity? The necessity to win the war? By any means? I read on. The next paragraph laid down that:

> "Any person without regard to nationality or the capacity in which he acted, is deemed to have committed a crime as defined in paragraph 1 of this article if he was (a) an accessory to the commission of any such crime or ordered or abetted the

same, or (b) took a consenting part therein, or (c) was connected with plans or enterprises involving its commission . . . "

The net which this "law" spread was clearly wide enough to catch a lot of people and its meshes were so narrow as to make it very difficult for the wrongdoer to wriggle through. I had certainly been all those things not once but many times. But whose "law" was it? The victors' law to catch guilty enemies? Or international law applying to everyone? "What is truth?" said jesting Pilate. No wonder he did not stay for an answer. I finished my wine and sandwiches without zest.

When I got back to England and reported to Bomber Command where our reports had a limited circulation I found the atmosphere gloomy. The war against Japan had been terminated after the atom bombs on Hiroshima and Nagasaki and the operation of sending "Tiger Force" including most of my old Group, No. 5, had naturally been abandoned. The whole giant organisation, which had been fighting from the first day of the war until the last, was now devoid of function, stranded like a whale on the beach. All the Headquarters had to do was to cut down, disband, discard and try to see that reasonable discipline was observed in difficult circumstances.

It was noticeable that I was accorded only the shortest and most formal interview by the C-in-C and received no second invitation to a ride in his Bentley or lunch at his house.

11

A Personal Assessment

'Withered is the Garland of the War'

For years I have put thoughts of the war aside; but with the coming of the fifty-year anniversaries people increasingly ask me: what happened? what was it like? who did what and why? Now that I am alone, I have thought to try to make some analysis of the limited sphere in which I was directly concerned. In particular I have thought and thought and thought again about the area of carpet bombing, the deliberate destruction of whole towns, which was such a large part of my active war. In 1941-42, area bombing, on the pattern set by the Luftwaffe in its attacks on British towns, and in particular on London, was inevitable if there was to be bombing at all. Later it was pursued as a deliberate option. I now feel I should set out, as far as I know it, the story of how the policy evolved in those dark days when Britain was alone and there was no way except by bombing of effectively striking at the victorious Nazis who controlled virtually the whole land mass of Europe west of the Soviet border.

The story has too often been simplified and portrayed in black and white, mostly black, as having been originated, refined and executed by Sir Arthur Harris and an image on these lines has become all too established in the public mind. This is arrant nonsense. Broad policies in wartime do not originate with Commanders in Chief although such individuals may have a powerful influence on the political and staff bodies which control the direction of war. Sir Arthur was, as we have seen, an enthusiastic advocate of the policy of area bombing and his energy and forcefulness led him sometimes to a broad interpretation of his instructions in his determination to hurt the enemy. But he did not invent area bombing nor could he have implemented it without a clear directive from his superiors and their continued support.

The seeds of the policy were sown in a desperate minute written on 8th July 1940 by Mr Churchill in his second month as Prime Minister. Britain was then probably nearer to terminal defeat than at any other time in her history. The Continent had capitulated to Hitler and, while two evacuations, the first from Dunkirk and the second from Brittany and Normandy, had preserved large numbers of fighting men, the soldiers had come home dispirited and without equipment. Britain was alone and there were some, even in the highest places, who thought it possible and desirable to sue for a negotiated peace.

But Churchill, by then Prime Minister and Minister of Defence, never flinched. In a minute, written only two days before the opening of the Battle of Britain, he wrote not of surrender but of ultimate victory and the document is significant enough to be quoted in full (the italics are mine):

PRIME MINISTER

TO MINISTER OF AIRCRAFT PRODUCTION

In the fierce light of the present emergency the fighter is the need, and the output of fighters must be the prime consideration till we have broken the enemy's attack. But when I look round to see how we can win the war, I see that there is only one sure path. We have no continental army which can defeat the German military power. The blockade is broken and Hitler has Asia and probably Africa to draw from. Should he be repulsed here or not try invasion, he will recoil eastward, and we have nothing to stop him. But there is one thing that will bring him back and bring him down, and that is an *absolutely devastating, extermination attack by very heavy bombers from this country upon the Nazi homeland. We must be able to overwhelm him by this means, without which I do not see a way through.* We cannot accept any lower aim than air mastery. When can it be obtained?

Although Sir Charles Portal was not Chief of the Air Staff when this was written, there can be no doubt that he, as C-in-C Bomber Command at the time, and all the most senior officers of the RAF, would have had knowledge of the gist of the minute. Its implication, that the war could be won by the RAF alone, inspired much RAF thinking, and all RAF wishful thinking, right up until a less famous minute in April 1945 put a stop to area bombing, not on humanitarian grounds nor to effect an earlier victory, but because more destruction would hamper the work of the occupation of Germany after her defeat.

As C-in-C Bomber Command, Portal had had first hand knowledge of the difficulties, possibilities and impossibilities of the bomber weapon in the early days of the war but when, as Chief of the Air Staff, he became head of the Air Force for the rest of the war, his attitude to bombing policy was curiously equivocal and could even be interpreted as having been at times hypocritical. He often talked and wrote in terms of attacking specific military objectives but he became increasingly interested in the effects of bombs which missed their targets. He well knew there would be very many and those bombs, he thought, should do damage, some damage. Any damage was better than no damage. There could be no "devastating, exterminating" element in throwing quantities of bombs onto green fields; any bomb dropped in a built-up area would do the enemy at least some harm.

Phrases like "the normal spread of a heavy attack would inevitably cause a high degree of devastation in the town" appear in early Portal correspondence. He is on record as having stated that "we have not yet reached the stage of desiring to burn down a whole town, but when this stage is reached we shall do it by dropping a large quantity of incendiaries first". The RAF reached that stage under his leadership.

His biographer writes of his attitude that "in destroying industrial towns his object was to demolish factories and . . . the amenities of major urban life. It was not to massacre civilians . . ." and quotes Portal as having said in a lecture at his old school, Winchester, after the war that, "the (German) loss of life through bombing, which amounted to some 600,000 killed, was purely incidental and in as much as it involved children and women . . . we all deplored the necessity for doing it." This is hypocrisy of a fairly high order. Everyone who had been in London during the blitz knew that bombing towns and the deliberate destruction of houses brings civilian casualties including women and children. British bombing, being far heavier than German, would bring much heavier casualties. These casualties were not really incidental because such casualties were, more honestly, inevitable. All evidence shows that Portal was in the van of those who pressed for and implemented the policy of area bombing.

I shall not burden the reader with descriptions of the vicissitudes of policy which, from 1940 to 1942 spawned a multitude of different, sometimes contradictory and often impracticable directives on bombing. These went far to confuse and never assisted the embryo offensive, struggling to achieve results in accordance with the Prime Minister's defiant minute of 1940.

As Chief of the Air Staff, Portal was responsible for the directive issued by Air Ministry to Bomber Command in February 1942 which, after detailing the main city targets, continued, "Operations should now be focused on the morale of the enemy civil population and in particular of industrial workers". Max Hastings records in his *Bomber Command* that the next day Portal reinforced this directive in a minute to Sir Norman Bottomley which stated:

> Ref: the new bombing directive: I suppose it is clear that the aiming points are to be the built-up areas, not, for instance, the dockyards or aircraft factories.

The policy circulated in February 1942 was far longer-lived than any of its predecessors and was not superseded until the spring of 1944 when the bomber effort, against the wishes of Churchill and Harris, was switched to direct preparation for, and participation in, the coming invasion and overall control was transferred to the Supreme Allied Commander with spectacularly successful results.

There are two reasons why the 1942 policy lasted so long. The first is that it was given respectability and an allegedly scientific basis by a paper written for the Prime Minister by his Scientific Adviser, Lord Cherwell, known as "the Prof". The argument of this paper, which its author claimed to be based on "careful analysis" of the effects of raids on British towns, stated that the destruction of housing and the rendering of people homeless was the most effective result of bombing. He estimated that "on average" a ton of bombs on a town centre demolished twenty to forty dwellings and "dehoused" one hundred to two hundred people. Taking fifty-eight towns in Germany with over 100,000 people "which should be easy to find and hit", and, assuming a high output of heavy bombers, he calculated that "the majority" of the inhabitants of these large towns, i.e. one third of the whole German population, "would be turned out of house and home".

"There seems little doubt," he concluded, "that this would break the spirit of the people."

This paper now seems to have been so riddled with nonsensical assumptions and bogus calculations that it is difficult to believe that it could ever have achieved any credibility, although it is always easy to believe what you want to believe. I do not think Mr Churchill recorded his reaction to Lord Cherwell's paper, but in an April 1942 minute to the Secretary of State for Air he wrote that "the Air Ministry's responsibility is to make sure that the maximum weight of the best type of bombs is dropped on the German cities . . . ", which is clear evidence that he had approved the policy. Max Hastings records that "the Air Minister, Sir Archibald Sinclair, and the Chief of the Air Staff found the paper simple, clear and convincing". The new C-in-C Bomber Command needed no reinforcement of his belief in a policy of which he was already the strongest advocate.

In the years up to 1942, press and wireless reports of Bomber Command's activities, often untruthful, nearly always equivocal, had played a significant part in the preservation of hope and

morale among the sorely distressed people of Britain, but in fact
nothing of real significance had been achieved in the bombing of
Germany. So it is understandable that the Air Force Chiefs
should have approved and welcomed a so-called scientific basis
for the theory of "de-housing" on a large scale. At last they had
a policy which they could be reasonably confident that they could
deliver. They could see, at last, an end to the long and sorry tale
of high hopes, failed forecasts and broken promises.

The second reason for the long life of the policy was that
1942 saw the first fruits of the considerable priority in both
research and production which had been accorded to the Bombers
by the decisions made in the dark days of 1940. Great strides had
been made in navigational aids and the new generation of heavy
bombers was coming on stream. The appointment of Sir Arthur
Harris to Bomber Command coincided with these improvements
and with the new directive.

Destructive attacks on Lübeck and Rostock soon made
headlines, although neither was a target of importance. But it was
in early summer that the new C-in-C made his real bid for the
continuance of the policy of "devastating, exterminating attack"
as envisaged in the Prime Minister's minute of 1940. He laid on
the famous thousand-bomber raids in which the first line bombers
were reinforced by aircraft and crews from the operational
training units. The Prime Minister was apprised of and
enthusiastically supported these operations, which were quite
clearly area attacks.

Mr Churchill reported to the House of Commons after the
Cologne raid that the results were of a devastating character and
went on to say that "German cities, harbours and centres of war
production will be subjected to an ordeal the like of which has
never been experienced in any country". The compliments of the
House were accorded to Air Marshal Harris, and the Air
Ministry on 11th June issued a second communiqué with a list of
factories known to be damaged or destroyed.

When Harris proposed a second effort after the raid on
Cologne had seemed successful, the PM, who seldom allowed
anything to take priority over the Battle of the Atlantic, gave his

support to the overruling of Coastal Command's objections to the use over Germany of aircraft loaned to them by Bomber Command. The raid on Cologne devastated much of the town, six hundred acres being reported destroyed, but later attacks on Essen and Bremen failed owing to unfavourable weather. The thousand bomber raids made a significant contribution to boosting morale in Britain which, for various reasons, was at a fairly low ebb at the time.

None of these operations, according to our researches after the war, had any pronounced effect on German production. They did, however, alert the enemy to the danger to his homeland, and were responsible for the change in his priorities which was later a major factor in the success of the Anglo-American invasion of France in 1944. The switch in aircraft production, from army co-operation and bomber aircraft to home defence and night fighters made necessary by the threat to the home front, denied the German armies much of the air support which had always been a prime factor in their success. This effect was seen at its most dramatic on 6th June 1944, D-Day, when allied aircraft flew some fifteen thousand sorties in support of the invasion against a mere one hundred by the Luftwaffe in opposition.

The other significant development in 1942 was the formation of the Pathfinder Force, to whom was given the sole responsibility for finding and marking targets. The main force now had to concentrate only on navigation to the target and on aiming their bombs at target indicators dropped by the Pathfinders.

Sir Arthur Harris fought tooth-and-nail against this concept, but when it was imposed upon him he did give it his full support and he can even claim some credit for its success through his insistence that the Pathfinder Force should be commanded by his protegé, the brilliant Imperial Airways pilot Don Bennett. Bennett had already distinguished himself in Bomber Command, but he was very much junior to other officers who were in line for the Pathfinder post and, although he had his drawbacks, all-in-all he amply repaid Harris' faith.

The crux of the story of Bomber Command came at the Casablanca Conference of Allied leaders in January 1943. It was the decisions taken there which were supposed to produce the overall guidance for all that was to be done by the Command and by the growing strength of the US 8th Air Force in 1943-44.

It is not difficult to find fault with the document on bombing policy which emanated from Casablanca. It was equivocal, subject to interpretation and consequently could be, and was, circumvented. But it must be remembered that there was a time limit to the conference: that it was necessary somehow to reconcile the opposing views of the American and British Air Forces and to present an agreed document before the end of the meeting.

The Americans, who had gone to Casablanca hoping for agreement to essay the invasion of Northern Europe in that year, had given in to British assurances that this would be disastrous and that 1944 was the earliest that invasion would be possible. Mr Churchill was much relieved at the American concession and was naturally prepared to give some *quid pro quo* to American views on other matters. He did not air the concept of defeating Germany by aerial bombardment alone, which Sir Charles Portal also seems not to have pressed. The American airmen were determined, against the advice and practical experience of the British, to pursue the aim of attack on specific targets, factories, shipyards and such. The British were convinced that such attacks would fail but, having achieved their objective of postponing the invasion, they were not prepared to oppose American ideas on bombing too strongly.

It was common ground that the air attack on Germany would be kept at the maximum and the final directive of the Chiefs-of-Staff to the Bomber Commanders ordered them "to embark on the demolition of a range of German targets as essential preliminaries to D-Day". Liddell Hart in his *History of the Second World War* writes that "The Casablanca Conference laid down the ancillary nature of strategic bombing as a forerunner of a land invasion". This may have been so but it appears that the decision was clothed in enough cotton wool for the British commander to be able to interpret it as not interfering with the detailed plan for destroying German towns which stemmed from the Air Ministry directive of February 1942.

Churchill in his memoirs quoted only the objective of "the progressive destruction and dislocation of the German military, industrial and economic system and the undermining of morale . . . ". Sir Arthur Harris recorded in his memoirs that the directive "allowed me to attack pretty well any German industrial city of 100,000 inhabitants and above." It is clear that he believed that the defeat of Germany could and should be brought about by the systematic destruction of German towns. It is less obvious that he was honestly convinced that this was the best possible method of using the bombing weapon "as an ancillary to land invasion".

At the time, as a new Commanding Officer of a main force Lancaster squadron, I naturally knew nothing of these top secret negotiations and documents and when, in June 1943, a refined version of the Casablanca directive reached Headquarters Bomber Command, I and my like were not conscious of any difference in the targets we were required to attack. This is not particularly surprising since, although the intention at Casablanca seems to have been to ensure and increase a co-operative approach to the concept of the offensive in preparation for invasion, the effect was to make the directive even more vague than its predecessor so that, in the words of the Official Historians, "for most of 1943 there was no combined offensive but a bombing competition".

I have said that my spell of research in Germany in 1945 convinced me that the efforts and losses of my squadron in 1943, all the blood, sweat and tears we expended, were, if not virtually wasted, certainly not cost-effective. All that was achieved from most of the effort in 1943 was the destruction of huge numbers of houses and the deaths and maiming of large numbers of Germans, including of course women and children. Civilian consumption was reduced and much capacity was converted to war purposes. Much equipment and many men were used in anti-aircraft defence, air-raid precautions, building shelters and repairing damage, who might have been employed on active service, but there is no evidence that this produced any shortages of either men or equipment in front-line units. And the total war production of the Reich actually increased in 1943.

So did Bomber Command obey the spirit of the directive from Casablanca that our efforts were to be "ancillary to the invasion of Europe"? Did the Battles of the Ruhr, of Hamburg and of Berlin do anything that directly smoothed the path of the invasion of 1944? Our greatest contributions were the attack on the V-weapon research establishment at Peenemunde which, with later attacks on the launching sites and storage units, postponed and reduced the V-weapon offensive. If that had transpired as originally planned, it might have disrupted or even prevented the invasion. Second was the effect of the switching of German production and attention to home defence, thus denying the Atlantic Wall some of the resources it needed to dispute the 1944 invasion of Normandy. Most of the rest emerges as waste of time, waste of valuable equipment, and of even more valuable people.

Could anything have been done which would have more certainly improved the chances of success in invading Normandy and overcoming the German armies in the West? Was there a different strategy available which would have saved us – and by us I mean the Prime Minister, the Air Minister, the Chief of the Air Staff, Air Marshal Harris, and down to the likes of me – from accusations that area bombing was an everlasting blot on the reputation of our country, for love of which we all planned and fought?

The ineffectiveness of Bomber Command in the first three years of war had left a deep scar on the Royal Air Force Command. The tales of how few bombers had found their targets, and how widely dispersed were the bombs when they did find them, were burnt deep into the consciousness of the RAF top brass. Time and again their predictions and promises had been exposed as no more than empty hopes. They were humanly determined not to be caught out again, as they were quite convinced their American counterparts were going to be caught out, in promising the destruction of individual targets. The accepted solution in 1942 had been that instead of futilely continuing to try to find and hit small targets in Germany the answer was to select targets so big that they couldn't be missed. That could only mean the area bombing of big towns.

The new aids to navigation and bombing, while a long step forward, did not promise results such as the US Air Force was promising of its daylight sorties. They could, however, be expected to make the area bombing of large towns much more effective. So Churchill's air advisers at Casablanca, led by Sir Charles Portal, Chief of the Air Staff, were content that the Prime Minister should put Britain's name to any document which, in their view, accepted for the RAF the realities of bombing which they had learnt the hard way. All they needed was something into which they could read a go ahead for the area bombing of towns which they were pretty sure they could do successfully.

Although the target in my first operational experience was stated as being the factory of Krupps of Essen, I now know, which did not occur to me at the time, that that aiming point was not selected because it was Krupps but because it was the geographical centre of Essen. It thus complied with Portal's minute that aiming points should be the built-up areas of towns. I had rather vaguely wondered about the preponderance of incendiaries in the bomb load, but I was too inexperienced at the time to have realised that the attack was intended as much or more to burn the town as to destroy the factory.

On other targets in 1943 the object was stated in such phrases as "to do maximum damage to an enemy industrial centre" (Dortmund and Cologne), although on Cologne I remember the aiming-points to have been on the west side of the Rhine, whereas the city's main industries were situated east of the river. On Stettin we were ordered "to do maximum damage to an enemy port" and on Düsseldorf and Berlin "to do maximum damage to an enemy city". It was on Hamburg that confidence in our power was enough to warrant, for I think the first time, the order "to destroy an enemy city". In all cases the aiming-point was in the centre of the town and the intention fell clearly within the category of "undermining the morale of the German people". There was only the most tenuous connection with any attempt to disorganise the building of aircraft or submarines, and none with the concept of preparation for the coming invasion.

It is right and proper in war not to place too much faith in unproven methods and weapons. At the time of the Casablanca meeting the new methods and weapons becoming available to Bomber Command were not fully tested in action. It would have been foolishly rash of the British delegation there not to have insisted on wording the bombing directive to allow for the possibility that the new methods might fail, making it inevitable that the British bombers would have to go on employing the methods so bitterly evolved over the years and set out in the directive of February 1942, to continue to essay the defeat of Germany by undermining civilian morale through area bombing of its greatest towns.

It was not at Casablanca but two months later, in March 1943, that it became clear that there was another path open to Bomber Command, a real alternative to the directive of February 1942, an alternative which would have complied with the spirit as well as the letter of the Casablanca decisions.

By that March the target marking device code-named "Oboe" had been well tested in action and it was clear that it could and did achieve its planned accuracy of placing a target indicator within a very few hundred yards of aiming-points within its limited range. That range included a large and important area of West Germany, but there were factors which dictated that, even with this degree of accuracy, a large proportion of bombs would not actually fall on a small target. For technical reasons only twelve "Oboe" markers could be dropped in an hour. That meant that, to ensure markers were available for the main force to aim at throughout the duration of an attack, the "Oboe" markers had to be "backed up" by markers aimed at them by the Pathfinder Force. This, together with inaccuracies in main force aiming, inevitably produced some scatter of bombing.

The fact remained, however, demonstrated in the two March attacks on Essen/Krupps, possibly the most heavily-defended target in Germany, that in both raids a considerable number of bombs did fall on the actual target and a large number fell in the immediate vicinity. This in spite of the poor aerodynamic qualities of the bombs used. I now know, as was shown in our researches when I was in Essen, that if we had really wanted to destroy Krupps we would have used many more medium and heavy cased high explosives as was done in the final destruction of the factory much later in the war. These would have done far more damage to the target and, the bombs having greater accuracy than those we did use, would have produced much more useful damage to the surrounding area by disrupting communications and utilities close to the target instead of indiscriminately burning houses.

However, at this time the theory of British bombing was dominated by two so-called axioms. The first, laid down by "the Prof", the gist of which was quoted on p.321 for the Prime Minister, was that "de-housing" was the most effective way of attacking Germany. The second, emanating from Sir Charles Portal and warmly endorsed by Sir Arthur Harris, was that every bomb dropped on Germany should do some damage. Any damage to anything was better than no damage.

It was paradoxical that these old axioms could be made to fit the new situation presented by the success of "Oboe". By putting aiming-points in the centres of large towns and using bomb loads of incendiaries backed up by four thousand pound blast bombs to discourage fire-fighters and break windows, huge fires would be raised, de-housing of large numbers effected and nearly all bombs could be expected to hit something. There would be relatively few cases with Oboe marking when a large town would not be marked with reasonable accuracy and seriously damaged.

Nobody seems to have questioned whether, in view of the new, if still less than total, accuracy of British night bombing, our efforts could or should have been harnessed to real compliance with the spirit of the Casablanca Conference which laid down "the ancillary nature of strategic bombing as forerunner of a land invasion". Still less did anyone question whether, with the experience of all the towns in Britain which had been attacked by the Luftwaffe, de-housing" really had an entirely negative effect on morale or much, if any, long-term effect on war production.

The Casablanca instruction to the Chiefs of Staff was expanded and supposedly clarified by the "Pointblank" directive issued to Bomber Command and the US 8th Air Force on 10th June 1943. This laid down in general terms the most desirable targets in support of the coming invasion but did not delete the phrase about "undermining the morale of the German people to a point where their capacity for armed resistance is fatally weakened . . ." It emphasised the importance of co-operation between the two forces, but the British blocked an American hope to unite them under one command. Nevertheless Max Hastings[1] states that it was agreed that "authority for the conduct of the Combined Bomber Offensive should be nominally vested in Sir Charles Portal". This was probably unfortunate since Sir Charles disbelieved in the American policy but did not have enough authority to change it. Equally he was not prepared to change the main thrust of British policy and consequently his influence in co-ordinating the effort of the two forces was remarkably small.

The two men whose duty it was to have continuously analysed how the now very large British bomber force should best be used in accordance with the spirit of the Casablanca directives were Sir Arthur Harris, C-in-C Bomber Command, and his superior, Sir Charles Portal, Chief of the Air Staff. It is abundantly clear that Harris never had any intention of doing any new analysis. He was a man of great strength of purpose and, with tunnel vision, intent on using his Command in the way he thought best, which was to win the war by the destruction of the city life of Germany. He honestly believed it could be done; he honestly believed that it would work; and he honestly believed that anyone who suggested otherwise was little more than a saboteur. His personality was so strong and his determination so great that his staff were scared stiff to demur, let alone to differ openly from

---

[1] Hastings, M. *Bomber Command*. p186.

him. Sir Arthur was determined to circumvent or ignore the spirit of the Casablanca directives which were supposed to tie the bomber forces to preparation for invasion. He was prepared only to interpret the directives in such a way that he could continue in his own preferred methods. The wording of the documents could be stretched to make this possible, but he could not have pursued this course, as he did for more than a year, without the concurrence or connivance of Sir Charles Portal.

Sir Charles left no memoirs and his real attitude at this time is not easy to gauge. He was, as we have seen, an early and passionate advocate of area bombing and, although he modified his views later in the war, in practice he gave Harris full support throughout the area offensive of 1943-44.

The role of the Prime Minister during this time is also very difficult to assess. He had undoubtedly realised that his 1940 idea of the bomber being the primary weapon with which Germany should be defeated had been overtaken by events. One gets the impression that he had so many other weighty matters on his mind that he was perhaps content to let the bomber offensive continue, propelled by its own inertia. Air Marshal Harris was still bidden to Chequers from time to time but there is no record that these meetings produced any significant discussions about bombing. Nevertheless the existence of these invitations and the statement in Harris' memoirs that "Winston was delighted by the way the offensive was developing during the Battle of the Ruhr"[1] suggests that the Prime Minister was fully aware of and approved of the area bombing carried out by Bomber Command in 1943 and early 1944.

As to the disastrous "Battle of Berlin" in the 1943-44 winter, Churchill had seen much of the London blitz in 1940-41 so it would not be altogether surprising if he had derived some satisfaction from reading reports of a reprisal blitz on the enemy capital. The weather was so bad that winter that no photographs were available to confirm the hopeful reports of crews who, in almost all cases, had bombed through cloud. This meant that both

---

[1] Harris, A. *Bomber Offensive*. p155.

BBC and official estimates of the damage caused were unjustifiably optimistic. There was no time for my research unit to make any proper examination in 1945 of what had happened in Berlin but my impression from a hurried visit was of a lot of scattered damage around the large area of the city but that the industrial effect was very small.

The policy and directives under which Bomber Command operated in 1943 did not change until April 1944 when, to quote Air Marshal Harris' memoirs, "all strategic bomber forces, both RAF and American, were placed under the direction of the Supreme Allied Commander, General Eisenhower, when these were engaged on operations connected with either the reduction of the German Air Force or with the invasion of Europe. All such commitments in preparation for, or support of, the invasion had absolute and overriding priority"[1].

This bland statement conceals, or does not admit, that both the Prime Minister and the C-in-C had serious reservations about releasing Bomber Command to attack the Railways and other targets on French soil whose destruction was demanded by the Supreme Allied Commander on the advice of his Deputy, Air Marshal Sir Arthur Tedder. Harris did not believe, or said he did not believe, his force capable of the accuracy required, while the PM, Francophile instincts to the fore at this pessimistic estimate, was fearful of the political damage which would result from the substantial French casualties he foresaw from inaccurate bombing of French targets. Mr Churchill gave way under American pressure and, in the event, the operations were outstandingly successful, resulting in relatively light casualties to the French and making an inestimable contribution to the success of the Normandy invasion.

It is clear now, and should have been clear in March 1943 to those with full knowledge of war planning and the technical factors then emerging, that any justification for Bomber Command continuing to rely on area bombing as proposed by the concept of 1940, the directive of 1942 and the axioms evolved

---

[1] Harris, A. *Bomber Offensive*. p191.

from previous failure, had vanished by April 1943. Britain was no longer alone and the balance of potential power was now so overwhelmingly in our favour that it was almost certain that the war could, would and above all should, be won by other methods than attacks on German civilian morale.

It was well-known that within and behind the evil of the Nazi movement which had taken control of Germany lurked the shadow of the German General Staff, obsessed with the knowledge that German arms, triumphant in 1866 and 1870, had in the First Great War defied the world for fifty months. After that war military circles in Germany encouraged the story that their armies in November 1918 were undefeated. Having imposed the Treaty of Brest-Litovsk, which stripped Russia of a quarter of her European territory and two-fifths of her population, with three-quarters of her iron and coal, and being still in possession of huge blocks of Eastern Europe and a sizeable slice of France, they considered that the Army had been betrayed from within the Reich and compelled to make peace. Such a belief was a certain recipe for fostering the worst strains of German militarism and it was a necessity for the Allies that the Germans should have no grounds this time for fabricating such a tale. In 1943 it was quite clear that the Anglo-Americans absolutely had to defeat the German armies in the West. They could not possibly allow the Soviet land forces, whose power was fast increasing, to be the sole conquerors of Germany on land. So, as was emphasised at the Casablanca Conference, it was necessary that the projected invasion of Europe should have first call on all, repeat all, resources.

To implement this, the alternative policy available to Bomber Command was to have concentrated operations on targets within Oboe range and to have attacked the same targets by night as the Americans had damaged or intended to damage by day. This would not have complied with the Cherwell/Portal/Harris axioms. De-housing would have been abandoned and, while it could be expected that many bombs would hit vital targets and many more spread havoc and damage to utilities very near those targets, a proportion of bombs would be wasted. The policy would have entailed a radical change in the bomb loads carried, away from the preponderance of fire and blast bombs used in de-housing, to medium and heavy cased high explosives. The switch of production needed to provide the bombs would have been a strain on industry but, in wartime conditions, could certainly have been effected. The result would have been damage to military targets in 1943 and early 1944 on a much greater scale than could have been effected by the Americans with their lesser bomb loads. If the bombs in the attacks on Krupps/Essen in March had been high explosives, instead of the blast-and-burn load we actually carried, the loss of production at Krupps would have been much greater and far more difficult to restore. But the de-housing of Esseners would have been far less. When the Americans had made a reasonably successful attack on a target within Oboe range, (and at this time they did not go further because of the lack of long-range fighter escort), the same target could have been marked by Oboe and attacked by Bomber Command with a far greater load of bombs. The total damage to the installation and its surrounds would very often have put it completely out of action.

This would have accorded with the spirit of the Casablanca directive and would have been in compliance with the stated, but not effective, British and American policies of co-operation and co-ordination of the two forces. It would also have restored the original British intent of not resorting to "terror" bombing.

Sir Charles Portal and Sir Arthur Harris did not even experiment with such a change because, apparently, they so passionately believed in their two bombing axioms and still thought of area bombing as a war winner.

It is quite clear, however, that the Prime Minister in 1943 did not any longer share that belief. He had probably begun to discard it as soon as the Americans made clear that they meant to give the European war priority in spite of their interests in the Far East. It is, therefore, much less easy to fathom why he did not have second thoughts about the area bombing campaign in 1943. Probably the bomber offensive no longer rated a very high priority among his tremendous and wide-ranging activities.

Nevertheless, he was always conscious of it and it is surprising that when he saw, as he must have seen, that Bomber Command was persisting in attacks on German town centres with the morale of the enemy population as a priority objective, he did not question it.

Naturally, I have no access to what was in his mind at the time. Perhaps the huge destruction wrought in Germany satisfied some instinct to appease the sufferings of Britain and the whole of Europe, by sufferings inflicted on the aggressor. Perhaps he remembered that when he was looking at air raid damage in London the crowd had shouted to him "Give it 'em back" and "Let them have it too" and he, in his own words, "had undertaken forthwith to see that their wishes were carried out"[1].

Had he bent his mind seriously to the problem in April 1943 one can imagine that one of his famous minutes might have emerged, perhaps on these lines :

PRIME MINISTER
TO: SECRETARY OF STATE FOR AIR AND CHIEF OF AIR
     STAFF
I am delighted to hear of the improved night bombing accuracy demonstrated in the two recent attacks on Krupps. Between the wars the German General Staff and the Nazis managed to fool the German people into believing that the German Army, Navy and Air Force were not defeated in 1918 but betrayed by the civil power. We need to be quite sure that there is no basis for such a canard being raised in Germany after this war. It was made clear at Casablanca that the war is to be won on the Continent by the utter defeat of the German land forces and that all available resources are to be directed to that end. Now that we have powerful allies and improved accuracy in our night bombing, there should be no more talk of direct attacks on the morale of the civil population. Please tell me on one sheet of paper how Bomber Command can best make direct attacks on the sinews of the German Armed Forces as required by the Casablanca Conference decisions.

---

[1] Churchill, Winston. *The Second World War* Volume II. "Their Finest Hour". p349.

It was a feature of Hitler's war that the prestige of Winston Churchill when Prime Minister was so high that his peremptory and often vague minutes would galvanise others in Britain to rise above their natural ceiling of enterprise or achievement. A minute on the lines of the above would have compelled Sir Charles Portal and Sir Arthur Harris to re-think the axioms by which they believed themselves bound. They might have looked at the idea that some bombs on targets which would directly affect the efficiency of the German forces occupying and defending France would be preferable to large amounts of inconsequential civilian damage.

To attack specific targets had been the British theory of bombing method before the war and up to the end of 1941. The fact that it was then discarded was not because the theory was proved wrong but because it was then impossible to carry out. If they had dusted down the theory and tried again when it was practicable they might have discovered that the bombs, which in 1941 missed their primary objective, would, given the right bomb loads, have made a better contribution to the defeat of Germany, than by the indiscriminate burning of houses. Serious damage would have then been caused to communications, utilities etc. near the primary objective, impeding repairs and delaying the resumption of efficient working.

They would surely have had second thoughts about the "Prof's" de-housing thesis, realising that London, Liverpool, Coventry, Bristol and the rest had lost little production through housing shortage, however inconvenient it was for the workers. Also, someone in the Intelligence world might have realised that nearly all German houses have a large cellar area in which it was not difficult to improvise adequate, if uncomfortable, shelter when the house above was burnt out.

All this, of course, is only might-have-been. It didn't happen, although the spectre of that might-have-been haunts me now because of what did happen. I live with the knowledge that in those hectic months of 1943 we fought the wrong battle and didn't even win it. I hate to write it but I am sure that almost all the blood, sweat and tears which Bomber Command expended and the majority of the deaths and injuries we suffered and inflicted in that time were futile. It has been proved by all research that the de-housing and deaths due to the bombing of German towns in 1943 served very little purpose in the defeat of the German armed forces.

The worst excess of the area bombing policy was in the so-called "Battle of Berlin" which resulted in heavy losses for Bomber Command with virtually no effect "ancillary to the invasion of Europe". For me, with my written warning against such a campaign hardly dry on the paper, it was an agony to have to despatch crews on what I believed to be totally futile, and knew to be very dangerous, sorties. And I hated to have to lie to the American journalists, Ed Murrow and Martha Gellhorn, both of whom became my friends, about the significance of what we were doing.

An extraordinary comment on this long campaign of area bombing, so expensive in the lives of men and the loss of machines, is that not only was there a reasonable alternative, but that a realistic plan for a truly "Combined Bomber Offensive" incorporating that alternative, actually existed and was promulgated by the Operational Committee charged with transforming the Casablanca directive into orders to the Bomber Commanders. This plan, called "Pointblank", stated that "when precision targets are bombed by the 8th Air Force in daylight, the effort should be completed and complemented by RAF attacks on the surrounding industrial area by night". Even more extraordinary is it that, as Max Hastings tells in his *Bomber Command*, Air Marshal Harris actually wrote to his opposite number in the 8th Air Force, US General Eaker, saying that he was "in complete agreement with the policy recommended".

However "complete" the C-in-C's agreement may have been on paper, I do not know of any single instance when the aiming point for a Bomber Command attack was the area surrounding a precision target which had been bombed by the 8th Air Force. The fact that the order (it was not a "recommended" policy as Harris' letter suggests) was ignored by the British is a heavy indictment of Sir Charles Portal in whom was "nominally vested authority for the conduct of the bomber offensive", whatever that may have meant. For me it is a misery that so much of what I did, tried to do and ordered others to do in that terrible year was to no purpose.

The tension in a bomber squadron at that time, born of the high casualty rate and the frequency of operations, made aircrew concentrate on the continuous war they waged against their immediate and close enemies, the German defences, the radar operators, the searchlights, the flak gunners, the night fighters and the weather. They thought about finding and bombing the target indicators and getting home. Except for routine answers to the Intelligence Officer's questions at debriefing, most aircrew didn't think too much about the, to them, impersonal targets on which the bombs were falling. What the target indicators were actually indicating was too remote, more than three miles below them, not really their business. As everyone who has had children knows, the human race is naturally destructive and fascinated with destruction. We knew that we were spreading destruction on an unprecedented scale, but it was all a long way away.

When I came to have the chance of a second tour of operations, I had had some time to think about bombing and the great changes which had taken place in the year since I left 49 Squadron. Almost always No. 5 Group now operated as a single force, targets being marked by a specialised technique used by its own Pathfinder squadrons, one of which I was to command. Very considerable accuracy was possible through the development of the low-marking system pioneered by Cheshire at Woodhall, and more accurate navigation was made possible since the allied invasion of France had driven back the German defences and early warning system with a corresponding advance in the ground stations for our own navigational aids.

With the Romanian oilfields, which had contributed a large proportion of German oil, in Russian control, surely, I thought, oil is the Achilles heel of the Nazis. We could now expect to hit oil installations really hard, even the considerable number of important ones in east Germany and Czechoslovakia. Surely,

I thought, we could start, and perhaps even complete, the strangulation of Hitler's forces through their dependence on oil. Although the German forces were no longer spread, as they had been eighteen months before, from Bordeaux to Leningrad and from Stavanger to the Caucasus, they were now fighting on two major fronts. It seemed to me obvious that the problems of supply, and of switching sources when oil plants were damaged, would soon become insupportable for Germany if one or more large installations were attacked on every day or night when it was feasible.

Thinking on these lines in September 1944, it was a shock when I took over command of No. 97 Squadron to read in the latest Intelligence report on Bomber Command's activities that in the last three months, oil targets had only taken up half the effort devoted to German cities. These Intelligence reports were prepared at Bomber Command Headquarters and the comments obviously mirrored the outlook of the Commander-in-Chief. The statement that from April to June the bombing effort had been "diverted" from the "strategic bombing of German cities", and that from July to September, in the crucial times of consolidation of the Normandy invasion, "only twenty per cent of bombs had been dropped on German cities" clearly reflected the C-in-C's disappointment that higher authority had, at least temporarily, insisted that his force should be used in direct furtherance of the mainstream effort to win the war by the defeat of the German armed forces.

His was an extraordinary standpoint at the end of the splendid six months when his Command had been in the forefront of the battle and had rendered a service to the invasion forces without which they could hardly have succeeded in their formidable task. I remember being shocked that anyone could have rated the genuinely huge achievements of Bomber Command during that six months as of less importance than the devastation of more German cities. It is fair to say that in his memoirs, *Bomber Offensive*, Sir Arthur, while admitting his early reservations about attacking French railway targets, or any railway targets at all, claimed for his force a very considerable share of the credit for the success of Operation Overlord, the great invasion plan, a share of glory to which it was richly entitled and with which it is seldom credited.

In August, with Allied forces fairly securely installed on the Continent, the selection of targets had reverted from being under the general direction of the Supreme Commander in Europe and his staff to normal RAF procedures. This meant that overall authority fell to the Chief of the Air Staff and the C-in-C Bomber Command resumed the day to day selection of targets. Urgent requests for assistance from the armies advancing towards the German frontiers would naturally be met and there might, of course, be major policy changes directed by those responsible for high strategy.

It has subsequently transpired that there were at that time three currents of opinion in the top ranks of the RAF. It seems that the Chief of the Air Staff favoured an all-out offensive on German oil as an absolute priority. Air Marshal Tedder, General Eisenhower's Deputy and the presiding genius of the great air contribution to the invasion force, who still naturally and rightly had considerable influence, believed that attacks on transportation targets could have an effect on the advance into Germany similar to the spectacular results achieved on the French targets before and during the Normandy campaign. Air Marshal Harris never swerved an inch from his desire and intention to continue and intensify the attack on the German population. He believed that he had destroyed forty-five out of the top sixty German cities and yearned to "finish the job".

The Chief of the Air Staff seems to have made an effort at this time to impose on his Bomber Commander a directive which would have ensured an absolute priority for oil and transportation targets but Harris' threats of resignation if he was subjected to too much interference seem to have carried the day. The C-in-C was at that time something of a hero in the country, his popularity stemming from the time when he was seen as a vigorous and successful commander bringing home to the Nazis some of the horrors that they had inflicted on London and other British towns earlier in the war. His resignation or transfer from

Bomber Command would have dealt a severe blow at general confidence in the direction of the war. Portal seems to have decided that things had already gone too far to risk the hassle of a showdown.

Knowing nothing of the controversies in high places, I was bewildered in my first weeks of commanding No. 97 Squadron by the diversity of the targets we were required to find and mark. We did, finally, deny to the enemy the use of the two great canal systems which connected the Ruhr, Berlin and the North German ports. But the attacks were spasmodic and the final blow was too late to affect the war. From time to time we attacked oil targets as far afield as east Germany and Czechoslovakia, often with success, and it was heartening when we were told that an incipient shortage of oil had contributed to the final collapse. Again it was too late to have been a decisive factor. And until April 1945, the month before the war ended, we were still attacking towns. I remember Darmstadt, Karlsruhe, Dresden, Chemnitz and, especially, Würzburg as targets for my own squadron. Many more towns were attacked by other Groups.

It was my misfortune that, although I was in Bomber Command from late 1942 until the end of the war, during the time in 1944 when the Command and No. 5 Group made their greatest contribution to victory, I was engaged in training. Important as I was told the job at Syerston was, it was galling indeed to have no part in that splendid phase of the bomber war. It was little consolation that I had made some small contribution by having helped and encouraged Wing Commander Cheshire, when he was under my command at Woodhall Spa, in his pioneering work on the low-marking system which ultimately proved itself one of the most successful steps towards accurate bombing. Even the difficult attacks on distant oil targets when I commanded No. 97 Pathfinder Squadron in 1944-45 were too late to exert any crucial influence on the result of the war, which by then was already lost for Germany even though it had not yet been won by the allies. Those useful operations have never obliterated my memories of the area campaign of 1943.

Of such attacks as those, when they were perpetrated by the Germans against London, the famous author J.B. Priestley wrote in the book *Defiant City*, from which I have already quoted, as follows:

The fact remains that this indiscriminate mass bombing is a terrible and obscene business. It belongs to the nightmare side of things. It is like some old, ugly dream come true. It cuts deeper, as I know from my own experience, than fighting at the front. And for this reason, that it is warfare at its foulest, all mixed up with women and children, with familiar surroundings, with houses and shops, libraries and hospitals. The mangled bodies of the young and innocent, the old and feeble, are dragged out of the huge rubbish heaps and carted down the street. There is something fundamentally obscene and revolting about the whole business."

Well, I took a fairly prominent part in the deliberate mass bombing of German towns. Liddell Hart, the famous English military historian and thinker, summed up the bombing campaigns in his *History of the Second World War* with a final comment that "there is ample evidence to show that the war could have been shortened, several months at least, by better concentration (of the bombing effort)". It is melancholy indeed to think of the lives which were lost in that unnecessary prolongation of the fighting. Liddell Hart's ultimate conclusion was that area bombing was pursued "long after there was any reason or excuse" and with "disregard for basic morality.

I have no doubt now that those actions have left a permanent stain on the long, and on the whole honourable, record of British arms. It is the worse that the actions were stupid as well as cruel. Nearing the end of my life I have to admit that even the post war revelations of the greater and more ghastly crimes of the Nazis, including my own experience of Belsen, do not, cannot, expunge that stain or my part in it.

It is the ignorant fashion to place most of the blame for this murky page in British and RAF history squarely on the broad and willing shoulders of Air Marshal Sir Arthur Harris, who commanded Bomber Command from early 1942 until after the war and under whose command all the substantial attacks on German towns were planned and executed. In particular, Harris' responsibility for the destruction of Dresden has been grossly and unfairly exaggerated. Never one to shirk responsibility, in his memoirs he records laconically that, although many thought that the destruction of "so large and splendid a city at this late stage of the war" was unnecessary, "the attack on Dresden was at the time considered a military necessity by much more important people than myself".

The Prime Minister had in fact minuted the Air Minister and the Chief of Air Staff in January 1945 asking "whether the east German cities should not now be considered specially attractive targets". When the Secretary of State, who was as much in awe of Churchill as anyone, replied pointing out that other targets also had priority, he received a considerable thunderbolt in answer to his timid demur. The Prime Minister pointed out ferociously that he had not intended to start a debate. He had merely asked whether certain targets should not be considered attractive. So "specially attractive targets" the east German cities, including Dresden, remained.

As the Nuremburg and lesser tribunals, and countless moral thinkers and legal authorities before and after, have found, it is not always easy to assign clear-cut responsibility for war crimes. At Nuremburg it was laid down that an individual could not, as many of the defendants had hoped, be relieved from blame by the plea that he was acting under orders from superior authority. Had such a plea been acceptable it was indubitably true that ultimate responsibility for all Nazi actions and crimes could be attributed to Hitler who was, conveniently or otherwise, dead. Allied authorities were naturally concerned that this ultimate responsibility should not be allowed to exonerate the criminals who exercised power and earned infamy under their beloved Führer.

This being so, anyone who has read this book must conclude that, if deliberate indiscriminate area attacks on German towns were criminal acts, although Air Marshal Harris' responsibility is great, he shares it with some, at least, of his juniors and with his superiors, Winston Churchill and Marshal of the Royal Air Force, Lord Portal. Originally, they ordered the attacks by clear and definite instructions and, until the run-up to the Normandy invasion, neither demurred at Harris' interpretation of the allied policies laid down at Casablanca. After the invasion was secure, Portal made attempts to make oil the main priority with transport in second place but, in the face of Harris' intense and threatening determination to continue on his course, Portal was not strong enough to suggest to Churchill that an edict be issued outlawing area bombing, even if he had really wanted to do so, which is uncertain. In any case, the Prime Minister's January 1945 minute calling for the bombing of East German towns must have destroyed any impulse he might have had to lay down a firmer and less equivocal directive for Bomber Command.

Churchill did not record this minute in his *Second World War* nor is there any mention of area bombing in the last two volumes of that magisterial work. The city of Dresden is only mentioned in the context of the advance of the Red Army and the possibility of allied forces reaching it first. When international dismay at the destruction of the city became too vocal to be ignored, the Prime Minister directed that the area bombing of towns should cease, but this was on the grounds that further destruction would add to the problems of the occupation forces in Germany after the war had been won. It was late in the day for such a thought.

So, if the deliberate area bombing of towns when a genuine alternative was available was cruel, inhuman, immoral and stupid, we were all in it together. According to the "Law" I read on the downs at Travemunde. those who gave the orders, those who relayed or transmitted them and those who carried them out were equally guilty. But let it be said that as far as I know no member of the Luftwaffe was indicted either at Nuremburg or by any lesser tribunal on these grounds.

Nevertheless for us and for them, truly *"Withered is the garland of the war"*.

C.B.S. LONDON FRIDAY DECEMBER 3, 1943.
BROADCAST AT:_____   EDWARD R. MURROW

THIS IS LONDON.   The pilot was called Jock. xxxOne day
while we were sitting around

    Last night some of the young gentlemen of the R.A.F. took
me to Berlin. The Pilot was called Jock.   One day while we
were waiting for the weather he drove me across a bit of England,
through small villages with greystone houses marching straight
on each side of a small common.   We passed innumerable airfields,
and/about the fourth he remarked: "It's a pity; not one but would
make two good farms".   He explained that night bombing was
really rather simple - there wasn't much real danger.   And then
we passed a field, and Jock remarked: "Last winter one of our
crews bailed out just over there, in a snow storm.   When their
parachutes opened it jerked off their boots, and they had to
walk home in the snow".   And he added, by way of reassurance:
"Now each time I fly I tie on my boots; for a man would have
no chance of walking home from Germany without his boots".

    Yesterday afternoon the waiting was over, the weather was
right, the target was to be "The Big City".   The crew captains
walked into the briefing room, looked at the maps and charts,
and sat down with their big celluloid pads on their knees.   The
atmosphere was that of a school and a church.   The weather man
gave us the weather;   the Pilots were reminded that Berlin is
Germany's greatest centre of war production;   the Intelligence
Officer told us how many heavy and light ack-ack guns, how many

Ed Murrow's Broadcast

searchlights we might expect to encounter.   Then Joek, the
Wing Commander, explained the system of markings - the kind of
flares that would be used by the pathfinders.   He said that
concentration was the secret of success in these raids - that as
long as the aircraft stayed well-bunched they would protect each
other.   ~~He urged them not to try to fly wide of searchlights
or ack-ack, but to keep dead on the course that had been set.~~
The captains of aircraft walked out.   I noticed that the big
Canadian with the slow, easy grin had printed Berlin at the top
of his pad, and then embellished it with a scroll.   The red-
headed English boy with the two-weeks' old moustache was the last
to leave the room.

     Late in the afternoon we went to the locker-room to draw
parachutes, Mae Wests and all the rest.   As we dressed, a couple
of the Australians were whistling.   Walking out to the bus
that was to take us to the aircraft I heard the station loud-
speakers announcing that that evening all personnel would be able
to see a film: "Star Spangled Rhythm" - free!

     We went out and stood around a big, black, four-motored
Lancaster, D - Dog.   A small station wagon delivered a thermos
bottle of coffee, chewing gum, an orange and a bit of chocolate
for each man.   Up in that part of England the xxxxx air hums
and throbs with the sound of aircraft motors all day.   But for
half-an-hour before take-off the skies are dead silent and

expectant.   A lone hawk hovered over the airfield, absolutely
still as he faced into the wind.   Jack, the tail-gunner said:
"It would be nice if we could fly like that".   Jock looked at
his watch, and moved toward the aircraft.   Nothing was said;
we all followed.   D - Dog eased around the perimeter track to the
end of the runway.   We sat there for a moment, the green light
flashed, and we were rolling ten seconds ahead of schedule.
The take-off was smooth as silk.   The wheels came up, and D - Dog
started the long climb.   As we came up through the clouds I
looked right and left, and counted fourteen black Lancasters
climbing for the place where men must burn oxygen to live.   The
sun was going down, and its red glow made rivers and lakes of fire
on top of the clouds.   Down to the southward the clouds piled up
to form castles, battlements and whole cities....all tinged with
red.

   Soon we were out over the North Sea.   Dave, the navigator,
asked Jock if he couldn't make a little more speed - we were
nearly two minutes late.   By this time we were all using oxygen -
the talk on the intercom was brief and crisp.   Everyone sounded
relaxed.   ~~Afterxaxwhilex~~   For a while the eight of us in our
little world in exile moved over the sea.   There was a quarter
moon on the starboard beam.   Jock's quiet voice came through the
intercom: "That'll be flak ahead".   We were approaching the
enemy coast.   The flak looked like a cigarette lighter in a
dark room - one that won't light....sparks but no flame ~~xxxxx~~ -

crackling just about level with the cloud tops.   We flew steady and straight, and soon the flak was directly below us.   D - Dog rocked a little from right to left, but that wasn't caused by the flak.   We were in the slipstream of other Lancasters ahead;   and we were over the enemy coast.   And then a strange thing happened. The aircraft seemed to grow smaller.   Jack in the rear turret, Wally, the mid-upper gunner, Titch the wireless operator - all seemed somehow to draw closer to Jock in the cockpit.   It was as though each man's shoulder was against the other's.   The understanding was complete.   The intercom came to life, and Jock said: "Two aircraft on the port beam"; Jack in the tail said: "Okay Sir, they're Lancs".   The whole crew was a unit, and wasn't wasting words.   The cloud below was ten-tenths.   The blue-green jet of the exhausts licked back along the leading edge, and there were other aircraft all around us.   The whole great aerial armada was hurtling towards Berlin.   We flew so for twenty minutes, when Jock looked up at a vapor trail curling across above us, remarking in a conversational tone that from the look of it he thought there was a fighter up there.   Occasionally the angry red of ack-ack burst through the clouds, but it was far away and we took only an academic interest.   We were flying in the third wave, ~~which meant that we would be in the last group of planes over the target~~.

Jock asked Wally in the mid-upper turret, and Jack in the

rear turret if they were cold.   They said they were all right,
and thanked him for asking.   He even asked how I was, and I said:
"All right so far."   The cloud was beginning to thin out.   Off
to the north we could see xxⁿxx the lights, ~~of the German searchlights~~,
and the flak began to liven up ahead of us.   Bosz, the bomb-
aimer crackled through on the intercom: "There's a battle going
on on the starboard beam".   We couldn't see the aircraft, but
we could see the jets of red tracer being exchanged.   Suddenly
there was a burst of yellow flame, and Jock remarked: "That's a
fighter going down - note the position".   The whole thing was
interesting but remote.   Dave, the navigator, who was sitting
back with his maps, charts and compasses said: "The attack ought
to begin in exactly two minutes."   We were still over the clouds.
But suddenly those dirty grey clouds turned white - we were over
the outer searchlight defences - the clouds below us were white,
and we were black.   D - Dog seemed like a black bug on a white
sheet.   The flak began coming up, but none of it close.   We
were still a long way from Berlin.   I didn't realise just how
far.   Jock observed: "There's a kite on fire dead ahead" - it
was a great golden, slow-moving meteor slanting towards the earth.

By this time we were about thirty miles from our target area
in Berlin.   That thirty miles was the longest flight I have
ever made.   Dead on time Bosz, the bomb-aimer, reported "target
indicators going down".   At the same moment the sky ahead was

lit up by bright yellow flares.   Off to starboard another kite
went down in flames.   The flares were sprouting all over the sky -
reds and greens and yellows; and we were flying straight for the
centre of the fireworks.   D - Dog seemed to be standing still,
the four propellers thrashing the air - but we didn't seem to be
closing in.   The cloud had cleared, and off to starboard a
Lanc was caught by at least fourteen searchlight beams.   We could see him
twist and turn, and finally break out.   But still the whole thing
had a quality of unreality about it.   No one seemed to be shooting
at us, but it was getting lighter all the time.   Suddenly a
tremendous big blob of yellow light appeared dead ahead, another
to the right, and another to the left.   We were flying straight
for them.   Jock pointed out to me the dummy fires and flares
to right and left, but we kept going in.   Dead ahead there was
a whole chain of red flares looking like stop lights.   Another
Lanc was coned on our starboard beam; the lights seemed to be
supporting it.   Again we could see those little bubbles of
colored lead driving at it from two sides.   The German fighters
were at him.

        And then with no warning at all D - Dog was filled with an
unhealthy white light; I was standing just behind Jock and could
see the seams of the wings.   His quiet Scots voice beat into my
ears: "Steady, lads - we've been coned".   His slender body lifted
half out of the seat as he jammed the control column forward and
to the left.   We were going down.   Jock was wearing

woollen gloves with the fingers cut off .   I could see his
finger nails turn white as he gripped the wheel.   And then I
was on my knees, flat on the deck, for he had whipped the Dog
back into a climbing turn.   The knees should have been strong
enough to support me, but they weren't; And the stomach seemed
in some danger of letting me down too.   I picked myself up and
looked out again.   It seemd that one big searchlight instead of
being twenty thousand feet below was mounted right on the wingtip.
D - Dog was corkscrewing.   As we rolled down on the other side
I began to see what was happening to Berlin.

The clouds were gone, and the sticks of incendiaries from
the preceding waves made the place looked like a badly laid out
city with the street lights on.   The small incendiaries were
going down like a fistfull of white rice thrown on a piece of
black velvet.   As Jock hauled the Dog up again I was thrown
to the other side of the cockpit, and there below were more
incendiaries glowing white and then turning red.   The cookies -
the four-thousand pound high explosives - were bursting below,
like great sunflowers gone mad.   And then as we started down,
still held in the lights, I remembered that the Dog still had
one of those cookies, and a whole basket of incendiaries in his
belly, and the lights still held us - and I was very frightened.
~~Finally was were out of the scene and leveled off~~xxxx While Jock
was flinging him about in the air, he suddenly flung over the

intercom: "Two aircraft on the port beam".   I looked astern and
saw Wally, the mid-upper whip his turret around to port, and then
looked up to see a single-engined fighter slide below us.   The
other aircraft was one of ours.   Finally we were out of the cone,
flying level.   I looked down, and the white fires had turned red;
they were beginning to merge and spread just like butter does on
a hot plate.

Jock and Bosz, the bomb-aimer, began to discuss the target.
The smoke was getting thick down below.   Bosz said he liked the
two green flares/almost dead ahead.   He began calling his
directions, and just then a new bunch of big green flares went
down on the far side of the sea of flame and flare that seemed
to be directly below us.   He thought that would be a better
aiming point.   Jock agreed; and we flew on.   The bomb doors
were opened - Bosz called his directions: "Five left....five left".
Then there was a gentle, confident upward thrust under my feet,
and Bosz said: "Cookie gone".   A few seconds later the incendiaries
went, and D- Dog seemed lighter, and easier to handle.   I thought
I could make out the outline of streets below, but the bomb-aimer
didn't agree, and he ought to know.   By this time all those
patches of white on black had turned yellow, and started to flow
together.   Another searchlight caught us but didn't hold us.
Then through the intercom came the word: "One can of incendiaries
didn't clear - we're still carrying it".   And Jock replied: "Is it
a big one or a little one?"   The word came back: "Little one I
think, but I'm not sure - I'll check".   More of those yellow flares

came down and hung about us.   I haven't seen so much light since
the war began.   Finally the intercom announced that it was
only a small container of incendiaries left, and Jock remarked:
"Well, it's hardly worth going back and doing another run-up for
that".   If there had been a good fat bundle left he would have
gone back through that stuff and done it all over again.

I began to breathe, and to reflect again that all men would
be brave if only they could leave their stomachs at home, when
there was a tremendous WHOOMP, an unintelligible shout from the
tail-gunner....D - Dog shivered and lost altitude.   I looked out
the port side, and there was a Lancaster/that seemed close enough to touch;
he had whipped straight over us - missed us by 25....50 feet -
no one knew how much.

The navigator sang out the new course and we were heading
for home.   Jock was doing what I had heard him tell his pilots
to do so often - flying dead on course.   He flew straight into
a huge green searchlight, and as he rammed the throttles home
remarked: "We'll have a little trouble getting away from this one".
And again D - Dog dove, climbed and twisted, and was finally free.
We flew level then, and I looked on the port beam at the target
area.   There was a red, sullen, obscene glare - the fires seemed
to have found each other.....and we were heading home.   In little
more than half-an-hour Berlin had received about three times the
weight of bombs that had ever fallen on London in the course of

a long winter night. For a little while it was smooth sailing -
we saw more battles, and another plane in flames, but no one could
tell whether it was ours or theirs. ~~Then~~ we were ~~somewhere~~ still
near ~~Hanover.~~ the target. Dave, the navigator, said: "Hold her steady
Skipper, I want to get an Astro sight". Jock held her steady,
and the flak began coming up at us. It seemed to be very close;
it was winking off both wings; but the Dog was steady. Finally
xxx Dave said: "Okay Skipper, thank you very much"; and a great
orange blob of flak smacked up straight in front of us. Jock
said: "I think they're shooting at us"; (I had thought so for
some time;) and he began to throw D for Dog up, around and about
again. When we/clear of the barrage I asked him how close the
were
bursts were, and he said: "Not very close. When they are
really near you can smell 'em"." That proved nothing, for I had
been holding my breath.

Jack sang out from the rear turret, said his oxygen was
getting low, thought maybe the ~~thing~~ lead was frozen. Titch, the
wireless operator, went scrambling back with a new mask and a
bottle of oxygen. Dave, the navigator, said: "We're crossing
the coast". My mind went back to the time I had crossed that
coast in 1938, in a plane that had taken off from Prague. Just
ahead of me sat two refugees from Vienna - an old man and his
wife. The co-pilot came back and told them that we were
outside German territory. The old man reached out and grasped

his wife's hand.   The work that was done last night was a
massive blow of retribution for all those who have fled from the
sound of shots and blows on that stricken continent.

We began to lose height over the North Sea.   We were
over England's shore.   The land was dark beneath us.   Somewhere
down there below American boys were probably bombing up
Fortresses and Liberators, getting ready for the day's work.

We were over the home field; we called the control tower;
and the calm, clear voice of an English girl replied: "Greetings
D - Dog, you are diverted to Mulebag."   We swung round,
contacted Mulebag, came in on the flarepath, touched down very
gently, ran along to the end of the runway/- and turned left and Jock, the
finest pilot in Bomber Command said to the control tower:
"D - Dog clear of runway".

When we went in for interrogation, I looked on the board and
saw that the big, slow-smiling Canadian, and the red-headed
English boy with the two-weeks' old moustache hadn't made it.
They were missing.

There were four reporters on this operation. Two of them
didn't come back - two friends of mine, Norman Stockton of
Australian Associated Newspapers, and Lowell Bennet, an American
representing International News Service.   There is something of
a tradition amongst reporters that those who are prevented fromx

by circumstances from filing their stories will be covered by their colleagues.   This has been my effort to do that.

In the aircraft in which I flew, the men who flew and fought
poured
it ~~hammered~~ into my ears their comments on fighters, flak and flares - in the same tone they would have used in reporting a host of daffodils.   I have no doubt that Bennet and Stockton would have given you a better report of last night's activities. ~~Theyxtriedx   Bathxwerexflownxbyxfirstxclassxpilots;xandxeveryonex whoxwasxairbornexlastxnightxwasxinterestedxinxonexthingxonly;x andxthatxwasxthatxthexbombsxshouldxgoxdownx~~

                    a
Berlin was ~~the~~ kind of orchestrated hell - a terrible symphony of light and flame.   It isn't a pleasant kind of warfare. The men doing it speak of it as a job.   ~~Yesterday~~ Yesterday afternoon, when the tapes were stretched out on the big map all the way to Berlin and back again, a young pilot with old eyes said to me: "I see we're working again tonight.   That's the frame of mind in which the job is being done.   The job isn't pleasant - it's terribly tiring - men die in the sky, while others are roasted alive in their cellars.   ~~Andxthosexwhoxarex endingxanxepochx~~   Berlin last night wasn't a pleasant sight. In about 35 minutes it was hit with about three times the amount
                    on
of stuff that ever came down ~~in~~ London in a night-long blitz. This is a calculated remorseless campaign of destruction.   Right now the mechanics are probably working on D - Dog, getting him ready to fly again.

Index

Index

Index